THE UNSHAKABLE KINGDOM
AND THE UNCHANGING PERSON

The 21st Century Edition Series
Series Editor: Anne Mathews-Younes, Ed.D., D.Min.

THE
UNSHAKABLE KINGDOM
AND THE
UNCHANGING PERSON

E. STANLEY JONES

DEDICATION

With gratitude to Duane and Nancy McNett,
whose vision and faithfulness have ensured that the
Unshakable Kingdom and the Unchanging Person
is available to new generations of seekers.

Contents

CONTENTS

CONTENTS

PREFACE TO THE 21ST CENTURY EDITION

By Anne Mathews-Younes

AMERICANS ARE BECOMING less religious, but feelings of spirituality are on the rise, according to a recent study by the Pew Research Center. At one time or another most of us have overheard others use the phrase "I am spiritual but not religious" to describe his or her position on faith. I am not sure how this plays out in practical life, given that it neither contains meaning nor offers evidence of any persuasion. I suppose it has to do with an individual's desire for an inspirational connection to the universe. We must admit that this pursuit can hardly be thought difficult, given that anyone looking up at the night sky cannot but be inspired by the vista of the stars. This is hide-and-seek spirituality. It is feel-good, safe, and politically correct. It says nothing about one's faith and cuts no ice in the foxholes of life. Yet this empty declaration is gaining traction even as it shuts down meaningful religious narratives about faith and the reality of God. I live in hope that the next person who utters this statement will not leave me hanging, and continue by saying "and the source of my spirituality is …!"

In this book, E. Stanley Jones dares to question this pervasive contemporary view. By questioning, he hopes to neutralize the harm it causes. It harms by proclaiming that the act of belief, no matter how aimless or ill defined, is enough to get us through the perils of life. Jones boldly declares the opposite by saying, "There is no deeper and greater need in the world today than the practical mysticism that Jesus brings to bear upon the problems of life." Further, he supports the integrity of this statement and others—equally provocative—in scripture. Which of these two positions describes your beliefs? Do you have faith?

This book is a safe place for you to explore your real questions about the existence and relevance of God, the reality of His Kingdom, and the realism of Jesus Christ. What do these deep questions have to do with you? Why should you care about finding answers, given the demands of your life today? Who has time for one more old theory done up in new packaging?

Do you think there is truth to the notion that humankind is hard-wired through every fiber and nerve to seek God? If the Kingdom of God holds the grand plan for the means to make life work, who wouldn't want to know the details of that plan? In these pages Jones unpacks the practical implications and applications of God's Kingdom on earth. He does this in understandable and discerning ways. He uses straight-talk to clarify the lingering, unresolved issues of faith and spirituality. He helps us discover the answers that transform our lives and teach us how to live in God's way.

You will be left to draw your own conclusions about the earthly reality of the Kingdom of God. But the pursuit this book challenges you to undertake lies in this question: "When we find the Kingdom of God, do we find real Life?" After all, isn't this what we really want—an abundant, real life?

The Kingdom of God fomented a revolution in Jones' life that sustained him throughout his life-long ministry. He said, "I see now, as I have never seen before, the eternal fitness of the gospel – it fits the soul like a glove fits the hand. It is the way that we are made to live, and to try to live some other way is not only foolish, but is also impossible. You cannot live against life and get away with it."

Jones tells a story on page 373 about Anne Byrd Payson, a highly sophisticated member of New York Society who found the way she was made to live! Payson had a dramatic conversion experience in 1930 after reading Jones' *Christ of the Indian Road*. While she felt that her life had changed, she could not determine what came next. "Now that I'm a Christian, how do I act as a Christian? What's the technique of being a Christian?" She soon discovered *the unshakable kingdom* and *the unchanging person* were the grounding for her faith journey. Jones watched her grow in and through her faith as she found the reality of the unshakable Kingdom. Anne Payson wrote a book about her experience that Jones found to be "the revelation of a soul that was following the gleam amid the complexities of modern life. Something redemptive had begun working at the heart of her life and she shared those results." I recently read Payson's book and it is an illumination of the power and reality of kingdom living and of a life following the

13

unchanging person, Jesus Christ. You will discover many other profound examples of transformed lives in this book.

In the course of editing this book, I learned from Patricia Saylor, a dear friend of E. Stanley Jones, that Jones wrote much of this manuscript while in her home and he even stayed a little longer than expected as he found the setting highly conducive to writing. Mrs. Saylor shared the following memories:

"It was not the first time that Brother Stanley had visited our home. Little did we know then that it was to be his last. So here we were, Brother Stanley and I, outside on this perfect summer day, sipping afternoon tea. Finishing our second cups, we put them aside and picked up our Bibles as was our custom when he visited. Brother Stanley turned to a passage he had been working on as he wrote, *The Unshakable Kingdom and the Unchanging Person*, and opened up that scripture to me. I had just had a taste of what the disciples must have felt listening to Jesus! Finishing the study, he laid his Bible back onto the table, and clearing his voice began to share a concern he had. "I've noticed," he said, "that my speech doesn't come as easily as it used to. I seem to be having trouble enunciating my words. I feel a slight thickening of my tongue." I hadn't particularly noticed. It seemed to be the same clipped almost British accented voice to me. About this same time, my husband Don, a Lutheran pastor, came home. Brother Stanley repeated his concern. Taking charge, Don asked if Brother Stanley would be willing to go to our family doctor the next day. He would and we did. After hearing his symptoms and doing an examination, our physician recommended that his patient undergo further testing at Riverside Methodist Hospital as soon as possible. Brother Stanley responded, "First, I'll have to ask." Upon arriving home, Brother Stanley went right upstairs and 'asked.'

In just a few minutes he descended the stairs holding a yellow legal pad and said, "It's a go!" Thrusting the legal pad into my hands, he smiled and ordered, "Guard it with your life. It's the manuscript I have been working on!"

We piled back into the car and drove to the hospital where he was admitted. After we helped settle him in and said prayers, we left him, but Brother Stanley was never 'alone.'

A few days later after the tests were done, the doctors determined that he had suffered a mild stroke. The orders were to take it easy (bed rest only) and to do nothing strenuous. Brother Stanley ignored all of this guidance. He had an Ashram to attend in Evansville, Indiana, and he would be there! We were running out of time. Evansville was not nearby. The patient needed bed rest yet insisted on keeping his promise.

We pulled down the seats of our Matador station wagon, placed two sofa cushions onto the now flat space and Brother Stanley sat upon them and piled pillows on both sides to keep him from rolling. I don't think this was exactly what the doctor had meant by 'bed rest," but it would have to do. I felt sad and concerned as I said goodbye this time All I could do was pray. They made it to Evansville, but Brother Stanley never made it back to our home, going a few years later to a far better one, his heavenly home. I don't know what work he has been given to do there, but I do know he will show up when he has promised to show up!

It was a moment that I will never forget and I am so grateful that this book is being reprinted."

This edition could not have been completed without the assistance of Rev. Shivraj Mahendra, whose publishing, editing and theological skills were essential to this project. In addition to working on his doctoral dissertation about E. Stanley Jones' theology, Shivraj has made time to assist in the designing and reprinting of this book with speed, expertise and precision. Nicholas Younes contributed his considerable content editing expertise and Barbara Ryder Hubbard brought her years as a teacher of reading and English to the task of copy editing this book.

I want to express particular gratitude to Duane and Nancy McNett, who single-handedly brought this book back into print in 1995. While they are not in the publishing business, they created a publishing house for the sole purpose of reprinting this seminal statement of Jones' theology. Thanks to the vision of Duane and Nancy, thousands of copies of this book have been shared across the world over the last twenty years and the E. Stanley Jones Foundation is honored to assume their mantle.

ANNE MATHEWS-YOUNES, ED. D., D. MIN.
President, E. Stanley Jones Foundation

A NOTE

From Duane McNett

LAST WORDS ARE important. Towards the end of his life, E. Stanley Jones embarked on a project to codify the Kingdom of God and its principles. As he launched this venture under Holy Spirit inspiration, he realized stunningly that the Kingdom cannot be separated from the person of Jesus. The results were what you read today, *The Unshakable Kingdom and the Unchanging Person.* Although not his last published work, this book represents a summation of a lifetime of over 70 years in ministry.

As a new believer in my early twenties, this book, then out of print, was recommended to me. It has been my constant companion now for 40 years. My wife Nancy and I had the privilege of publishing this book for over two decades and making it available to many thousands of Christians. We are honored to be associated in this way with E. Stanley Jones, his family, and now the E. Stanley Jones Foundation.

A NOTE

This book will lead you on a magnificent journey to an ever-increasing knowledge of God's order and God Himself. E. Stanley Jones brings grandfatherly wisdom as he reveals eternal spiritual truths.

Not many authors can bridge the cultural divide from one generation to the next. However, you will see that the concepts he presents are universal. These concepts are just as relevant today as they were when this book was written.

The Unshakable Kingdom and the Unchanging Person will help you, the reader, bridge the gap between the seen world (the natural world) and the unseen supernatural world (the Kingdom of God). It will arm you with tools to live the abundant life that Jesus offers us. Scripture implies that we are in the world, but not of it. E. Stanley Jones offers us a supreme knowledge of life and how to live it, even though this world is not our natural homeland or our final destination.

While many have no controlling purpose in their lives, this book offers dramatic guideposts that we all need on our journey. E. Stanley Jones, in my estimation, is unique in his approach and the revelation he presents. I believe he joins the ranks of classic Christian authors like Spurgeon, Chesterton, and Tozer in longevity and certainly inspirational content.

DUANE V. MCNETT
McNett Press, Washington

FOREWORD

By Tony McCollum

IT IS RARE TO FIND a voice that can speak with authority, clarity and compassion to an entire generation. However, when you encounter a voice that speaks not only to his own generation, but also to the generations that follow with the same clarity and authority, you know you have discovered a true gift from God. Without a doubt, this book epitomizes the teaching mantle of the life and ministry of Dr. E. Stanley Jones. His understanding of the Kingdom of God shaped his ministry with such precision and purpose that he spoke to world leaders, children and the common man alike regarding the Good News of eternal and unchanging truths.

Change shapes our human existence in absolute and profound ways, and yet we are a people internally wired to resist change. The rise of technology has increased the rate and scope of change we must deal with on a daily basis. Using a cell phone to watch movies, for example, or to make a charitable contribution, while commonplace today, was beyond our imagination less than a decade ago. Instantaneous communication with people around the world has allowed us to see in our brothers and sisters the joy on their faces or a tear in their eyes. Our world is smaller and yet our responsibility to care for our neighbors has greatly increased. How do we deal with such change? Are there laws to govern a world that is changing faster than we can adapt? Is God immune to change?

Writing to a world almost two generations prior, Dr. Jones' use of the words "Unshakable" and "Unchanging," suggests a stability and security found in the Kingdom of God that is nothing less than transcendent. This understanding has the power to both answer our deepest questions today, and at the same time upset every social structure we have created to order a world that runs contrary to the Kingdom of God.

Dr. Jones points out that one of the great weaknesses in the teaching of the Christian faith is that we have separated Jesus Christ the King from the Kingdom over which He rules. We tend to think of the Kingdom of God as a future hope, rather than a present reality. We miss the abundant life of power, freedom and peace that can be ours here and now by living as disciples of the Kingdom. Ours is not the first generation to lose a proper understanding of the Kingdom, but thankfully an individual decision is all that is necessary for you and me to realize the Kingdom of God in our lives. In *The Unshakable Kingdom and the Unchanging Person*, Dr. Jones gives indispensable instruction for experiencing, teaching and sharing the blessings of God and His Kingdom. His work is as vital today as it was 45 years ago when readers first poured over the words of this senior statesman of the faith.

You will find encouragement in the pages of this book as Dr. Jones offers extraordinary insight for the individual and the church, which dares to live as disciples of the Kingdom of God. Dr. Jones' personal observation and belief that Jesus is the Unchanging King over an Unshakable Kingdom is still on target today. It is my belief and my prayer that our lives, our families and our world will be blessed beyond measure if we follow the teachings of Jesus and "seek first the Kingdom of God."

TONY McCOLLUM, D.MIN.
Senior Pastor
Cypress United Methodist Church
Cypress, TX

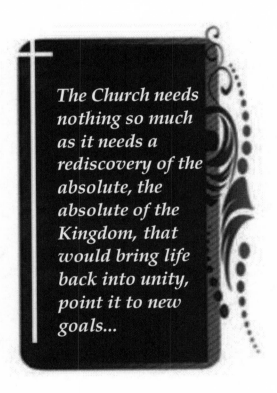

The Church needs nothing so much as it needs a rediscovery of the absolute, the absolute of the Kingdom, that would bring life back into unity, point it to new goals...

INTRODUCTION

THIS BOOK WAS triggered by the suggestion of a prominent pastor on the West Coast of America who spoke on over eighty radio stations each week. He heard me speak on the Kingdom of God and said: "Why don't you codify the laws of the Kingdom of God. They are too hazy. If the kingdom of God is God's total answer to man's total need, as you say and the Scriptures say, then they must be put into a form which we can see and obey." My reply was, "I'm not a lawyer and I'm not a theologian. Technically, I'm a bearer of the Good News. I must stick to my focus." "Yes," he replied, "but you possess the Kingdom and the Kingdom possesses you." I slowly replied, playing for time and a legitimate way out of such a task, "Let me go over the New Testament to see what it says about the kingdom of God. I've done it before, but this time I will do it intensively and it will take about a year. If at the end of the year I feel that there is no way to avoid this requested task, then I'll do it." Well, I've spent the year with a rising excitement at what I found. There were many question marks at the beginning, but as I have gone along, these question marks have become straightened out into exclamation points.

A modern girl in the jargon of the day said to me, "You tell it like it is!" But as I have gone along, I have had a growing question, "Are you telling it like it is?" For almost the whole of the New Testament is on the kingdom of God. Is this the theme of the book? Then I saw that the person of Christ was just as important as the message of Christ — the Kingdom of God. The two were linked, inseparably linked. So in midstream, I had to change horses. Instead of the total emphasis on the order, I had to make both the Kingdom and Jesus my message — the order and the Person. So I had to change the title of the book from *The Laws, Principles, and Attitudes of the Kingdom of God* to *The Unshakable Kingdom and the Unchanging Person.*

An Anglican bishop once said, "Stanley Jones seems to be obsessed with the kingdom of God," and my inner reply was: Would God that I were, for it would be a magnificent obsession. Jesus was obsessed with it, and to be obsessed with his obsession is to be on safe and universal ground. But I'm also obsessed with the person of Jesus, Jesus Christ. A Hindu said to me in India, "Jesus has got into your blood, hasn't he?" And my reply was, "Yes, and he has raised my temperature. I'm excited over him." Now that the kingdom of God and the person of the Son of God (the message and the Man) have come

24

together in a living blend, I'm doubly excited. For they are both absolutes — and they have taken absolute possession of me. At eighty-seven years of age, one is supposed to slow down and take life easy and calmly. I do, for his yoke is easy and his burden is light, and I do take things calmly, too, for this fire that burns in one's bones is like the burning bush of Moses which was afire but not consumed. This divine fire does not consume. It consummates. You walk out of it like the Hebrew captives without the smell of smoke upon you.

To change the image, there is no smoke from the exhaust. It does not exhaust, it exhilarates. If this is the gushing of an evangelist, then listen to the considered conclusion of historian, H. G. Wells who, when fumbling through history in search of the "relevant," came across the fact of the kingdom of God and was shocked as by an electric shock, "Why here is the most radical proposal ever presented to the mind of man, the proposal to replace the present world order with God's order, the kingdom of God." It is. So I'm excited with a divine excitement. As a possible last fling, I'd like to fling my blazing torch of the Unshakable Kingdom and the Unchanging Person amid

> *Then I saw that the person of Christ was just as important as the message of Christ — the Kingdom of God.*

25

the burned out heap of extinguished or dying enthusiasms, to set them ablaze again with the relevant — the really relevant, the fact of the kingdom of God on earth exemplified in Jesus.

I find myself with an inner compulsion, bolstered with confidence by the fact that the best and most influential man who ever lived, Jesus Christ, made the kingdom of God his central emphasis. I can't go very wrong if I stick close to him. If I fail, I fail in the right direction. I would rather fail with him than succeed with anyone else.

Another element in this compulsion: If Jesus made the kingdom of God the center of his message and the center of his endeavor, then the greatest need of man, as I see it, is to rediscover the kingdom of God. Man needs nothing so much as he needs something to bring life together into total meaning and total goal. Life for the modern man in East and West needs something to give total meaning to an otherwise fragmented life. Modern man needs an absolute from which he can work down to the relativisms of the day, a master light of all his seeing. Modern man is being pushed, pulled, beckoned, enticed and bludgeoned from all directions. He is being pushed from relativism to relativism. He is confused — the most confused, and yet the most intelligent person that ever existed. Modern man knows everything about life, except how to live it.

The modern man stands between two worlds — one dead and the other not yet born. And he stands there empty, for meaning has dropped out of life. He could stand anything if there were meaning, purpose, goal, especially if that meaning, purpose, goal were worthwhile, worth living for and worth dying for. But he sees no such worthwhileness at the heart of things. Life is like the tale of an idiot, full of sound and fury, signifying nothing. A woman arose in a spiritual meeting and asked: "Is there anyone with a car going anywhere?" She didn't care where, just so it was out of there. She was so bored with the here and now. A maid resigned a good job in a good household and when asked why, she replied with a sigh, "Life is so daily here."

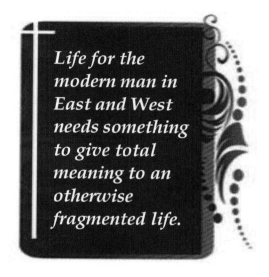

Life for the modern man in East and West needs something to give total meaning to an otherwise fragmented life.

These two illustrations are among the comparatively inconsequential, but suppose this becomes the mood of youth—the coming generation— and among the leaders in literature, among industrialists and those who guide the nations? Suppose it becomes the climate of an age, and suppose it has become the sincere mood of that age, for the members of that age are really convinced that there is no goal, no purpose, no real meaning to life? Then it is no longer an irritable rash on the skin of humanity. It is a creeping paralysis of the heart. We are dying where it counts—at the heart.

Since the sickness is radical, the remedy must be radical; not verbally radical, but vitally radical. The sickness is that mankind as a whole is losing, or has lost, an absolute from which to work down to all the relativisms of the hour, a master light of all its "seeings." We have no starting point and hence no goals.

But the modern man sighs and says, "The sickness is more serious still, for there are no absolutes. They have all been dissolved in the acids of modern thinking. More deeply, there are not supposed to be any absolutes. We are born into the relative, live in the relative, and die in the relative. Life is a vast question mark. There are no exclamation points. It is all inherently uncertain — the way it is supposed to be. We are all doomed to be like blind men, with white sticks tapping our way along the pathway of life to feel out a way of least obstructions. Life is made that way."

The god that would put drives within us, drives that have heaven or hell wrapped within them as results or consequences, and then gives us no plan and power for the handling of these drives, would not be my god. He would be my devil.

A professor said to his students, "Young men, play the game of life." A student spoke up and said, "Sir, but there are no goal posts. There is nothing to shoot at." Are there no goal posts? Is there nothing fixed in this moral and spiritual universe? No goal posts that are our guideposts? It is unthinkable. A meaningless universe would be a mean universe. And the god behind it would be a mean god, which would mean: no god.

In the physical universe, the same laws are seen in the cell and in the farthest star. The universe has the marks of one creative God upon it — it is a universe and not a multiverse. Then the plan for the universe must be one plan, valid and vital for all men everywhere. For we are discovering that humanity is one. Therefore, there must be one plan for this one humanity.

Has that one plan been provided for and has it been revealed? We believe that it has. However, for the revealing of that plan, there must have been a period or periods of preparation for revealing that plan. If the plan should be given without preparation, unprepared man could no more have understood it than a rabbit could understand higher mathematics. There are signs that intimations have been given of that total plan to all peoples and nations, enough intimation that when the plan is presented, it does not sound foreign, but as fulfillment.

> *A meaningless universe would be a mean universe. And the god behind it would be a mean god, which would mean: no god.*

But these intimations are not enough. The intimations had to become instructions, definite enough to understand

and to follow. But how? A universal man must come to reveal in himself the one universal God, and the one universal Kingdom, the kingdom of God.

We think that has happened and happened in history and is verified in experience, verified to the degree that it has been tried. In that verification, there is the growing feeling and conviction that this is it—a feeling and conviction that this is my native land, the land for which I was born, that everything for which I was born is now fulfilled. It is a sense of universality and total acceptance. Such an experience could not be anything but the kingdom of God.

However, this revelation of God and the kingdom of God must not be a verbal revelation. It must be the Word become flesh, the idea of God and the idea of the kingdom become real, become flesh. We must see it as well as hear it. We have.

Jesus was at once the revelation in flesh of what God is like and of what the kingdom of God is like. Both are important, all important. For what God is like in character we must be like in character. We cannot be at cross-purposes with ultimate reality without getting hurt, vitally hurt. But how could we know what God is like unless we saw it—saw it lived out before us? We must see God's character in a human character and see it in operation in human relationships, under the storm and stress of those relationships. Everything must fall on that character that falls on us. We must see his motives and actions and reactions, and then we will know what God is like in character. We have seen it. "He that hath seen me hath seen the Father." Then God is Christ-like. If so, he is a good God and trustable. I could ask nothing higher. I could be content with nothing less. One thing about the universe is settled and settled satisfactorily: There is a God, our heavenly Father, and he is Christ-like in character. Nothing could be settled more satisfactorily.

But one thing remains: What is the nature of the Kingdom of God? After God's personal character, nothing is more important than the nature and character of God's reign, his kingdom. For this is where the whole impinges upon us. His kingdom must be by its very nature a total kingdom, for God is not a half-god ruling over a half-realm, ruling over

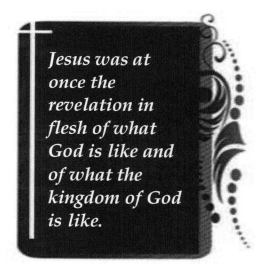

Jesus was at once the revelation in flesh of what God is like and of what the kingdom of God is like.

the personal but not over the social, or ruling over the social and not over the personal. Nor must he be a god who fits into the unexplained facts of nature and not into the total facts of nature, with its regularity and its unexplained mysteries. He must be totally present and totally relevant or totally absent, and hence, totally irrelevant. He must be God and not a mere half-god. And his kingdom must be totally present and totally relevant or totally nothing, hence, totally irrelevant. There is no middle ground. You cannot tuck God into the unexplained gaps in nature, for those unexplained gaps in nature have a way of being filled up and then where is God? He must be God of all or not God at all. And his kingdom must be a total kingdom or no kingdom.

There are two possible ways of revealing the nature and extent of that kingdom. One is to inaugurate it with a fanfare of physical accompaniment that would impose that rule with thunder and lightning and earthquakes which would say to quivering man: "Obey — or else." That would create not men, but slaves. The other way would be for God to hide the Kingdom in the facts of nature and life and gradually reveal it as man developed sufficiently to see that kingdom and adopt it as his own. Then in the fullness of time, when God could find a people or nation most likely to be the people or nation to accept that kingdom and make it its own, he would overtly reveal the nature and the implications of that kingdom in understandable form — human form and in human relationships.

We think that God chose the second way, he stole up on us in a disguised form — the Babe, the Boy, the Carpenter, the Prophet, the Son of man, the Son of God, the Redeemer, the Crucified, the risen and alive Redeemer, the One who sat at the right hand of ultimate power in the universe — thus he revealed the Kingdom in a Person.

Would men take that kingdom in such a form? Some did and were transformed and showed a quality of life and power far beyond the ordinary. But many did not, and as a consequence live half-lives by half-lights, or fumbled and stumbled in the dark.

However, many who took the Kingdom took it in a modified form, as a personal spiritual refuge into which they could run and be safe now or as a place of reward in heaven; they didn't reject it—they reduced it. And in reducing it, they rendered it innocuous now. It wasn't "the Kingdom," God's total answer to man's total need. It wasn't God's total plan and program for life, all life, now, but a reward thrown in at the end.

And now life has become so physically dynamic, so mentally and emotionally free, and so morally irresponsible that it is bursting at the seams; it is going to pieces at the very moment of our greatest triumph in so many fields—in every

We know everything about life except how to live it. We need nothing as desperately as we need something to bring life into total unity and coherence and meaning and goal.

field except the field of living. We know everything about life except how to live it. We need nothing as desperately as we need something to bring life into total unity and coherence and meaning and goal. We have become ripe for a rediscovery of the Kingdom of God.

Everything else has broken down or is breaking down. The totalitarianisms, fascism, Nazism, communism, oligarchies have broken down or are breaking down. Fascism made the state supreme; Nazism made race supreme; communism made the proletariat supreme, oligarchy makes money supreme. All are half-gods and, hence, no gods.

I was speaking in a cathedral in West Germany on the Kingdom of God. On the front seats were prominent German leaders. As I spoke they kept pounding their benches with their fists. I was puzzled. I did not know what it meant—was it in support of my comments or against them? But at the close they revealed what the beating of the benches meant: "You seem to sense why we turned to Nazism. Life for us was at loose ends— compartmentalized. We needed something to bring life back into wholeness, into total meaning and goal. We thought Nazism could bring that wholeness. But it let us down, let us drown in blood and ruin. We chose the wrong totalitarianism. We now see that what we were seeking was the kingdom of God, but we didn't know it. That's why we pounded the benches, we missed the kingdom of God." That opened my eyes. I saw as in a flash the meaning of these various revolts—the totalitarian revolts, the revolts of youth, the revolt of the races. Are they not all seeking for the kingdom of God and don't know it? The answer is yes. We can see what they are revolting against—various injustices in society—but we cannot understand what they are revolting for. That is undefined and hazy. The key seems to be: They are seeking for the kingdom of God, but they don't know it. Someday it will all dawn upon them and then we will have the greatest spiritual awakening that this planet has ever seen. For men need nothing so much as they need an absolute from which they can work out to the relativisms of the hour — some master light of all their seeing.

Psychologists say there are three basic needs inherent in all human nature: the need to belong; the need for significance; and the need for reasonable security. The first need is to belong. Behavioral health experts say that ninety-five percent of delinquencies among youth come out of broken homes. When the security of the home is broken, youth feels that he doesn't belong, so he turns

> *For men need nothing so much as they need an absolute from which they can work out to the relativisms of the hour — some master light of all their seeing.*

to crime and delinquency. A Chinese proverb says: "In a broken nest there are no whole eggs." The rogue elephants in Burma, India, and Ceylon are elephants that have been put out of the herd by the younger males. They then turn rogue, tearing up huts, gardens, villages — anything in their pathway. Why? They don't "belong." The central and acute sickness of this age is that people do not belong—do not belong to anything significant. It was found up on the death of a certain man that he belonged to twenty-seven clubs; he tried to make up in quantity for what he lacked in quality. The sum total had no significance. Hence the man had no significance, hence no security. We must belong to something that gives a sense of belonging and a sense of significance and security for now and forever.

Call the roll of the possible memberships and I know of none, except one, the kingdom of God, that promises and brings a sense of total belonging and a sense of belonging now to ultimate significance and ultimate security. If there is another such possibility for belonging, let men trot it out and people will follow it by the millions if it is real. Then why hasn't the Church offered it? The answer is simple and tragic: the Church has lost it. The Church has lost the Kingdom of God.

Call the roll of the tragedies in history and they all root in that loss of the Kingdom. Take Israel, when it was said of her: "The kingdom of God will be taken away from you and given to a nation producing the fruits of it" (Matt. 21:43 RSV). That refusal on the part of Israel began the long tragedy of a frustrated nation. Take the Crusades— men of violence tried to take that kingdom by force and succeeded in laying the foundations of hate and conflict through the centuries. Take Genghis Khan's request through Marco Polo to the Pope: "Please send us a hundred teachers, well learned in the seven arts and well

36

able to prove that the way of Christ is best." Marco Polo, seeing the request was of great significance, hastened back to the Pope. Two years later, two teachers instead of a hundred were sent with this message, "Become politically and ecclesia-stically attached to Rome." They didn't offer the kingdom of God, a universal kingdom; they offered a political and ecclesiastical attachment to Rome. Genghis Khan turned it down, accepted Islam, and spread blood and fire through Asia and Europe.

When Russia was in the throes of a revolution instead of the church offering the kingdom of God on earth, a church council was debating the question of whether garments of a certain color should be used in a certain time and place in the church service —

Call the roll of the possible memberships and I know of none, except one, the kingdom of God, that promises and brings a sense of total belonging and a sense of belonging now to ultimate significance and ultimate security.

debating that trivialty when Russia was moving toward communism. In Italy, the nation was not offered a universal kingdom, the kingdom of God, but a papal ecclesiastical system instead, so Italy made the state supreme, chose Fascism, and brought the nation into defeat and collapse. Germany chose Nazism, making the race supreme; when the church offered a kingdom in heaven hereafter, it brought on its own ruin. When in the welter of conflicts, America arose supreme out of the chaos, we offered the American way of life, instead of God's way of life, the kingdom of God, and are ending up plagued by our own racial, class, and economic conflicts, with little to offer the world.

The Church is largely to blame because the Church, instead of offering the kingdom of God, offered various conflicts (fundamentalist-modernist; the social gospel — the individual gospel; racial integration; the secular church; long hair; short hair; beards and non-beards; the church-building orgy; then vestments and candles and robes; conversion; abolition of poverty and the ghettos) every issue except the kingdom of God.

If the Kingdom of God is missing in the magnificent and in the minute, then the key to meaning, goal, life-redemption, and life-fulfillment is missing. Life turns meaningless and sick, becomes a problem instead of a possibility. But if you have the key to the Kingdom, you find it a master key, the key to life now and hereafter, life individual and collective. That is important to the modern man: You have the key to relevancy in every situation. If you know the Kingdom by experience, then you know what to do in every situation. Do the kingdom thing and you are relevant and you are attached to the relevant and you do the relevant thing. You are at the center of relevancy.

So for the Church to be relevant the answer is simple: Discover the Kingdom, surrender to the Kingdom, make the Kingdom your life loyalty and your life program; then in everything and everywhere you will be relevant. For the kingdom of God is relevancy, ultimate and final relevancy. When you have it, and it has you, then you are relevancy itself.

Without the Kingdom, the Church is irrelevant, except marginally. With the Kingdom, the Church is relevant centrally and marginally. By its very nature it is relevant. It doesn't have to try to be relevant by adopting little dabs of relevancy here and there. It is relevant when it is attached in loyalty and love to the relevant — the Kingdom.

> *If the kingdom of God is missing in the magnificent and in the minute, then the key to meaning, goal, life-redemption, and life-fulfillment is missing.*

Take two illustrations of what happens when the Kingdom is lost. The Christian Church founded by the apostle Thomas has existed in India since the first century. The evangelical portion of that church is alive and advancing. They have the largest Christian convention in the world—from fifty to seventy-five thousand persons participating. But many of the Christians had become communists. When I asked them why, they replied, "Christianity gives a social conscience, but no social program. So we are taking the communist program without its ideology and without its compulsions and tyrannies." I spoke to thirty thousand men on Christianity and communism at the convention. The communist officials were there, many of them Christians. The atmosphere was electric and tense. I spoke for an hour, and they asked questions for two hours afterwards. Two years later I spoke to the same number of people, in the same convention, on the same subject. They gave a pin-drop silence, but the tense electric atmosphere was gone from the audience. When I asked what had happened they replied: "The Christians have given up communism and have turned to the national congress and to socialism, because they said, 'We could not obey two totalitarianisms; both communism and Christianity demand a total allegiance. So we decided to remain Christians, and we are shifting politically to socialism and the national congress.'"

Now note, the Christians turned to communism because they had no absolute allegiance to an absolute order—the Kingdom of God. So they changed tentatively to communism. Then they returned tentatively to Christianity. They adopted the national congress and socialism as their medium of political expression, both of them sub-Christian and often in practice anti-Christian.

But they had no alternative. They had lost the absolute of the kingdom of God; hence, they turned to other relativisms for guidance and received half-lights.

Take another example. In the World Conference of Missions in 1938, a time when fascism, Nazism, and communism were rising to ascendancy and when the ecumenical movement was rising amid the Christian churches, the thought of the missionary conference in Madras began flowing toward the ecumenical church as the answer to those earth-born totalitarianisms. I pleaded that we make the Kingdom of God our stand and thus match against these earth-born relativisms God's absolute — the Kingdom. They preferred to make the ecumenical church their stand — to match against relativisms another relativism, the ecumenical church. "Suppose," I said, "you go out and cry, 'Repent for the ecumenical church is at hand,' what would be the reaction? The people would laugh at you, as they do laugh when I suggest it to audiences. But you don't laugh when I say, 'Repent for the kingdom of God is at hand,' that is, if you have any sense, you don't laugh, you bend the knee."

So the Church having lost its absolute — the Kingdom of God — is now in a welter of conflicting relativisms, all bidding for the Church's attention and loyalty. So the Church leaves a blur instead of a mark. Where Paul could say, "This one thing I do," the Church says, "These forty things I dabble in." The Church needs nothing so much as it needs a rediscovery of the absolute, the absolute of the Kingdom, that would bring life back into unity, point

41

it to new goals (individual and collective), discover new power, the power of the Spirit, to move on to those goals, and give it nerve to face a hesitating and confused world with, "Repent for the kingdom of God is at hand."

When I say that the Church has lost the Kingdom, I do not mean that it has totally lost the conception of the Kingdom. It has it as a marginal concept, something you get into for security by the new birth now, something you will inherit hereafter as a reward in heaven, something you receive at the Second Coming, something to which you point to as an ideal. These conceptions of a kingdom are generally dehydrated because they are marginal. They are not the starting point and the ending point, not the total program now for all life, not the head-on and total answer to man's total need, individual and collective. In other words, we do not seek first, last,

What we have lost is God's redemptive totalitarianism, the Kingdom of God. That is the central sickness of our age.

and always the kingdom of God as our way of life now, and we do not offer it to the world as our answer to the world's ills now. What we have lost is God's redemptive totalitarianism, the Kingdom of God. That is the central sickness of our age. Until we find that all our endeavors for amelioration are a sprinkling of rose water on a cancer.

Not that we do not appreciate attempts at amelioration — we do. But if we substitute attempts at amelioration as a substitute for the kingdom of God, then it must come under the rosewater condemnation.

- E. Stanley Jones
1971

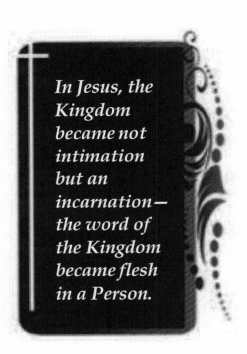

In Jesus, the Kingdom became not intimation but an incarnation— the word of the Kingdom became flesh in a Person.

I

THE UNSHAKABLE KINGDOM
AND THE
UNCHANGING PERSON

WE TURN NOW to the nature and meaning of the Kingdom and to the Person, the Person who brought it as good news. They belong together, for they are together. Others in the Old Testament have brought intimations of that kingdom, but they were intimations, stray descriptions. In Jesus, the Kingdom became not intimation but an incarnation — the word of the Kingdom became flesh in a Person. This sets off the Kingdom, which Jesus announced and revealed in his own Person so that it was not merely a difference in degree, but a difference in kind. The content of the character of Jesus has gone into the Kingdom so that it turned out to be something quite different and other than what the prophets announced. One modern writer spent 187 pages on the pre-Christian intimations of the Kingdom in the Old Testament and about fifty pages on the actual announcement of and revelation of the Kingdom in Jesus. One talked in stray references about the Kingdom, while the other showed the life of the Kingdom in the Person of Jesus. One showed the relationship of the Kingdom to a nation (Israel) a glorified nationalism; the other showed the Kingdom in relationship to humanity, a universal kingdom. "The kingdom of God shall be taken away from you, and given to a nation bringing forth the fruits thereof" (Matt. 21:43). Note, "bringing forth the fruits thereof." The test of possessing the Kingdom was to bring forth the fruits thereof. That lifted the Kingdom out of identification with any existing nation and any existing church or movement and placed it in the hands of those who bring forth the fruits thereof. This universalized the Kingdom. It is offered to all and yet identified with none, none except those who brought forth the fruits of the Kingdom. To make it more specific, Jesus said, "Many shall come from the east and west, and shall sit down with Abraham, and Isaac, and Jacob, in the kingdom of heaven. But the children of the kingdom shall be cast out" (Matt. 8:11, 12). "The children of the kingdom" are apparently those in the line of the kingdom of God — Jews and Christians — who have inherited the kingdom of God by birth, but those who have not brought the fruits thereof will be cast out. This includes all to the degree that they bring forth the fruits of the Kingdom and excludes none except those who exclude themselves. This is a fair exclusion and a fair inclusion. This is a worthy openness and a worthy exclusion, worthy of a kingdom of God, our Father. And it is a worthy basis of inclusion or exclusion, to bring forth the fruits thereof. It is not based on a marginal issue. It is based on a fundamental issue: fruits. The outcome, the fruits, is the criterion.

And the fruits were not in quantity, but in quality. The fruits were the extension of his life, the Kingdom was Christlikeness universalized. He used interchangeably "for my sake" and "the Kingdom's sake." He was the Kingdom, not merely expounded, but exposed. Men saw it and did not merely hear it. He was it. That is of vast and significant importance. For it saves the kingdom of God from being identified with, or colored by, other kingdoms — the kingdom of socialism, the kingdom of capitalism, the kingdom of communism, "the commonwealth of God," the kingdom of the Church. The kingdom of God may gather up into itself anything good in each of these, but in itself it is more than and other than any or all of these. It is unique in quality and quantity and goal and

> *Jesus used interchangeably "for my sake" and "the Kingdom's sake." He was the Kingdom, not merely expounded, but exposed.*

scope and objective. It is the most radical proposal ever proposed to the mind and allegiance of man. This is *radicalism.* Nobody and nothing is beyond its scope and purview and redemption. This makes sick and irrelevant all the earth-born totalitarianisms. And this is *conservatism*. It gathers up everything good in any system of thought and every religion anywhere, fulfills the good, cleanses the evil, and goes beyond anything ever thought or dreamed anywhere. This is the desire of the ages — if men only knew it. All life, rational and sub-rational, is on tiptoe of expectancy for the kingdom of God, if men only knew it!

Let us back up a bit. The best and wisest and most powerful man who ever lived — Jesus — made the kingdom of God his message. He called it the Good News — the Gospel. It is the only thing he called the Gospel: "He went out preaching the gospel of the kingdom" (Matt. 4:23). He sent out his disciples to preach the gospel of the kingdom of God. Jesus used the phrase "the kingdom of God" or its equivalent a hundred times. This is important, for the marginal, the unimportant, and the unworthy never misled him. He made the kingdom of God the center — the heartbeat of his message. Anything he said a hundred times is important, for the most important person who ever lived was speaking. That makes his choosing "the Kingdom" important, for it was a life choice, a life emphasis. Jesus summed up his life purpose in these words: "I must give the good news of the kingdom of God to the other towns also, for that is what I was sent to do" (Luke 4:43 NEB). Note, "I must give the good news of the kingdom of God for that is what I was sent to do" — it was his life purpose given to him of God.

What did he mean by the Kingdom? He made it the first petition in the Lord's Prayer: "When you pray say: Our Father ... Thy kingdom come. Thy will be done, on earth as it is in heaven." Prayer is the deepest thing we do and in that deepest thing we do, the coming of the Kingdom is the most important. It is the foremost and the uppermost—without it the prayer is comparatively meaningless. This focus on the Kingdom is the framework and the core of everything. Rauschenbusch says, "The Kingdom is the vertebrae on which all things in the body hang."

The key words are these: "Thy kingdom come. Thy will be done, on earth as it is done in heaven." The second phrase explains the first. The coming of the Kingdom was the doing of the will of God on earth as it is done in heaven. How is the will of God done in heaven? In the individual will? Yes. In the collective will? Yes. In the total social arrangements of heaven? Yes. It is a complete totalitarianism, a total way of life in this life now. But wouldn't that be total bondage? Strangely enough, No. Here is a complete totalitarianism in which, when you obey it totally, you find total freedom. I do not argue. I

All life, rational and sub-rational, is on tiptoe of expectancy for the kingdom of God, if men only knew it!

49

only testify: When I belong to Christ and his kingdom I am most my own. Bound to the Kingdom I walk the earth free. Low at his feet I stand straight before everything. This is the difference between the earth-born totalitarianisms and God's heaven-born totalitarianism: If you obey the earth-born totalitarianisms, fascism, Nazism, communism totally, you find total bondage. If you obey God's kingdom totally, you will find total freedom. This is a profound difference — the universe backs one and blocks the other. This is important, all-important, for if it were otherwise, the kingdom proposal would be a hopeless proposition. But if the kingdom proposal brings freedom now and ultimate triumph then it is the only hopeful proposition. All other proposals are disqualified from the beginning, for you cannot buck the universe and get away with it. The dust heaps of the centuries are witness to that.

As a passing reference of how the Church through the centuries has lost the kingdom of God, the New English Bible puts in alternate readings of "Thy kingdom come." One manuscript puts it, "Thy Holy Spirit come upon us and cleanse us." Another: "Thy will be done on earth as in heaven" (Luke 11:2, note).

Since the destiny of individuals, nations, mankind in general, and the whole of creation was involved, Jesus stayed with his disciples for forty days after his resurrection. To talk about what? To have a long, last farewell conversation about everything in general and about nothing in particular? No. He emphasized what he began with — the kingdom of God — and what he continued to emphasize through his ministry, and what he specially emphasized during these last forty days. Jesus talked to them about the kingdom of God. Talked to them in world-determining terms for the whole of the future of life was in these conversations. "Get this straight," he was saying, "for if you get this straight then the whole future of the human race will go right with you; but if you get this wrong, then the whole of the future will go wrong with you." Did they get it straight? No, for the proposal was too big for their small hearts. They were still Jewish in thought and outlook and revealed it in their reply: "Lord, wilt thou at this time restore again the kingdom to Israel?" (Acts 1:6.) His heart must have sunk within him. Here, after three years of intensive teaching and illustrating, he had presented the Kingdom, and for forty days he dotted his i's and crossed his t's, and they responded: "Do we get back our self-government?" The disciples were trying to jam a universal order into a nationalistic mold! They didn't reject the Kingdom, they reduced it! They tried to make the universal into nationalism. The Kingdom was to be the key to the future

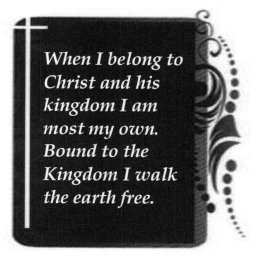

When I belong to Christ and his kingdom I am most my own. Bound to the Kingdom I walk the earth free.

and we, like the Disciples, have not rejected the Kingdom. We have reduced it. We have made it innocuous by reducing it to ecclesiasticism (the Church is the Kingdom); denominationalism (a particular denomination is the Kingdom); the nation is the Kingdom; the particular type of experience is the Kingdom; and so on. The constricting hand of littleness has been at the throat of the Kingdom, so when it spoke it was a squeak instead of a world-shaking call to acceptance and action. That constricting hand must be taken away. It is being taken away, for necessity demands it. We are perishing for just such a clear-cut voice that will command us and free us and unite us — and save us. We need that clear voice of the Kingdom.

We see the progressive loss of the Kingdom message in the wording of the historic creeds, which were written in the second and third centuries. The Apostles' Creed and the Athanasian Creed do not mention the kingdom of God. The Nicene Creed mentions it once, beyond the borders of this life — "His kingdom shall have no end." This kingdom was spoken of as something beyond the general resurrection, as a heavenly kingdom. The three historic creeds, summing up Christian thought and doctrine among them, mentions once what Jesus mentioned a hundred times. The greatest loss that has ever come to the Christian movement in its long course in history was this loss of the Kingdom. For the thing that Jesus called the Good News, the Gospel, has been lost. Not silenced, but lost as the directive of the movement. The Christian movement went riding off in all directions without goal and without power to move on to that goal. The substitutes became the goal. The Church became the Kingdom, the Church with all its manufactured claims to infallibility. The reaction to this claim of infallibility was that the Kingdom was made to retreat within and the Christian experience became the refuge, the citadel to hold against the world. A crippled Christianity went across the Western World, leaving a crippled result. A vacuum was created in the soul of

> *The greatest loss that has ever come to the Christian movement in its long course in history was this loss of the Kingdom.*

Christendom. The kingdom of God became an individual experience now and a collective experience in heaven. Between that individual experience now and the collective experience hereafter in heaven vast areas of life were left out, unredeemed: the economic, the social, and the political. Into that vacuum the earth-born totalitarianisms moved and said to us: "We will give you your inner experience now and your collective experience hereafter in heaven, but we will take over the rest—the economic, the social, and the political— and we will direct them to our ends with our means."

We were shocked, badly shocked, for an alien philosophy of life had moved into the soul of

Christendom. We are still in a state of shock. It may be that God is applying shock treatment to shock us back into the discovery of our own totalitarianism — the Kingdom of God. If that should happen, there would be the greatest spiritual awakening that this planet has ever seen. For the half-answers are all breaking down and will break down progressively. And this includes the half-answer of secularism, the making of mammon the answer, "What do I need of God, I have three million dollars in the bank," said a confident devotee of mammon to Christian Ashram Bible teacher, Estelle Carver. Her reply was: "You had better go and read the parable of the rich fool." He replied: "Isn't that harsh?" Not as harsh as life itself — it says the same thing. "At the heart of every earthly thing there is a sting and that sting is that man is too great to be satisfied entirely with things. "The two things I wanted to do when I retired were to play golf and smoke cigarettes," said a disillusioned man, "and now the doctor says I can't do either one because of my physical condition." Life was empty, meaningless, and valueless. He couldn't put his weight down on life, for it was empty.

Man needs nothing so much as he needs something upon which he can put his whole weight down in time and in eternity, something which will not turn sour or stale through sickness, old age, or death and which will give him something to sing about when there is nothing outwardly to sing about, nothing except the fact of an Unshakable Kingdom and an Unchanging Person.

I found the power of the Unshakable Kingdom and the Unchanging Person in the context of Marxian communism in Russia during a visit in 1934. The setting was important. When Jesus went to Caesarea Philippi he went deliberately to ask his disciples a question, a question that held the destiny of the world in it. And he asked it at this particular place, for in a white grotto in Caesarea Philippi there was a statue of Caesar where Caesar was worshiped as God. With that background, Jesus asked his disciples, "Who do men say that I am?" When he got their answers he became more specific: "Who do you say that I am?" This was a question that compelled them to consider the nature of God, life, and destiny. Is the ultimate power in the universe like Caesar? Does force and might have the last word in human affairs? Is God like Caesar, a cosmic Caesar? Or is God like Christ? And, is the ultimate power in the universe love — self-giving love? Does God rule by a rod of iron or by a cross?

It may be that God is applying shock treatment to shock us back into the discovery of our own totalitarianism — the Kingdom of God.

This question was raised anew in my mind when I saw the communists in Russia building up a civilization without God and doing it enthusiastically. The young people carrying earth out of the subway were chanting: "We are making a new world." I was shaken. I needed reassurance. I was given it. There in Moscow as I went to my Bible the first verse my eyes fell upon was this one: "Let us be grateful for receiving a kingdom that cannot be shaken" (Heb. 12:28 RSV). It seemed so personal, so straight to the point. Did we have a kingdom, the kingdom of God, that cannot be shaken? The answer was clear and unmistakable. Yes, the one Unshakable Kingdom is the kingdom of God. And not only will it not be shaken, it cannot be shaken, for it is ultimate reality. All other kingdoms are shakable. The kingdom of communism is shakable. They have to hold communism together by force. Relax the force and it goes to pieces.

The kingdom of capitalism is shakable. President Eisenhower had a heart attack and the stock market lost four billion dollars in an instant. The stock market goes up and down daily with the events of the day, it is shakable. The kingdom of personal health is shakable. The doctor gives you a checkup, shakes his head and says: "You've got cancer." Shakable. Everything is shakable, except one thing — the Kingdom of God. There is one thing and only one thing that is unshakable and that one thing is the Kingdom of God. To be able to say that and to be able to say it in a world of relativisms and to say it without fear of contradiction from any source, scientific, religious or philosophical is important — all-important.

A Hindu chairman at the close of one of my addresses said, "If what the speaker has just said isn't true it doesn't matter, but if it is true then nothing else matters." If what

I have just said about the Kingdom isn't true, it doesn't matter, but if it is true then nothing else matters. Then all science, all knowledge, all achievements, all nations, all persons, and all things must be related to this Unshakable Kingdom in surrender, obedience and alignment or else end in frustration, failure and decay. I have never penned a wilder or a wiser statement than I have just penned. Nor has anybody else. And I can pen it because it is true!

I lived on that verse (Heb. 12:28 RSV) exultantly that day in Moscow and kept saying to myself, this is it! But there was more to follow. The next day I went to my Bible hungry for another message. This verse, a few verses below the previous, was the "another message:" "Jesus Christ, the same yesterday, and today, and forever" (Heb. 13:8). In a world of flux and change is there one unchanging person and is that one unchanging person Jesus Christ? And the answer came back, yes—an unhesitating full-throated, yes. Jesus Christ is not changing. Our views about him may change, all the way from myth to Master, but he himself is not changing—not changing, except unfolding from age to age until the more we see in him the more we see there is to be seen. He is the unfolding miracle of relevancy, "the Pioneer of life." He is always the same and yet forever new; unfolding, but always the same.

Everything is shakable, except one thing—the Kingdom of God.

57

I saw that I had discovered two absolutes: the Unshakable Kingdom, the absolute order, and the Unchanging Person, the absolute Person. There were two absolutes then, but now they have coalesced and have become one. Jesus used interchangeably "for the kingdom of heaven's sake" and "for my name's sake" (e.g., Matt. 19:12, 29). Was Jesus the kingdom of God, embodied? Yes, and this was necessary and all-important. For without the embodiment of the Kingdom in a person we would have read into the term "kingdom of God" our preconceptions of the Kingdom, which would all be wrong or at the very least inadequate. We had to see the Kingdom in operation in a person. It had to be made concrete or it could not be conceived. Jesus is the kingdom of God taking sandals and walking. The Kingdom and the Person belong together, for without the Person illustrating the Kingdom, the kingdom pattern would have taken many directions with all sorts of meanings, as it has done through history when the kingdom and the person were separated.

The rediscovery of Jesus without the rediscovery of the kingdom of God would be a half-discovery—a king without a kingdom, a lone figure unrelated to a larger reality. But a rediscovery of the Kingdom without the rediscovery of the King would also be a half discovery, for it would be a kingdom without a king. But since it is a kingdom of God and a kingdom among men, then only the God-Man could be the illustration of its meaning. Jesus shows us what God is like and also shows us what the Kingdom of God is like in operation. The kingdom of God is Christ-likeness universalized. Was there any better way to introduce the meaning of the Kingdom than to introduce it in a person and was there any better person through whom it could be introduced than Jesus? The ages are silent. For there is no better.

Here then come together two uniquenesses—two absolute uniquenesses: the Unshakable Kingdom and the Absolute (Unchanging) Person. It is a sign of our having lost the kingdom of God as the working force, and the working conception and the working plan of the Christian faith when in all our apologetics for the uniqueness of the Christian faith I cannot remember having seen the kingdom of God set forth as the center of that uniqueness. And yet it is the one outstanding lack in the non-Christian faiths. They all lack, with no exception, any conception or plan comparable to the Christian conception of the kingdom of God. Mahatma Gandhi put forth the conception of Rama Rajya— the kingdom of Rama, a Hindu hero—as his objective in the struggle for independence. But it has faded out, for it lacked content and illustration. And it was entirely Hindu

> *Jesus shows us what God is like and also shows us what the Kingdom of God is like in operation. The kingdom of God is Christ-likeness universalized.*

and nationalistic. This lone and faint attempt to produce something to match the kingdom of God is eloquent of the lack of such a conception and proposal in any non-Christian alternative.

But the Christian faith as an organized system, while it inherited the kingdom of God, cannot lay claim to the Kingdom of God as its exclusive possession. For as Jesus broke the Jewish mold and universalized the kingdom of God so He broke the organized Christian mold and made the kingdom of God open to anyone who would bring forth the fruits thereof.

The Christian Church, while it holds within itself the best life of the Kingdom, is not the Kingdom of God. The Kingdom is absolute, the Church is relative—relative to something beyond itself, the Kingdom. The Kingdom judges and redeems the Church, and the Church is potent to the degree that it obeys the Kingdom and embodies the life and spirit of the Kingdom. The Church is not an end in itself, the Kingdom is the end. Jesus never said, "May thy church come on earth as it is in heaven." He did say, "Thy kingdom come . . ., on earth." He made the Kingdom and his will identical: "Thy kingdom come, Thy will be done, On earth as it is in heaven."

During his last days on earth Jesus relentlessly and decisively tore the mask of outwardness off the face of organized religion: "Besides, all they do is done to catch the notice of men" (Matt. 23:5 Moffatt). This referred to the personnel of the organized religious system. The system itself centering in the temple went down under the withering words: "See, your House is to be left desolate" (Matt. 23:39 Moffatt). Not only left, but left desolate. So the personnel and the place crumbled into a wailing wall— then and now. Jesus' own little flock crumbled under the onslaught of the Crucifixion, one betrayed him, another denied him—"they all forsook him and fled." And yet Jesus and his kingdom stood intact, unshaken. "Art thou a King then?" asked Pilate, the voice of imperial might. And Jesus quietly said: "You have said it." The King and the Kingdom were unshaken and the Resurrection put its stamp of approval on the Unshakable Kingdom and the Unshaken King.

The Christian Church, while it holds within itself the best life of the Kingdom, is not the Kingdom of God. The Kingdom is absolute, the Church is relative—relative to something beyond itself, the Kingdom.

And now two thousand years have gone by, and today we are in the midst of the greatest shaking, ideologically and outwardly, that this planet has ever seen. It means the removal of that which can be shaken—the cosmic sifting hour. What does the cosmic score board say? Weighed and found wanting. It says this about everything except about the "Unshakable Kingdom and the Unchanging Person." They stand unshaken and intact and occupy the field, not by claim and propaganda, but by trial and error. Every alternative to Jesus and his kingdom has broken down, is breaking down, and will break down. The ages and the present say so. Every revolt against Jesus and his kingdom has turned out badly and sadly, in the individual and in the collective. There is a way to live and Jesus and his kingdom are that way. We have missed the way, hence, our present chaos and confusion. What we have refused to take by choice, we must now take by necessity. The alternatives are fast dwindling. They won't work. The nature of reality determines it. And Jesus and the Kingdom represent the nature of reality revealed. Is this a partisan claim? Then listen to this word of a Hindu historian: "My study of history has shown there is a moral pivot in the world and the best life of East and West is more and more revolving around that moral pivot. That moral pivot is the life and teaching of Jesus. There is no one else bidding for the heart of the world. There is no one else on the field." And the facts of life say a deep-throated, "Amen."

So let not our cry be, "Save the Church," but "Seek the Kingdom," seek the Kingdom, first, last, and always, and "all these things will be added unto you," including the Church, redeemed and reoriented and single-pointed toward—the Kingdom. If the Church should perish the Kingdom would remain. But another church would take the place of the present structure, for the Church is a deep necessity as long as men want and need a corporate expression of their religious life. And they do, inherently. But if the Church concentrates its endeavors in saving itself it will lose itself, for it will break a law of the Kingdom: "He that saveth his life shall lose it and he that loseth his life shall find it." The Kingdom has the last word—now and always.

However, before we go further, let me declare my faith in, and appreciation of, the Christian Church. With all its faults it is the greatest serving institution on earth. It has many critics, but no rivals in the work of human redemption. There isn't a spot on earth from the frozen north to the tropical islands of the sea where we haven't gone with schools, hospitals, orphan and leper asylums, churches, everything to lift the soul, the mind, and the body of the human race. But the Church is relative, not absolute. The Kingdom is absolute.

Every alternative to Jesus and his kingdom has broken down, is breaking down, and will break down. The ages and the present say so.

This Unshakable Kingdom and this Unchanging Person belong together. If we present the Person without the Kingdom, then the Person may have individual relationships, but would lack social relationships. Or if we present the Kingdom without the Person then the Kingdom would have social relationships but would lack personal relationships. But if you put them together you have a complete and total relevance and meet man's total need.

Hitherto, we have had the slogan "Jesus is the Answer," but Jesus is not the answer unless we give Jesus' answer — himself *and* the Kingdom.

The wonder of the Unshakable Kingdom and the Unchanging Person is that Jesus did not merely preach this kingdom, He was the illustration of what the Kingdom is. That fixed the character of the Kingdom. He fixed it and yet unfolded it. For just as Jesus is a fixed point, he is an unfolding pattern, "I have yet many things to say to you, but you cannot hear them now. When the Spirit of truth comes, he will guide you into all truth; ... for he will take what is mine and declare it to you" (John 16:13-14 RSV). So the Kingdom and Jesus are fixed and unfolding. The more you see the more you will see what there is to be seen. It is an exciting adventure, a surprise around every corner, never a dull moment, horizons cracking, new horizons looming, every possession an invitation to possess more, every solution gives the key to further solutions. You're on the tiptoe of expectancy, life beckons!

This identification of the order, the Unshakable Kingdom, the kingdom of God and the Unchanging Person, the same yesterday, today, and forever, the Son of God, is unique, and He is unique at the very highest level. Never did the highest order and the highest Person ever come together before. And they came together, not by divine fiat or divine contrivance, but they came together because they belonged together, intrinsically so. We could never have understood the one without the other. Since this was the most important junction ever seen upon our planet with the greatest consequences for the future of the race, it had to be an illustrated junction; it could not be merely verbal. It had to be vital, acted out, lived out, and proclaimed.

This unity of the order and the Person is not something imposed on the account. It is its warp and woof. "But when they came to believe Philip with his good news about the kingdom of God and the name of Jesus Christ, they were baptized" (Acts 8:12 NEB). The order, the kingdom; and the Person, the name of Jesus — both of them are called the Good News. Again the final emphasis of Paul, the chief exponent of the Good News: "He dealt at length with the whole matter; he spoke urgently of the kingdom of God (Moffatt: "from personal

The wonder of the Unshakable Kingdom and the Unchanging Person is that Jesus did not merely preach this kingdom, He was the illustration of what the Kingdom is.

testimony") and sought to convince them about Jesus" (Acts 28:23 NEB). The order, the kingdom of God and the Person, Jesus, were one. Again: "with a welcome for all who came to him, proclaiming the kingdom of God and teaching the facts about the Lord Jesus Christ quite openly and without hindrance" (Acts 28:31 NEB). "Proclaiming the kingdom of God" (the order) and "teaching the facts about the Lord Jesus" (the Person). Thus the Acts of the Apostles closes on that dual note of the order and the Person.

So what was given to Paul in his Roman prison as his message to the world was given to me (no comparison!) in the "larger" prison at Moscow, behind the Iron Curtain. The message had to be in the context of an earth-born totalitarianism for me to get its full significance. The issue was dramatically set — man's organized attempt to place man on the throne for some men (communists) and call it communism, and God's offer of a total redemption for all men through a new order, the kingdom of God, and the absolute order and offered by the Son of man, the absolute person. Through total obedience to communism, man finds total bondage; through total obedience to the kingdom of God, man finds total freedom. The stage was dramatically set — it was a cosmic setting with cosmic consequences for the future life of man on this planet now and beyond!

I pick out Russian communism as dramatizing the conflict between the kingdom of God and the kingdom of man. (There are clearly other examples from history about ill-advised examples of the kingdom of man.) But the facts would widen and deepen the conflict. It is a choice between the kingdom of God on earth and the kingdom of man on earth—wherever you have man at the center instead of God —you find mammon; self-seeking; things-seeking; pride—individual, group, race; hate; lust; lack of love (the list can be enlarged interminably). When you have something other than the kingdom of God as the center, then you are on one side and the kingdom of God is on the other and the choice has to be made. The imperative is this: "Seek first the kingdom of God and all these things (including yourself) will be added unto you." Seek first something other than the kingdom of God and everything else, including yourself, will be subtracted from you.

An individual gospel without a social gospel is a soul without a body and a social gospel without an individual gospel is a body without a soul.

I came out of Russia with a suppressed excitement within me. I had a gospel, the gospel of the Unshakable Kingdom and the Unchanging Person. I had a gospel for the total man, individual and collective. I was no longer interested in an individual gospel or a social gospel. An individual gospel without a social gospel is a soul without a body and a social gospel without an individual gospel is a body without a soul. One is a ghost and the other a corpse. You can take your choice. I didn't want either one. I wanted both. I had it in a living blend: A Gospel that lays its hand upon the individual and says: "Repent, be converted, obey, live in the new order, the Kingdom." That gospel also lays its hand upon the collective will, the social, and says, "Repent, be converted, obey, live in the new order, the Kingdom." This was a total answer to man's total need, a head-on answer, and one gospel for all men and for the total man and his total environment. This gospel is relevant in every situation for all men, everywhere, at any time, in any and every condition. And it was no modern imposition on the Gospel, it was the revelation of the basic nature of the gospel I had always believed in. It was not reversing anything, but regenerating everything.

I was to become a disciple *of* the Kingdom of God — and a disciple *to* the Kingdom of God — what a name and what an affiliation! A disciple to the ultimate order, the Unshakable Kingdom; this is radicalism par excellence, a radicalism that makes the man-made radicalisms look inconsequential and anemic and irrelevant. No wonder the account says: "Every scribe who has been trained for the kingdom of heaven is like a householder who brings out of his treasures what is new and what is old" (Matt. 13:52 RSV). A scribe, a dry as dust copyist, begins to bring forth the new. He becomes creative for he is dealing with the revealed drama of creation, the unfolding of the Kingdom of God, the revealing of the very purpose, goal, and intention of the creation. That is exciting! It reveals an intention in every happening, for in every happening it says, "The Kingdom is coming, and the Kingdom is!"

But this ultimate order is also conservative, for the scribe who is a disciple to the Kingdom also brings it forth from his treasures of things old. This is conservatism, par excellence, for it brings everything packed into the old into completion in the new. "Gather up the fragments that remain that nothing be lost" was said of fragments of bread, but here is a gathering up of the fragments of truth found everywhere and completing and fulfilling them in the truth.

We need both the new (the radical) and the old (the conservative). If we were all conservative, we would dry up; if we were all radical, we would bust up. Between the pull back of the conservative and the pull ahead of the radical we make progress in a middle direction. A French philosopher said, "No man is strong unless he bears within his character antitheses strongly marked." So the severely radical man is weak and the man who is severely conservative is also weak; the man who is conservatively radical and who is radically conservative is strong. But note the new was first, things new and old. The Christian faith leans toward the new, for it stands for the great change—the Kingdom. This points to the Kingdom of God man as the man of the future.

I have mentioned a Hindu who said to me, "Jesus has gotten into your blood, hasn't he?" "Yes," I said, "and he has raised my temperature." Since then I can add, "Jesus and his kingdom have gotten into my blood and he and the kingdom have raised my temperature, my emotions, and also my thinking, my outlook, my confidence, my allegiance, my everything."

A very modern young man hearing me in a sophisticated drawing-room meeting turned to his host and said, "That old cat knows where it is at." His comment was no credit to me. I had been sniffing around the world for half a century, sniffing for reality, and when I got a whiff of this, I pounced on it. This was it—I did know where it was "at."

So the Unshakable Kingdom and the Unchanging Person have me with the consent of all my being. All my question marks have been straightened out into exclamation points.

But there is a fly in the ointment. Will this Unshakable Kingdom work in a world like this one? Isn't it an idealism, which breaks its delicate wings on the hard facts of life? Is the Unshakable Kingdom idealism and not realism?

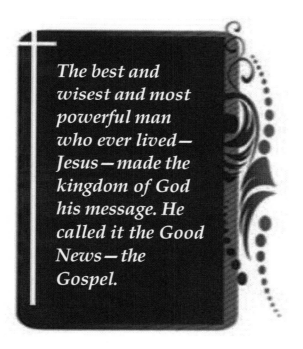

The best and wisest and most powerful man who ever lived — Jesus — made the kingdom of God his message. He called it the Good News — the Gospel.

I went to my Bible to see whether as a Christian I was an idealist or a realist and came out at the end of two years of investigation convinced that if I am to be a Christian, I have to be a realist, for Christianity in its essential nature is realism.

II

DO THE UNSHAKABLE KINGDOM AND THE UNCHANGING PERSON REPRESENT IDEALISM OR REALISM?

THE REDISCOVERY of the Unshakable Kingdom and the Unchanging Person came to me in Russia. No more hard-faced and relentless confrontation could have been found. I am glad I discovered it there and not in a cloistered theological seminary. Strangely enough the question raised in the title of this section was raised in Russia and the quest for the answer began in Russia. The circumstances were these: I was on a train and in a compartment with an intelligent Russian actress. She asked me straight off, "I suppose you are a religious man?" And when I answered, "Yes, I suppose I am," she replied, "You're religious because you are weak. You want God to hold your hand to give you comfort." And she took my hand to show me what she meant! I replied, "My sister, I believe you are totally wrong. I don't want religion as comfort, but as adequacy, adequacy to stand anything that can happen, adequacy because my faith can stand not only anything that can happen, but supports my 'using" whatever happens to me for the good. I don't want God to hold my hand, but I want him to strengthen my arm that I might reach out a helping hand to others." Seeing that she was on the wrong track, she asked, "I suppose you are an idealist?" More hesitatingly, I replied, "Yes, I suppose I am." With an air of finality she waved her hand and said, "*Au revoir*, goodbye, I'm a realist." Communism was realism and Christianity was idealism! This was my second great shock in Russia. And it shocked me forward. I went to my Bible to see whether as a Christian I was an idealist or a realist and came out at the end of two years of investigation convinced that if I am to be a Christian, I have to be a realist, for Christianity in its essential nature is realism. If I were to pick out the most important verse in Scripture, to me, I would pick out this one: "And the Word became flesh" (John 1:14 RSV). In all other religions, it is the word become word, a philosophy or a moralism. Once, and only once, the Word became flesh, the ideal became real. Everything, which Jesus taught, he embodied. You cannot tell where his words ended and his deeds began, for his words were deeds and his deeds were words and, together with what he was the Word became flesh.

When he finished the Sermon on the Mount — which many people think is impossible idealism — the multitudes were astonished at his teaching for "He taught them as one having authority, and not as the scribes" (Matt. 7:29).

The Scribes quoted authorities, the authority of the past. Jesus, however, spoke with authority, the authority of the past, present, and future, the authority of reality. The Greek word for "authority" is *exousia* — "out of the nature of things." The sum total of reality was behind Him. Jesus was not a moralist, imposing a moral code upon men, a code for which humanity is badly made. He was a revealer of reality. He seldom used the imperative, almost never the subjunctive, almost entirely the indicative. He kept saying "This *is*, and you must come to terms with it."

I don't want God to hold my hand, but I want him to strengthen my arm that I might reach out a helping hand to others.

With that key in my hand, I emerged from my two-year scriptural quest convinced that if I were to be a Christian I had to be a realist, for the life and teaching of Jesus was stark realism. During that time I got hold of certain passages of Scripture, or rather they got hold of me. They were passages such as these, which opened my eyes wide: "The Word, then, was with God at the beginning, and through him all things came to be; no single thing was created without him. All that came to be was alive with his life, and that life was the light of men" (John 1:3, 4 NEB). Two things jumped out at me: (1) "Through him all things came to be" — the touch of Christ was upon all creation. All things were created by him and for him. (2) That fact was the light of men — the fact that gave men the key to life and creation — all things were made by and for Jesus Christ and that fact is the light of men, the master light of all their seeing. Get that fact and you have the key; miss that fact, you stumble in the dark as to what life is all about. Another verse was: "He was in the world; but the world, though it owed its being to him, did not recognize him" (John 1:10 NEB). "The world owed its being to him" — the world and everything in it is structured by him and for him, destined by its very make-up to be his. Here is yet another verse: "But in this final age he has spoken to us by a Son whom he hath made heir to the whole universe, and through whom he created all orders of existence" (Heb. 1:2 NEB). Here man and nature were created by Christ and for Christ. And now the most comprehensive verse: "He is the image of the invisible God; ... In him everything in heaven and on earth was created, not only things visible but also the invisible...: the whole universe has been created through him and for him" (Col. 1:15, 16 NEB). Not only created through him but for him — everything is destined to work in his way.

Three writers, all important and prominent — John, Paul, and the author of Hebrews — all say with varying terminology that man and nature and the whole universe were made by Christ and for Christ, that a destiny is therefore, written into the structure of new things, and that structure and that destiny is a Christian destiny.

Whom he did "predestinate to be conformed to the image of his Son" (Rom. 8:29). We are destined by our makeup to be made into his image. When we work in his way we work well; when we work in some other way we work our own ruin.

Could anything more important and more consequential be said about human nature and human destiny? If so, I do not know of it, nor have I heard of it. It sounds too good to be true, but it is too good not to be true. But if it is true, do facts and experiences of life justify these words and back them? The facts of life say yes. (But some theology stands in the way: "human nature is against it.") But theology—all Christian theology—says that God made man in his own image. We are naturally made by God and for God. "So God formed man in his own likeness, in the likeness of God he formed him, male and female he formed both" (Gen. 1:27 Moffatt). Man's freedom has spoiled that image, corrupted it. But it is not natural. If it were natural, why should it corrupt him, and spoil him? The fact is that sin does corrupt man and does

> *We are destined by our makeup to be made into his image. When we work in his way we work well; when we work in some other way we work our own ruin.*

spoil him. That fact proves that sin is not natural. If it were natural, it should fulfill and make man complete. Carlyle says, "Sin is, has been, and ever shall be the parent of misery." Sin is a foreign body in the body of humanity. The word "evil" is the word "live" spelled backward. So the idea that you can have a good time in sin and evil is pure illusion. It will keep the word of promise to your ear and break it to your hope. In the book of Revelation it says: "I took the little scroll . . . and ate it, and in my mouth it did taste sweet as honey; but when I swallowed it my stomach turned sour" (Rev. 10:10 NEB). That is the history of sin—in the mouth it tastes sweet as honey, "I'm free, I can do as I like." But when you try to digest it, assimilate it into life, then human nature rejects it. Human nature is allergic to sin and evil. You do as you like and then you don't like what you do; you have your way and then you don't like your way. You express yourself, and you don't like the self you express. All going away from Christ and his Kingdom has the feeling of estrangement upon it. All coming back to Christ and his kingdom has the feel of a homecoming upon it.

There are several passages, which seem to say the opposite— that sin is natural: "But the natural man receiveth not the things of the Spirit of God" (I Cor. 2:14). However, Moffatt and other translators put it this way: "The unspiritual man rejects these truths of the Spirit of God," and the Greek bears it out— it is *pneuma*— "unspiritual," not "unnatural." Another passage is quoted: "Jesus, however, would not trust himself to them; he knew all men, and required no evidence from anyone about human nature; well did he know what was in human nature" (John 2:24, 25 Moffatt). But this passage is neutral. We do not deny that sin is in human nature. It is there, and deeply so, it has corrupted man, and deeply so. But we do deny that it is natural. If it were natural, why should it corrupt him? If it were natural, man should blossom and bloom and be fulfilled in sin. Is he? Quite the opposite is true. A man inevitably goes to pieces under sin. "If that man is not a bad man, then God writes an illegible hand," said one man of another. "As ugly as sin," is an adage, coined from observation.

All going away from Christ and his Kingdom has the feeling of estrangement upon it. All coming back to Christ and his kingdom has the feel of a homecoming upon it.

A young man who had halfheartedly tried the Christian way determined that he would try the un-Christian way, as an experiment. He did everything in the book that was un-Christian. At the end of a year he said in disgust to a friend, "Help me to get back home." The Christian way was home, the way of sin was alienation, rebellion against himself. If you won't live

79

with God, you can't live with yourself. For when God goes, goal goes. When goal goes, meaning goes, and when meaning goes, value goes. This thing called life turns dead on your hands. A friend was sent some poetry, which he had written when he was a Christian, and a colleague asked about it. The person wrote back: "Oh, I'm sorry, but I don't believe in that anymore." Why did he say, "I'm sorry"? Why didn't he exult and say, "Hallelujah, I don't believe that any more"? They all, like the rich young ruler, go away sorrowful. The modern revolt against Christ and his kingdom sings, but it is in a minor key, with evident strain, trying hard to be happy. When I am in his kingdom, I don't try hard to be happy. I just *am* happy. There is more joy to the square inch in being a Christian than there is to the square mile in being a non-Christian. It is pure unalloyed joy with no hangover from it. I won't wake up tomorrow morning with a hangover and say to myself, "Stanley Jones, why were you a Christian last night, what made you do it?" I said that to an audience of two thousand and though it was a Sunday morning service and the listeners didn't do this sort of thing, the audience broke out in applause with loud laughter. Why? It was so absurd— having a hangover from being a Christian! But a hangover is the natural accompaniment of sin. "He who spits against the wind spits in his own face" — an unnatural thing to do.

I went to see the stone put up to the memory of Aaron Burr in a cemetery in Princeton, New Jersey. At first the citizens would not allow any stone to be put up in his memory, but a man stole in one night and put up a stone with just the name carved on it. And yet Aaron Burr had once been within one vote of the presidency of the United States. He died unwept for and unsung and unmentioned —except with execration. Why? A spiritual awakening was on at Princeton University while Burr was a student there. He was moved by it. He went to the president of the university and asked what he should do about it. The president advised him to wait till the emotions died down and then settle it. He never really settled it. He neglected it, and thereby, said no to Christ and his kingdom. Later he said it in decisive words, "If you'll let me alone, Christ, I'll let you alone."

> *For when God goes goal goes, and when goal goes meaning goes, and when meaning goes value goes— and this thing called life turns dead on your hands.*

Sadly in midcareer Burr said, "I'm afraid he has let me alone."

Aaron Burr became his own God, a completely self-centered man. Burr provoked a duel with Alexander Hamilton and killed him. He was so repudiated by his countrymen that he fled to Europe and was a man without a country. Worse, he tried to destroy the country which he could have governed as president had he not rejected Christ and his kingdom. He only succeeded in destroying himself.

So man's nature and man's society is allergic to sin, both in the individual and in society. Life will not work except in God's way, and God's way is Christ's and Christ's way is the kingdom of God. Just as Jesus was called the Way, so the Kingdom is called the Way. "Then Paul entered the synagogue and for three months spoke out fearlessly, arguing and persuading the people about the Reign [i.e. kingdom] of God. But as some grew stubborn and disobedient, decrying the Way in the presence of the multitude, he left them" (Acts 19:8, 9 Moffatt). Here the kingdom of God is called the Way, and Jesus called himself the Way. "Jesus replied, I am the way; I am the truth and I am the life" (John 14:6 NEB). Here, Jesus and the Kingdom are called the Way — Jesus and the Kingdom are the same. He is the Kingdom embodied. Again, Jesus uses "life" and "the kingdom of God" interchangeably: "Better get into life a cripple, . . . better get into God's Realm [i.e. kingdom] with one eye" (Mark 9:45, 47 Moffatt). Jesus said, "I am the life." So both Jesus and the Kingdom were called interchangeably the Way and the life.

If God created the world by and for Jesus Christ, then he created the world for the Kingdom. This throws light, an important light, on the passage: "Come, ... inherit the kingdom prepared for you from the foundation of the world" (Matt. 25:34 NEB). The Kingdom was prepared for man not merely in a point of time, but prepared for man in that by its very nature it fits man. Man and the Kingdom are affinities. When we obey the laws of the Kingdom, we obey the laws of our own beings. So the Kingdom is written not merely in the New Testament and in the message of Jesus, it is written into our blood, our nerves, our tissues, our organs, our relationships— in our whole makeup. We are structured for the Kingdom.

Jesus and the Kingdom are the Way and the life, and therefore, the truth.

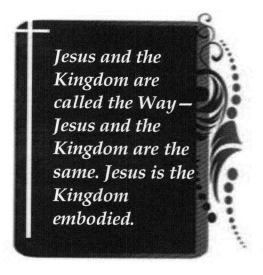

Jesus and the Kingdom are called the Way— Jesus and the Kingdom are the same. Jesus is the Kingdom embodied.

When we say that Jesus and the Kingdom are the Way, we don't merely mean they are the way to get to heaven. They are, but the account does not say so. The Kingdom and Jesus are the Way unqualified, the Way to think, to act, to feel, to be—in every relationship, in the individual and in the collective, for God and man. There are just two things in life—the Way or not the way. If God should do anything against the Way or fail to act according to the Way, he would be wrong and off-center. He wouldn't be God! I said that to a group in the Ashram at Sat Tal in India and a Hindu wrote me a letter afterwards and said: "When you said that I gasped. You said that if God should do anything contrary to anything in Jesus, your guru, then

God would be wrong and no longer God. That is Bhakti (devotion) par excellence." No, not Bhakti, just simple fact. Jesus is the revelation of what God is like, what we may be like, and what the kingdom of God is like. The kingdom of God could not come until Jesus came, so we could see what the Kingdom would be like—Christlikeness universalized.

That answers the question raised by the theologians: "Did Jesus bring the Kingdom, or did the Kingdom bring Jesus?" Jesus brought the Kingdom, for the Kingdom could not come until the character pattern had been set in Jesus. This was true as well of the Holy Spirit, which had not yet been given. "He was speaking of the Spirit which believers in him would receive later; for the Spirit had not yet been given because Jesus had not yet been glorified" (John 7: 39 NEB). The Spirit had not yet been given because the pattern of Jesus-likeness had not yet been set in Jesus. So Jesus had to live and teach and die and rise again and then, and then only, could God give the Spirit. Before then, God could give the Spirit with pinches between thumb and finger, but with the pattern of Jesus fixed, God could give the Spirit with both hands. Before Pentecost it was intimation, now after the pattern was fixed, it was inundation! So before Jesus came we had intimations in the Old Testament of a coming kingdom, but in Jesus the Kingdom was here—in his person. Now God could back the kingdom pattern and program with the sum total of his almightiness, so the Kingdom is God's all-out answer to man's total needs.

We can bet our lives on this answer with no question or fear of being let down. It is the destined way, the natural way to live—the supernaturally natural way to live. His way is our freedom. My way against his way is my bondage. Jesus said, "My meat is to do the will of him that sent me" (John 4:34). His will is my food—it feeds me. My will against his will is my poison. It poisons my health, my usefulness, my present, and my future.

And yet we think the opposite: "Were I to write for him my laws, he would but think them foreigners' saws" (Hos. 8:12 Moffatt). A very able book on the kingdom of God cancels its effectiveness by saying in the ending: "But human nature is against it." God's laws were "foreigners' saws"—foreign sayings, foreign to human nature. Therefore, he concludes that "the Kingdom is an uphill way, all the way." This is false. The non-Christian way is an uphill way all the way, and ends in being unworkable. It is living against the grain of the universe. Nothing could be more false. Tertullian said the soul is naturally Christian. Reinhold Niebuhr says the soul is

> *The kingdom of God could not come until Jesus came, so we could see what the Kingdom would be like— Christlikeness universalized.*

naturally pagan. Dr. Walter Horton says the soul is naturally half-pagan and half-Christian. I vote with Tertullian. Jesus said, "My yoke is easy and my burden is light." Why? Is it because he puts nothing on you? On the contrary, when you follow him, he dumps the world and its troubles into your heart. Then the Christian way is the hard way? No. What is the law of happiness in this world? It seems to be this: The most miserable people in the world are the people who are self-centered, who won't do anything for anybody, except for himself or herself. They are centers of misery, with no exceptions. On the contrary, the happiest people in the world are the people who deliberately take on themselves the sorrows and troubles of others. Their hearts sing with a strange wild joy, automatically and with no exceptions. We are structured for the outgoingness of the love of the Kingdom. It is our native land.

John says: "For to love God is to keep his commands; and they are not burdensome" (I John 5:3 NEB). His commands are not burdensome for what he commands our human nature demands. At the close of the morning session just before the lunch period, I say to the Ashram group: "I am going to give you a command and you tell me whether it is burdensome: Go to lunch." The audience breaks into laughter, for my command is their demand. We are made for each other, the command and the demand, as the eye is made for light, as the heart is made for love, as the aesthetic nature is made for beauty. When we find the Kingdom, we find ourselves.

I was talking to a great surgeon and he said to me, "I've discovered the kingdom of God, discovered it at the end of my scalpel. It's in the tissues." When I asked him to go on, he said, "The right thing morally, the Christian thing, is always the healthy thing physically." "Then," I replied, "morality is not merely written in the Bible — it is written in our blood, our nerves, our tissues, our bones, our organs, our relationships." "Yes," he said, "and therefore, inescapable. You can't jump out of your own skin." I quoted that in a public address and an economist said to me: "The right thing morally, the Christian thing, is always the healthy thing economically." Then I said, "So there is a way to get along with material things and that is the Christian way." The Japanese have found this out. A Japanese banker said to me: "Before the war we had a saying that 'Business is like a folding screen. It won't stand unless it is crooked. 'Make it straight and it will fall.' We acted on that. The consequence was that we had a very bad reputation for our goods — beautiful, but shoddy. Then at the close of the war, we decided to change and adopt the Christian idea of loving your neighbor as yourself and doing unto

the happiest people in the world are the people who deliberately take on themselves the sorrows and troubles of others.

others as you would have them do unto you. We did this nationally, and the government supervised all the goods manufactured in Japan and made them conform to the new pattern. Result? Our reputation went up and now Japanese manufactured goods are "tops" and our economy is humming." There is a way to get along with the material—love your neighbor as you love yourself. This is an ultimate. It will never be improved upon. Again I quoted the surgeon's statement and this time a leading sociologist said, "I'd like to put it this way: The right thing morally, the Christian thing, is always the healthy thing sociologically." There is a healthy way to get along with your neighbor—love your neighbor as you love yourself. You don't have to love your neighbor as you love yourself, but if you don't, you won't be able to get along with your neighbor and you won't be able to get along with yourself. So God has us hooked.

The modern man, drunk with the idea that he is free to do as he likes, says, "I'm free. There is no morality except the morality of doing as I like. I'm free." Then God slowly reels him in. He's hooked. He still says, "I am free," but the line is getting shorter. He's hooked. A banker started kiting checks. Every morning for fifteen years he had to kite checks to cover the kited checks of the day before. When it finally caught up with him and he was being taken to jail he said, "Now, for the first time in fifteen years I'm free." He didn't break the laws of the kingdom— they broke him. The laws of the kingdom are self-executing; the payoff is in the person. He tied himself in knots for fifteen years before the outer law caught up with him. The head of a Dutch college said in the Open Heart session of the Ashram: "I'm the only black sheep here. I'm not a Christian." Later in private conversation I said to him: "You are a marked man, marked for God." He said, "That got me. I knew it was true, I was marked for God." He gave himself to Christ, and when we chose someone to head the Ashram, the group chose him. He went from nothing—to everything.

I sit here in our Florida home after seven months of intensive evangelistic work, preaching the Unshakable Kingdom and the Unchanging Person in India, Europe, the United States, and Canada—preaching to villagers, to drawing rooms full of the affluent society, and to crowds seventy-five thousand strong in Kerala, India. I sit here within a few miles of Cape Kennedy, from where the expeditions went out to land men on the moon and return, a marvelous achievement in obedience to physical law. I am reminded of what Immanuel Kant, the philosopher, said: "Two things strike me with awe, the starry heavens above and the moral law within." The dependableness of the physical laws that govern the outer universe is proved and verified by the trip to the moon and back—they conquered outer space by obedience. This fills me with awe. But the dependableness and amazing sweep of the moral law within strikes me with even greater awe. Wherever men—or women or youth or old age—come in conflict with this Unshakable Kingdom they are broken. Civilization goes to pieces at the seams to the degree that it breaks these moral laws written into the nature of things. There is no exception. I pick up my newspaper and I read of a youth of sixteen sentenced to life imprisonment for murder and rape, and as he was led away after the sentence was pronounced, he muttered, "What a life." Yes, what a life — he will be behind bars for his whole life. Had he not been caught and sentenced, the result would have been the same; he would have been in the hell of a guilty conscience, afraid every moment that he would be caught.

A culprit who has not been found will be in the hell of guilt and fear from the moment the evil deed was committed. The kingdom-of-God law had been broken, and the breaker (of that law) was and is broken. "And whosoever shall fall on this stone shall be broken; but on whomsoever it shall fall, it will grind him to powder" (Matt. 21:44).

Are the self-centered comfortable — do they escape? No, the story is told of a man who received instantly everything he wished for. He wished for a palatial house and it was there. He wished for the latest and most expensive car and it was there. He wished for a liveried chauffeur and he was there. No matter what he wished for, it was immediately there. He grew tired of this and said to his attendant, "I'd rather be in hell than this." The attendant said, "Where do you think you are?" The steady decay of the self-centered is a visible sign of the operation of the law of the Kingdom: "He that saveth his life shall lose it."

So the starry heavens above and the moral law within speak of the dependableness and utter surety of the Unshakable Kingdom. And that kingdom is outside us and within us— "the kingdom of heaven is within you," —therefore when you break its laws written within you, you get broken. On the other hand, when you obey its laws and its principles and its attitudes at any period of your life, and in any circumstances, you can say to yourself, "What a life!" The young man of sixteen said it from the prospect of an entangling hell, and I say it at eighty-seven from the prospect of an ever-opening heaven.

> *The laws of your being are the laws of the kingdom of God— the kingdom of God is within you, in your nerves and tissues, your organs, your relationships.*

The laws of your being are the laws of the kingdom of God—the kingdom of God is within you, in your nerves and tissues, your organs, and your relationships. A man, whose story has often been told by others and me, was shot through the stomach. When the wound healed, an aperture was left so they could look in and watch the process of digestion. When he was in a good humor with everybody and with himself, digestion was normal; the

91

stomach blushed a rosy red, digestive juices poured down the walls of the stomach like sweat down one's face, the stomach would go into churning movements — digestion was normal. But the moment he became angry and bad tempered and ugly spirited, the color of the stomach would change. It would become ashen, the gastric juices would stop and digestion would be at an end. The stomach obviously is made for good will, not for ill will. In other words, you have a Christian stomach. It works well in a Christian way and badly in an un-Christian way. The same can be said of every organ of your body. You have Christian nerves, Christian brain cells, a Christian heart, Christian tissues — Christian everything. They work well in a Christian way and badly in an un-Christian way. No exception! A man was berating another man over the phone. A friend listening in said to him as he laid down the receiver: "You'd better look out or you'll get an ulcer." He replied, "I don't get ulcers, I give them." Perhaps the lining of his stomach was tough, but his personality had suffered — he was an "ulcerous" person.

I read somewhere that if you could upset the secretions of a person's glands, you could change a person's character — a good man would lose all moral sense. This, I said to myself, is serious: Morality must be in the glands, so we had better go out and preach the gospel of good glands! But one day I asked a doctor: "Do states of mind and emotion and action upset the secretion of glands?" "They certainly do," he said decisively. Then I asked: "What kinds of states of mind, emotions, and actions upset the secretion of glands?" He named them off. My eyes opened wide. Everything he named was un-Christian, the whole list. I then asked: "Suppose a person's glands were normal and suppose the person lived in a truly Christian way, would his glands function well?" His reply: "They would function perfectly." I replied, "Then, doctor, we have Christian glands." "I couldn't say anything against it," was his thoughtful reply. Dr. William Sadler, the psychiatrist, put it this way: "If we lived in a truly Christian way, half the diseases of the people of America would drop off tomorrow morning and we would stand up a new healthy people." A psychiatrist went around the world in search of the attitudes toward life, which made for health, came back and came to the conclusion that the Beatitudes contain the list that makes for health. I would amend it by saying, "The laws, principles, and attitudes of the kingdom of God" are the built-in basis of health—obey them and you fulfill yourself as a person and your body will be at its maximum best.

Dr. Adler, a Jewish psychiatrist, put it this way: "I suppose all the ills of human personality can be traced back to one thing—not understanding the meaning of the phrase: 'It is more blessed to give than to receive.'" But, Dr. Adler, who was Jewish, could scarcely be biased in favor of this saying of Christ. How did he come to that conclusion? The answer: The facts. The facts are slowly but surely catching up to the fact—the fact of Jesus and his kingdom.

I once watched a crow teach one of its young to forage for food on its own. The parent crow put a morsel in the young crow's mouth and then flew up on the palm leaf thatched roof and stuck another morsel in between the leaves of the roof in the sight of the young crow and then flew up on the ridge pole to await developments. The young crow flew to the place where the parent crow had hidden the morsel, discovered it and swallowed it on its own. The parent crow flapped its wings in approval. I think God our Father, the Creator, must have done something like that. He hid secrets amid the leaves of creation and as he hid them, he must have said to himself: "I wonder how long it will take men to discover that. I hope they will be morally prepared to handle it wisely." He hid electricity and wondered if men when they discovered it would electrocute themselves or use it to light their way around the earth and to lift men's burden from their backs and put electricity on wires to be transported. When God hid the atom, he must have drawn a long breath and said, "This is one of the most dangerous powers I have entrusted to man. I hope they will have developed in character sufficiently to handle it for the collective good. If not . . . ?"

Then God tucked within the leaves of creation his greatest secret and his most precious gift — the Unshakable Kingdom, the Kingdom of God, and the Unchanging Person, the Son of God. "I must put them together," he must have mused, "so men will know that this kingdom of God on earth means after the pattern of the Son of

God, on earth. It will be his spirit and his method universalized. It will all be so different, reversing all their values in religion and in politics and in commerce that they will all combine to crucify him and his kingdom." I continued the musing: "But Jesus and his kingdom will arise from the dead and slowly permeate the world. Then will come a world crisis for the powers that crucified him will try to set up on earth a replica of the Kingdom on a world scale, but this time the kingdom will be earth-born, with no morality and no God, but with force at its center and domination as its objective. They will be the earthborn totalitarianisms — man in revolt against God and his kingdom. They will fail, for nothing will be behind them except man, and mankind in increasing disillusionment. Then will come the period of the rediscovery of the Kingdom of God, the Unshakable Kingdom, and the rediscovery of the Son of God as its illustration. This rediscovery could not have

God tucked within the leaves of creation his greatest secret and his most precious gift—the Unshakable Kingdom, the Kingdom of God, and the Unchanging Person, the Son of God.

happened except in the flickering light of the totalitarianisms. It will take their rise and failure to let men see the need, the absolute need of God's totalitarianism — something which will command them totally and free them totally. This is so because the Kingdom is written into the nature of man and his environment and is his homeland. The central sickness of man is homesickness. But a powerful ally is arising, an ally of the Kingdom — science is preparing a world climate in which men will reject all substitutes and take only those based on facts, and facts which will work here and now in human relations. And the facts of life are driving men inevitably to the fact of the Unshakable Kingdom and the Unchanging Person."

I know it is absurd to put words like that in the mouth of God, but God is increasingly putting these words into the mouths of human beings. If we sputteringly try to decipher them here and there but miss the real message, nevertheless we are saying what men will more and more say and are saying as the facts unfold.

Someday science is going to put it down on the table and say: "This and this and this is the way to live. And this and this and this is not the way to live." And we are going to look on those two lists and our eyes will open and open wide for we are going to say: "Why, Brother Scientist, the way you say to live is the Christian way. Every item is Christian in its essence and in its object. And the list you give as the way not to live is the un-Christian way, every item is un-Christian." And the scientists will reply, "We don't know anything about that, but this is the way that life works and that way is the way that life does not work."

The two approaches to life, the Christian and the scientific when truly Christian and truly scientific, are coming out to a common conclusion and more and more rendering a verdict on life. That verdict is a Christian verdict—the facts are coming out at the place of Christ.

These 'facts" are the distilled essence of experience—distilled from the entire world. Let me put it in the language of today, the language of a hardboiled newspaperman. I once said to him: "If you don't believe in the Christian way then why don't you go out and try some other way and put it under life and see what life will say. I suggest this: Go out for a week and say the un-Christian thing, think the un-Christian thing, do the un-Christian thing, and be un-Christian in every situation for a week and then come back and tell me what you have found, and how it has worked." "Shucks," he snorted, "You'd be bumped off before the end of a week."

> *And the facts of life are driving men inevitably to the fact of the Unshakable Kingdom and the Unchanging Person.*

I was talking to a politician in India trying to persuade him to give up a relationship he was having with a woman who was not his wife. He had been challenged by the Oxford Group Movement (now the Moral Rearmament Association) with its four absolutes—absolute honesty, absolute purity, absolute unselfishness, and absolute love. He was challenged by these absolutes, but wasn't prepared to build his life upon them. In order to ward off my appeal, he told me of a British general who also was challenged by these absolutes, but he, too, hadn't been prepared to build his life on them, so half seriously and half humorously he said, "I suggest we organize another movement, the Cambridge Group Movement, and let us have four absolutes too, but the opposites— absolute dishonesty, absolute impurity, absolute selfishness, and absolute hate." When the politician waited for me to laugh, I looked him straight in the face and said: "Why not? If you believe in sin, why do you not go out and make it absolute? Why are you so tentative in evil? Why don't you sin with the stops out? Why not go out and organize a society on absolute dishonesty, absolute impurity, absolute selfishness, and absolute hate?" He looked at me in astonishment and said, "Oh no, we couldn't do that—it wouldn't work." "Oh," I replied, "you've given away the case for sin. The only way to keep sin and evil going is to throw enough good around it to keep it going. I challenge you to build a society on absolute dishonesty—nobody would trust anyone else; on absolute impurity—it would rot; on absolute selfishness—no one would think in terms other than himself; on absolute hate—it would be so divisive it wouldn't hold together over night."

Then to what conclusion must I come? This: Every dishonest man is a parasite on the honesty of some man whose honesty holds together the situation long enough for him to be dishonest in it. Every impure man is a parasite on some pure man whose purity holds together the situation long enough for him to be impure in it. Every selfish man is a parasite on some unselfish man whose unselfishness

The only way to keep sin and evil going is to throw enough good around it to keep it going.

holds together the situation long enough for him to be selfish in it. Am I rubbing this in? Yes, but life is rubbing this in harder. Evil is an attempt to live life against itself, and it cannot be done. So evil is not only bad—it's stupid. Evil is trying the impossible, namely, to live life against itself and to get away with it.

There is one other passage in the New Testament that seems to imply that the state of sin is natural: "We were objects of God's anger by nature, like the rest of men" (Eph. 2:3 Moffatt). Man is corrupted by his own sin and the sin of society in which he is born and lives, but it is not natural to human nature. The context says: "You were dead in trespasses and sins" (Eph. 2:1 Moffatt) — trespasses and sins produced death — why should it, if it were natural? Note later Paul says: "For we are God's handiwork, created in Christ Jesus to devote ourselves to the good deeds for which God has designed us" (Eph. 2:10 NEB). God has designed us by our makeup to be in Christ and "to devote ourselves to the good deeds for which God has designed us." So we fulfill the design of our creation when we live in Christ and for Christ. His kingdom is our native land. In it we are supernaturally natural.

A Hindu, after visiting our Ashram at Sat Tal, wrote a letter to the group: "I expected to find Brother Stanley in deep *tapasiya* (bodily and mental and emotional austerities — punishing the body on behalf of the spirit as the Hindu holy men do), but instead I found him a God-intoxicated child of nature." A God-intoxicated child of nature — what a description of one who lives in the Kingdom of God now, not fighting his nature, but dedicating it to the purposes for which God designed it. Not holding up my right arm until it withered away, but reaching out my arm to help my fellow stragglers in a restless and stormy sea. Not killing the mind, as a famous Swami advised his followers so they could meditate on their being God, but dedicating my mind as a disciple to the kingdom of God. So the end was not desecration of nature, but its dedication to kingdom-purposes.

Sadly, man has become naturalized in unnatural sin. But it isn't natural; accustomed, but not natural. A pastor told me that he had ridden his bicycle so long with crooked handlebars that when somebody straightened them he fell off. He was naturalized in the unnatural. A woman who had lived all her life in the dust-laden atmosphere of New York City went into the country in upper New York State. "Why the air was so clean it made me sick." In South America they put in a new sanitary market, but the occupants of the old market wouldn't move to the new: "It's too clean. It reminds us of the hospital." They were naturalized in dirt, but not natural.

we have been told so long and so often that sin is natural that we have become brainwashed with this idea so that we sin to fulfill ourselves.

However, and this is the point and it is an important one, we have been told so long and so often that sin is natural that we have become brainwashed with this idea so that we sin to fulfill ourselves. It is false—the great delusion. Sin is anti-life. The good is pro-life. The good is not only good—it is good for us. A youth was being sentenced to jail for participating in a break-in. The judge noted the tattoo on the youth's arm: "Born to raise hell." We have unwittingly tattooed that message on the mind of this freedom-obsessed age, and since we are born to it, we've got to do it! Instead, we have got to tattoo on the mind of this age: "Born to the kingdom of God." For if we are not reborn to the Kingdom, it was better that we had not been born at all.

So I came out of Russia with three life convictions indelibly impressed on me — tattooed on my mind and heart, if you will — namely; the Unshakable Kingdom, the absolute order; and the Unchanging Person, the absolute person; and both of them are realism — the ultimate realism."

If the Church will make these three things the center of its message and endeavor, then the Church will be relevant anywhere and everywhere, on all matters great and small. It will be relevant — the only relevancy.

Then passages like these will no longer sound like nostalgic dreams: "Go forth therefore and make all nations my disciples" (Matt. 28:19 NEB). Note, "my disciples" — who else? No one else is on the field. And for what? To learn from Jesus the Unshakable Kingdom. What else is on the field? It is this or chaos.

Here is another passage: "So pray the Lord of the harvest to send laborers to gather his harvest" (Matt. 9:38 Moffatt). Note, "his harvest." Is the future his future? And is the future gathering up of the fruits of human living, his harvest? Does it all come out at his feet for disposal and distribution? If so, then this is big business, nations becoming his disciples and the future of the world coming out at his feet for disposal — this, I repeat, is big business, the biggest business. But nothing less than this is in the cards, if Jesus Christ represents the Unshakable Kingdom, the one Unshakable Kingdom and if he is the Unchanging Person, the one Unchanging Person.

We turn now to ask whether this Unshakable Kingdom can be shaken. Will this Unchanging Person be changed by a future that promises to be choosy — scientifically so? We are entering the period of the removal of all that can be shaken, and then all that cannot be shaken will remain. Are we dealing with ultimates here — with reality, or are we dealing with the passing or the trivial? The future of the world is in the balance.

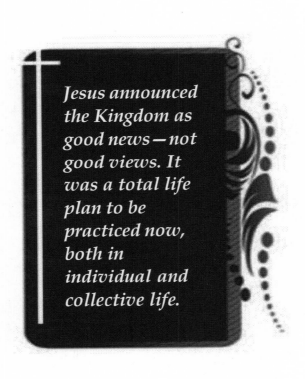

Jesus announced the Kingdom as good news — not good views. It was a total life plan to be practiced now, both in individual and collective life.

III

A STUDENT OF THE KINGDOM OR A DISCIPLE TO THE KINGDOM — IS THE KINGDOM OF GOD SOMETHING TO BE STUDIED OR TO BE FOLLOWED?

JESUS ANNOUNCED the Kingdom as good news — not good views. It was a total life plan to be practiced now, both in the individual and collective life. We saw that the kingdom of God was used interchangeably with life — enter into life now, and enter the Kingdom now. If the Kingdom is life, then it is something to be lived, lived now, not merely in the hereafter. We also saw the Kingdom was used synonymously with the Way — then the Kingdom is something to be followed, not a road map to be studied with no journeys taken. "If any man will do his will, he shall know of the doctrine" (John 7:17). We know as much as we are willing to practice — and no more. Your creed is your deed. Your creed is not something you point to in a book or something you repeat on Sunday morning as a part of a ritual. It is a road map, which you follow — or you get lost.

A South African pastor went with me from city to city in his country and then commented: "You preach a troublesome gospel. We preach a kingdom in heaven hereafter that upsets nothing now. But you preach a kingdom now on earth and that upsets everything." I laughed, for the Kingdom upsets everything that doesn't conform to the Kingdom now and it upsets the world to set it up on another level, the level of life from the level of anti-life, from the unworkable to the workable. I asked a Japanese driver what his greatest headaches were. He replied, "Two things: traffic lights and traffic policemen. Get rid of them and we would be free." Free — to be in a citywide and nationwide traffic jam in ten minutes. The Kingdom does have its restrictions, but they are all restrictions that lead to release, release to freedom. The freest people on this planet are the people who follow the Kingdom and its restrictions in order to follow life and its releases. The Kingdom says stop in order to say go when it is clear.

Before we take up the nature and scope and open possibilities of the Kingdom, we must look at the position of the kingdom of God in relation to the total Christian belief and movement. What place does the Kingdom occupy? Luke, after writing his gospel (which has been called the most beautiful account ever written), starts to write the Acts of the Apostles where everything that Jesus expounded and exposed in him was to be transferred into the lives of his followers. They were but pauses on the threshold of that account to sum up the meaning of what Jesus taught and brought in the Gospel. It is the Gospel of Luke condensed under seven headings into five verses: "In the first part of my work, Theophilus, I wrote of all that Jesus did and taught from the beginning until the day when, after giving instructions through the Holy Spirit to the apostles whom he had chosen, he was taken up to heaven. He showed himself to these men after his death, and gave ample proof that he was alive: over a period of forty days he appeared to them and taught them about the kingdom of God. While he was in their company he told them not to leave Jerusalem. 'You must wait,' he said, 'for the promise made by my Father, about which you have heard me speak: John, as you know, was baptized with water, but you will be baptized with the Holy Spirit, and within the next few days'" (Acts 1:15 NEB).

The freest people on this planet are the people who follow the Kingdom and its restrictions in order to follow life and its releases.

First: *The Word became flesh*—Jesus began to do and teach. The Gospel begins with Jesus, the Incarnate. You cannot say "God" until you have first said "Jesus," for

Jesus puts character content into God — His own character content. You cannot say "Christ," "the kingdom of God," "the Holy Spirit" until you have first said "Jesus," for Jesus puts his own character content in all of each of these. The Gospel lies in his person — he did not merely bring the Good News — he was the Good News.

Second: *The Word became deed* — Jesus did and taught. The Word was a deed before it was an exposition. Therefore, it was not a philosophy or a moralism — it was a fact, a deed, vital not verbal. But his words were an expounding of what he was doing. So his deeds became words, and his words became deeds and, coming together with what he was, the Word become flesh.

Third: *The Word became atonement* — Jesus, after his death, became atonement. When this Word came in contact with the sin of man it crimsoned into sacrifice. Jesus gave himself for our sins. The outer cross lighted up the nature of God as self-giving love.

Fourth: *The Word became victorious* — *Jesus . . . "showed himself to these men . . . and gave ample proof that he was alive."* Death could not hold him. The keepers were like "dead men."

Fifth: *The Word became ultimate and final authority and pattern for the new world* — *Jesus "over a period of forty days . . . taught them about the kingdom of God"* — The Kingdom became the Unshakable Kingdom and Jesus the Unchanging Person, the absolute order and the absolute Person.

Sixth: *The Word became the center of final power —* *Jesus was taken up — taken up to the right hand of God —* So the earliest Christian creed was: "Jesus is Lord."

Seventh: *The Word became inner adequacy —* Jesus told them not to leave Jerusalem. *"You must wait for the promise made by my Father . . . you will be baptized with the Holy Spirit"* — for this world revolution by the coming of the Holy Spirit within them. The Holy Spirit was the applied edge of redemption.

These seven things constitute the seven pillars upon which the Christian structure rests, each of them necessary and essential. Jesus made the sixth the center of his message. It was his first emphasis — "From that day Jesus began to proclaim the message: 'Repent, for the kingdom of Heaven is upon you.' ... He went round the whole of Galilee . . . preaching the gospel of the Kingdom" (Matt. 4:17, 23, NEB). Between that beginning and the last forty days with his disciples he made the gospel of the kingdom the framework and the center of all he said and did. Everything revolved around that center — He was the embodiment and illustration of that kingdom.

> *You cannot say God until you have first said Jesus for Jesus puts character content into God — His own character content.*

109

We lost the gospel of the kingdom in three ways: (1) By making the Kingdom and the Church the same. In Protestantism we sang:

> I love thy kingdom, Lord,
> The house of thine abode,
> The Church our blest Redeemer saved
> With his own precious blood.

"I love thy Kingdom, Lord . . . the Church."

(2) The Roman Catholic Church made the Kingdom synonymous with the Church and therefore had to make the Church infallible. That infallibility is falling to pieces — from within. In both instances, Protestant and Roman Catholic, the attitude of humanity was this: If the Church and the kingdom of God are the same, then the kingdom of God doesn't matter much, for the Church doesn't matter much; it is irrelevant. But suppose the Church takes its true position and points to the Kingdom and its total relevancy, then the Church becomes relevant in the Kingdom's relevancy. It stands for the big — the ultimate, and then it becomes big and ultimate because of what it stands for. It loses its life and finds it again in kingdom-greatness. The attitude of the world then changes: If that's what you stand for, then we stand for you.

(3) We lost that kingdom in binding it up with the *Parousia* — the return of Christ. We can do nothing about the Kingdom until Jesus returns, nothing corporately. We can redeem individuals now, but the Kingdom won't

come until the King comes. Now there are two sets of passages that tell of how the Kingdom of God is to come. One set tells that the Kingdom will come as a gradualism: "first the blade, then the ear, then the full grain in the ear"; the kingdom is also likened to a grain of mustard seed which, though beginning tiny, becomes a tree (Mark 4:28, 31 RSV). The Kingdom of Heaven is like leaven which, hid in the dough, leavens the whole lump (Matt. 13:33). These and other passages teach the coming of the Kingdom by gradualism — person-to-person, clime-to-clime, and nation-to-nation. On the other hand, there are passages such as the parable of the nobleman who went abroad to receive a kingdom and return, depicting Jesus going to the Father to receive a kingdom and return. This refers to the apocalyptic or sudden coming of the Kingdom when Jesus returns to set it up. Some people take the gradualist set of passages; others, the apocalyptic, the sudden. I can't do that, for both sets seem integral and related parts of the account. So I take both — the gradualist set gives me my task. I can be the agent of the coming of that kingdom now. The apocalyptic gives me my hope — my hope that the last word will be spoken by God and that last word will be victory. However, I have no timetable, nor map of the future. And Jesus said, "It is not for you to know the times and seasons, which the Father hath put in his own power" (Acts 1:7). "No one knows, . . . not even the Son; only the Father" (Mark 13:32). This interpretation of the Kingdom as in the future, when Christ returns, makes the Kingdom innocuous now. We

111

can do nothing about it until Jesus comes. Then we don't do anything, he does it all. This ignores the fact that Jesus after his resurrection talked to his disciples for forty days about the kingdom of God, or as the New English Bible puts it, "taught them about the kingdom of God" (Acts 1:3). Evidently, it was not a future kingdom with future implications, but a kingdom now, with now-implications. This we repeat for emphasis. Philip and Paul both preach "the kingdom and the name of Jesus" as issues now. "But when they came to believe Philip with his good news about the kingdom of God and the name of Jesus Christ, they were baptized, men and women alike" (Acts 8:12 NEB). The kingdom of God was an issue now and when they believe the good news, they were baptized. Paul said: "I have gone about among you proclaiming the Kingdom" (Acts 20:25 NEB). It was a proclaiming of the Kingdom for a decision now. Then "he spoke urgently of the kingdom of God and sought to convince them about Jesus" (Acts 28:23 NEB). Paul was preaching urgently and for a verdict concerning the Kingdom now. The decisive word is this: "From morning to evening he explained the Reign of God to them from personal testimony" (Acts 28:23 Moffatt). Note the Kingdom was preached to them from personal testimony—then the Kingdom was not a hope, bound up with Jesus' *Parousia*, his Second Coming, but it was something to be experienced now, and therefore, an issue now.

So the gospel of the Kingdom of God is an issue, the vital issue now, as a head-on and total answer to man's total need now. And never have we needed to preach the Unshakable Kingdom of God as now, for never were the pillars of civilization so shaken as now. We need as never before some total answer to man's total need, for civilization is going to pieces for the need of a total answer. Out of sheer necessity, we must turn to it. "The gospel of the Kingdom is coming back — coming back out of sheer necessity," said a leading churchman. If we hold our peace, the stones, the hard bare facts of life, will cry out for the Kingdom. The Kingdom of Heaven is within you — in the very laws of your being; but it is among you — in the relationships, which we have with others; it is at

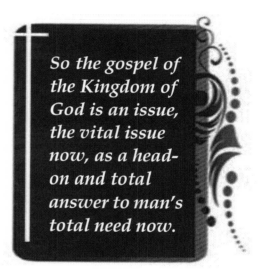

So the gospel of the Kingdom of God is an issue, the vital issue now, as a head-on and total answer to man's total need now.

your doors — ready to break into you and your relationships and remake you. So it is all three — within you, among you, and at your doors. It is present. "But if it is by the finger of God that I drive out the devils, then be sure that the kingdom of God has already come upon you" (Luke 11:20 NEB).

Jesus didn't define the Kingdom in precise terms, perhaps because he was its definition. We may define the Kingdom since he has shown us what it is — shown us in

113

his own person, as: The Kingdom of God is God's total order, expressed as realm and reign, in the individual and in society; and which is to replace the present unworkable world order with God's order in the individual and in society; and while the nature of the Kingdom is social, the entrance into it is by a personal new birth now; the character of that kingdom is seen in the character of Jesus — the Kingdom is Christlikeness universalized; while it comes on earth in the time process it is eternal and is the same rule which is in heaven and because it is Christlikeness that makes it heaven — there and here; and while it is a total order demanding a total obedience, it brings total freedom. The Kingdom will be consummated when Jesus returns; he came once and he will come again; but of that consummation I have no timetable. Jesus said nobody knows, only the Father.

Jesus did not gradually come to the point, by an oblique approach, but came straight to the point without preliminaries: "'The people that lived in darkness saw a great light, light dawned on the dwellers in the land of death's dark shadow.' From that day Jesus began to proclaim the message: 'Repent, for the kingdom of Heaven is upon you'" (Matt. 4:16, 17 NEB). It was a straightforward, head-on answer to the people who lived in darkness, to the "dwellers in the land of death's dark shadow" — a great light dawned — that great light was the kingdom of God. So I, too, will not be round about, but come straight to the point and will make my first kingdom unfolding this:

1. THE DIVINE CONFRONTATION

"Seek first his kingdom and his righteousness, and all these things shall be yours as well" (Matt. 6:33 RSV). All these things will be added—all your needs will be met, if you make the kingdom of God your supreme loyalty. Not only will your needs be met, but when you belong to the kingdom of God you have the significance of that kingdom. I was being introduced to a large public meeting by an African-American minister and he introduced me in these words: "I will introduce the speaker by quoting from one of his books in which he said, 'The significance of Mahatma Gandhi is not in the man, but in the cause with which he is identified, the cause of India's freedom. He is so identified with that cause that when he speaks, the cause of India's freedom speaks through him.' The significance of the speaker tonight is not in the speaker as a person, but in the cause with which he is identified— the kingdom of God. When he speaks, the cause of the Kingdom of God speaks through him—he has that significance." I gasped—is that true? I felt like going to my knees instead to the platform to speak. It is true and it can be true for every one of us through no credit of our own, but through grace.

But suppose you do not seek first the Kingdom of God, but make yourself God, seeking first the kingdom of self. Then all these things will be subtracted from you, for even if you get them, they soon end by owning you instead of your owning them. Things get in the saddle and ride you

115

to your ruin. A spectacular case arose recently in Ghana, Africa. Kwame Nkrumah was well educated and had the chance of bringing the Kingdom of God into developing Ghana. Instead, he brought himself. He tried to be a messiah of a new political order centered on himself. The people arose and banished him, tore down the monument to him and its inscription which, substituted him in place of the kingdom of God. This was dramatic. Usually such a story ends not in drama, but in decay. Three things contributed to Nkrumah's downfall — he, in trying to be God, only succeeded in being a poor man, inwardly decayed; second, the people felt the incongruity of a man trying to be God — their moral nature revolted; and third, the nature of the universe — the Kingdom, written into things and men, revolted, for it knew only its Master's voice. So Nkrumah under these blows went down — and was out.

But, and this is the point and a real one, every attempt by the individual and by society to seek for (and to substitute anything in the place of) the kingdom of God will end in dramatically swift or slow corrosive failure. It runs against the imponderables. Seek first the kingdom of God and all these things will be added to you. Seek something else first and all that you need will be subtracted. Your biggest need is cosmic backing, and when that is lacking, the house of man's-soul is empty — empty of meaning, purpose, goal... It is — empty.

2. THE OFFER OF HIS ALL FOR OUR ALL

The Kingdom is an absolute; we receive it or we get hurt. Science has learned that secret, hence, its achievements. Huxley once wrote to Kingsley: "Science seems to me to teach in the most unmistakable terms the Christian conception of surrender to the will of God. Science says 'Sit down before the facts as a little child, be prepared to give up every preconceived notion, be willing to follow to whatever end science will lead you or you will learn nothing.'" To the degree that science is humble and receptive — knows that it is poor — and poor enough to receive, to that degree the kingdom of facts is theirs.

So when we come to the greatest facts ever revealed to man — the Unshakable Kingdom and the Unchanging Person —, how do we get into the realm of supreme facts? We do it the same way science does. We surrender — surrender of the inmost self to the Divine Self, our all for his all. Then the Kingdom belongs to you. Let me repeat it again for it sounds too good to be true: "How blest are they who know they are poor; the kingdom of heaven is theirs." If it had said: "Then you belong to the kingdom of Heaven" — that would have been wonderful, but this is so wonderful that it is incredible, the kingdom of Heaven belongs to you! All its unshakableness, all its forgiveness, all its at-homeness, all its freedom, all its joy, all its everything — belongs to you. That can't just be classified under good views — that is the Good News — not a philosophy, but a fact — verifiable fact; not then — now!

117

3. THE KINGDOM—A DEMAND OR AN OFFER?

"Never . . . a . . . greater than John the Baptist, and yet the least in the kingdom of Heaven is greater than he" (Matt. 11:11 NEB). Why? A theological professor in England was teaching his class when he asked this question: "Young men, is the gospel you preach a demand or an offer?" With one accord they replied: "A demand." "Think again." "Well, a demand and an offer." "Think again." They came to the conclusion that if it were the Gospel it was an offer. And the offer turns out to be nothing less than the Unshakable Kingdom and the Unchanging Person.

This, then, gives us the clue as to why the least in the kingdom of God is greater than the greatest in the Kingdom of man. In the pre-kingdom period, John the Baptist represented the gospel of a demand— don't do this and do that. It was the whipping-up of the will. The kingdom of God is the gospel of an offer; not the whipping up of the will, but the surrendering of the will, the coinciding of the will of God with our surrendered will. Then we are free —free to accept the Kingdom and thus make all its resources our own.

I once was invited into the cockpit of a four-engine plane going out to India at the close of World War II. "Have you ever flown a plane?" the pilots asked me. "No, but I'd like to try it—once." "Then do what we tell you." They pointed out two white parallel lines representing level flight and two white parallel lines representing the angle of the plane. The point was to get those four lines to coincide, and when you did, the plane went along evenly. There were many things I didn't understand about the mechanism of the plane, but I knew one thing: Keep these lines coinciding and I will be on a straight, even course. For the time being, it was all reduced to simplicity. Keep the lines coinciding and then the course and the power were under control. I relaxed and enjoyed the next ten minutes. I had also learned a secret for my spiritual life: Surrender your will to his will and you will be on a kingdom-course with all the resources of the Kingdom behind it. It's simple!

Dr. Radhakrishnan, the great Hindu philosopher and ex-President of India, once said to me: "John the Baptist tried to make people better. Jesus made them different." Tried to make people better — that was reformation; Jesus made them different — that was regeneration. It was not a difference in degree merely — it was a difference in kind. One produced the tense, striving-hard-to-be-good-type, sincere but uncertain and preoccupied with, "Have I done

> *They came to the conclusion that if it was the Gospel it was an offer. And the offer turns out to be nothing less than the Unshakable Kingdom and the Unchanging Person.*

enough?" These souls live on a question mark. The other produced the receptive, relaxed, humble but certain persons, concerned not about what they have done, but what He has done in them, assured, living not on a question mark, but with all the question marks turned into exclamation points, regenerated and rejoicing. The least in the kingdom of receptivity is greater than the greatest in the kingdom of reformation.

There is the difference between two worlds in those two words — demand and offer. The one ends in "nerves," tense jittery nerves; and the other ends in nerve, nerve to face anything with joy.

4. THE KINGDOM — HOW ARE WE TO ENTER?

"In truth, in very truth, I tell you unless a man has been born-over again he cannot see the kingdom of God" (John 3:3 NEB). Or, "be converted" (Matt. 18:3). The first passage says "cannot see," the other "shall not enter" — both very decisive and decisively spoken. "In truth, in very truth, I tell you." That was no chance remark — it was a life conviction. What did he mean by it? Note the framework in which it is placed — it determines the nature of that new birth, which is to be born — re-born into the kingdom of God. If the new birth were set in the framework of the Church, it would probably mean the one undergoing the new birth will be baptized and join the Church and be a faithful attendant and supporter of a church. In certain cases there will be fringe benefits — prayer, Bible reading, renunciation of wrong habits and associations, and a strong witness to this new way of life. But — and this is the point — all this is within the framework of the church, a particular church. He is not born-into the Kingdom. The framework of the conversion was not the framework of the Kingdom. Hence, the conversion is a church-conditioned conversion, a limited conversion, limited to the outlook and spirit of that church. In other words, it is a sub-conversion, even at its best.

But suppose the one undergoing the new birth is born-to the kingdom of God. He sees everything in a new perspective, the kingdom-perspective: the Church is no longer an end in itself, everything it does is relative to the Kingdom, and it succeeds as it becomes a cameo of the new order and has interests and attitudes as wide as the Kingdom. Would trifles wither into insignificance in the light of changed perspective? They wouldn't be solved — they would be dissolved. Nothing would matter except the Kingdom. The Church would lose itself and find itself in something higher than itself.

The entrance into that kingdom is personal and by a new birth, but the nature of that kingdom is social; everything comes under its purview, for all life, individual and collective, is to become subject to the Kingdom. Then conversion in that setting is important, for it has important results — cosmic results, for it has cosmic backing.

We gave the few helpers we had in the Sat Tal Ashram a holiday one day a week, and we volunteered to do their work, including the sweeper's work, which included cleaning the latrines by hand before the days of flush latrines. No one but an outcaste would do it. I had volunteered with an ex-superintendent of police, who said: "Now that I've done that, I'm ready for anything." I turned to a Brahmin convert and said: "Brother Chandy, when are you going to volunteer to do the sweeper's work?" He drew a deep sigh and said, "Brother Stanley, I'm converted, but I'm not converted that far." Many of our conversions are limited conversions—not "that far." Conversion to the kingdom of God is conversion unlimited.

5. THE KINGDOM OF GOD — INDIVIDUAL AND COLLECTIVE RESULTS

We have seen that conversion to the Kingdom would mean conversion unlimited.

For many there is a kingdom of race. A large proportion of the problems of the world revolve around the problem of race. The solution is very simple. It is contained in this verse: "In it [i.e., the Kingdom] there is no room for Greek and Jew [racial distinction], circumcised and uncircumcised [religious ritual distinctions], barbarian and Scythian [cultural distinctions], slave or free man [social or economic distinctions]" (Col. 3:11 Moffatt). In another list is added: "male and female" [sex distinction] (Gal. 3:28 Moffatt). Here there is the simplest of solutions: *There is no room.* That is the simplest and profoundest of solutions—no room. In the Kingdom we are occupied with and dealing with matters that transcend these issues that deeply divide the world. So there is no room.

But aren't these racial distinctions important and aren't they inherent? No, down underneath there is one basic humanity. We have found in the Nurmanzil Psychiatric Center, Lucknow (the first of its kind in India), that the people of India go through the same emotional conflicts as the people of the West, modified slightly by the cultural context. Moreover, while there are developed races and underdeveloped races, there are no permanently inferior or permanently superior races. Given the same stimulus and the same incentives, the brain of humanity will come out about the same. There are infinite possibilities in everybody, everywhere. The climate of the Kingdom is the climate of belief and faith in God and in man. Faith in God creates faith in man. So under this kingdom-impact, the nobodies become the somebodies, fishermen become the teachers of humanity. Note the sneer of the Sanhedrin: "By what power, ... or by what name have such men as you done this?" (Acts 4:7 NEB.) Such men as you—the contempt of the ages was in that sneer—the hope of the ages was in that drama, a new humanity had come into being before their very eyes: "They were astonished to see how outspoken Peter and John were, and to discover that they were uncultured persons and mere outsiders; ... but as they saw the man who had been healed standing beside them, they could say nothing" (Acts 4:13-14

Moffatt). Two stark miracles stood before that whole system of class and race embodied in the hierarchy: the miracle of the healed man and the miracle of the men who were the agents of the healing. A new type of humanity had suddenly come into being to whom class and race were as nothing—they had no room for what the hierarchy counted of supreme importance; race and class were suddenly dissolved— a man was a man for whom Christ died. That was revolution— revolution upward!

I stood in the living room of one of the world's great scientists, Dr. George Washington Carver, a son of slaves, who out of the lowly sweet potato created one hundred and fifty commercial products, and out of the lowly peanut three hundred commercial products. As we stood there we held hands as we prayed for each other. At the close of the prayer I lifted the back of his hand to my lips and he lifted the back of my hand to his lips in recognition and gratitude that we both belonged to a kingdom in which there was no room for trivia like race and class. We were in the presence of the future—the man who is to be. We both stood in a kingdom that was race-blind and color-blind. There was no room for the idols of yesterday.

6. THE KINGDOM OF GOD — MORE APPLICATION OF THE MEANING OF IT

The next barrier: the surrender of outer differences as barriers — circumcision and un-circumcision. That difference between circumcised and uncircumcised, a religious rite, went deep in its consequences; as race separated, so religious rite deepened the separation — cut off all communication. Until the new order, the Kingdom, came and with this: "Circumcision is nothing; un-circumcision is nothing; the only thing that counts is new creation!" (Gal. 6:15 NEB).

I must confess that long hair in today's youth once repelled me as much as a religious rite repelled in that day. My prejudices went deep, until in Sweden I went to a youth meeting, and they were talking sense — talking about walking from Uppsala to Stockholm, forty-five miles, holding meetings on the way to gather collections for Africa. Then this verse came back to me translated: "Long hair availeth nothing, nor unlong hair but a new creation!" So that barrier went down from my side and when I quoted the above an especially longhaired and bush bearded young man on the front row got up and embraced me before everyone!

There is no room in the Kingdom for divisions based on the extraneous, provided there is the new creation.

7. THE KINGDOM OF GOD—
CULTURAL DIFFERENCES

By the surrender of cultural differences—barbarian or Scythian. The Scythian was cultured and the barbarian was not, so this created a cleavage. But in the new order, the Kingdom, there is no room for that cultural division.

A noted writer tells how as a boy in England he was walking with his tutor down a lane on his parents' estate when a tenant's little girl came out to greet them with a bouquet of flowers. He refused the flowers, turned away snobbishly, and left the little girl still holding her flowers, but now in tears. The writer commenting on it said: "That was the first time in my life that I authentically rejected the kingdom of God."

A British official, high up in the Civil Service, during the period of the British occupation of India, hated India and loathed Indians. He thought only of one thing: to retire at fifty-five, get his pension, and live the life of an English gentleman in England. As a result of his mentality, he was plagued with aches and pains and numerous maladies, brought on by his mental and emotional attitudes. Then in England during a furlough, he met Christ, and became a changed man. His wife, too, caught the contagion of the Kingdom. They came back to India and found themselves loving India and loving Indians and finding a deep response from the Indians—the Indians loved them in return. It was during the struggle for independence and feelings were running high. He and his wife stayed at the Government House in Naini Tal, ten miles from the Sat Tal Ashram where we had all types, including followers of Mahatma Gandhi. The couple oscillated between the Government House and the Ashram and partook of all our activities, including the work period when with our hands we all undertook manual labor. They were both at home with the Government House people and with the Ashram group.

His wife summed up their attitudes in these words to me: "Before we met Christ, we used to pick and choose our friends. Now we let God pick them for us." They had more and better friends and their ailments were forgotten. There was no room for barbarian and

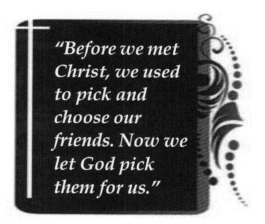

"Before we met Christ, we used to pick and choose our friends. Now we let God pick them for us."

Scythian and for the uncultured and the cultured. Everybody was a person, a person for whom Christ died.

Some of the deepest lessons of life I've learned are from persons with limited education. When I think of freedom from loneliness, I think of going past a log cabin in Virginia. We paused to greet the African-American woman who stood in the doorway. I asked: "Sister, who lives here?" And the cheerful reply: "Nobody, but me and Jesus."

Whenever I am asked to say Grace at meals, I am tempted to use this one, for I could not think of a better one. A Texas cowboy was converted and after his conversion was asked to say Grace at a pastor's home: "Lord, I ain't askin' you for nothing, but I'm a thankin' you for everything." Not much so-called culture, but a sound insight.

Africans when asked in greeting: "Are you well?" will answer: "I am, if you are." It would be hard to improve on that gentle fellow feeling.

So when the Kingdom says, "There is no room for barbarian and Scythian" — uneducated or uncultured and education or cultured — these are all persons for whom Christ died, it has solid basis for that no-roomness, for there are infinite possibilities in everybody, everywhere. When I was eighteen, a year after my conversion, I was seated in a streetcar in a southern city, my home city, Baltimore, with a very dignified and greatly beloved teacher, Miss Nellie Logan, when an African-American woman got in the car. Instinctively I arose, lifted my hat, and offered her my seat. My teacher friend blushed and a titter went through the streetcar. That just wasn't done! But I was taking off my hat to the future and greeting it from afar — sixty-eight years before it happened. I was in the Kingdom, a kingdom that is culture-blind and has no room for snobberies based on culture. So when we put on the wall as you enter the Sat Tal Ashram a motto: "Leave behind all race and class distinction ye that enter here," we were on kingdom ground, for that same motto is over the door of the Kingdom itself. "There is no room."

8. THE KINGDOM —
SOCIAL AND ECONOMIC DIFFERENCES

By the surrender of social and economic differences, there is no room for slave or free man in the kingdom of God. This cuts deep into our problems of today, for when you touch the economic nerve you touch the "touchiest" nerve in our society. For the economic determines status. And the status-seekers are the hungriest seekers of all in our society. Jesus said, "Which of you by taking thought can add a cubit to his stature?" And yet we try to make ourselves taller and more prominent by display, in houses, in dress, in social climbing. And yet there is no higher status in this world or the next world than to be a son of God, and to be made in the likeness of the Divine Son and to belong to the Unshakable Kingdom and to the Unchanging Person. That makes trivial and tinseled any other status.

A college president was about to introduce me to his student body when he asked me if I remembered writing a letter twenty years ago to a young pastor who felt inferior because his father had disgraced the family name. I not only remembered, but I remembered my reply: "In the genealogy of Jesus was this item: 'Solomon was born of David by Uriah's wife.' Did that ugly patch in his ancestral past break Jesus or cloud him? No, for he was more conscious of his heredity from his Father God, the heredity upward cancelled the heredity backward. You can have a blood transfusion from the Son of God that will cancel the tainted blood of ancestors. You can be born from above and not be born back there." "Yes," he said, "I saw it and took it and all my inferiorities dropped away and that's why I am a college president."

In the Unshakable Kingdom there is no room for inferiorities based on heredity or on economic circumstances. I do not care one rap where a person has come from—I'm only interested in where he is going! Jesus said: "No man who puts his hand to the plow and looks back is fit for the kingdom of God." For the Kingdom is forward looking, not backward looking.

"Is not fit"—"cannot fit into," as it could be translated. The Kingdom is interested in the present and the future and leaves "the dead to bury its own dead." The past is buried in the love of God, the present is guided by the love of God, and the future is unfolding under the beckoning of the love of God.

I have just returned from a short trip on which an African-American woman had volunteered to be my chauffeur. On the way through the traffic, she sang me this spiritual: "He woke me up and started me on my way. He didn't have to do it, but he did it." "He woke me up"—made me have a sense of his acceptance. I was at home in the Kingdom—I am a daughter of the Kingdom. "He sent me on my way"—for my way was his way, and his way was the Way—the way of the Unshakable Kingdom, which is the open way into the present and the future. He didn't have to do it—the Lord of heaven and earth was interested in me an individual, a nobody? But He did it—the universal became the particular, the promise became a performance.

The woman with the singing heart brought me to the house of a lady who couldn't sing a note, but she has a singing mind and a singing life. She had been two years on her bed, an invalid with a bad heart. She came to our Ashram, but on the way her heart began to act up and she thought: "How expensive it will be to send my body back the five hundred miles to Charleston, West Virginia." But nevertheless she attended, arrived as she describes it, "with my life hanging over a cliff by a frayed rope, all frayed out except one last frail strand." To complicate things, the doctor said she might have a malignant cancer of the breast, which must be operated on at once. She surrendered herself to Christ, and as she let go of the old frayed rope, she dropped into the Unshakable Kingdom. In two days she was up—normal, so free from fears that she said, "I was afraid." She had been with her fears so long. After a week, she felt for the lump in her breast, it was gone! She drove back the five hundred miles in one day without any weariness. She showed herself to the doctor who exclaimed, "If three-quarters of my patients had what you have, they needn't come to me at all. You better tell them." He verified the absence of the lump. A pastor said to me on a later visit to Charleston, "Do you see that little woman? She is the greatest spiritual power in this city." It was the woman whose life, such as it was, was held by the last strand of frayed rope over an abyss of fears. She is now cured and assured and ready for anything, for she has already met **no room for** fears or inferiorities based on anything.

9. THE KINGDOM—THE CRUX OF THE PROBLEMS: BY THE SURRENDER OF THE KINGDOM OF SELF

Here we come to the crux of the blocks to the Kingdom: all else is marginal, this is central; all else is symptom, this is disease. It was so when Jesus presented the Kingdom as God's total answer—it is so today—the kingdom of self-versus the kingdom of God. And strangely enough, self is made by its inner structure for the kingdom of God. When man opposes the kingdom of God, he opposes himself.

Take the crucial moment when Jesus asked the crucial question of his disciples: "Who do you say that I am?" Upon the lips of Peter trembled the great confession: "Thou art the Christ, the Son of the living God" (Matt. 16:15, 16). It was the great moment. They had followed him on the basis that he was a good man, a prophet; now they saw he was God's redemptive invasion of us—God manifested in the flesh. From that moment one would have thought that everything would have fitted into that fact — God incarnate had visited and redeemed his people. But strangely enough, nothing goes right — everything goes wrong in the whole of the rest of the chapter. Why? They knew that Jesus was the Son of God, but they did not know that self-giving love was at the center of his being the Son of God, and hence, at the center of the kingdom of God. They expected him to ride into Jerusalem, assert his power and set up his kingdom, and they would ride in with him. It would be self-assertion with him and with them. Two of the disciples even picked out the seats they wanted to occupy.

Jesus, always frank and honest, proceeded to let them know that at the center of his being, the Son of God was self-giving love. He was going to Jerusalem to lay down his life. They must take their crosses and follow. Then he said the most important thing that was ever said in history: "Whosoever will save his life shall lose it; and whosoever will lose his life for my sake shall find it" (Matt. 16:25). Nothing was ever said more important about human life and its relationships than that. "But they understood not the saying, for it was hidden from them." Why? Because they didn't want to understand it. His self-giving involved their self-giving, and it was the one thing they were not prepared to do. So Peter, leading in the great confession that Jesus was the Son of God, now led in the rejection of the central thing in his being the Son of God — self-giving love at a cross. "Be it far from thee, Lord, this shall never be" — never be to you because we don't want it to be for us. Jesus said the most devastating thing ever said to any

133

man: "Get thee behind me, Satan:... for thou savourest not the things that be of God, but those that be of men" (Matt. 16:23). Your whole life is out of gear with God and his Kingdom! And it was. "Self" had turned Peter from the Way to a by-lane that led to nothing but entanglements.

"A dispute arose among them as to which of them was the greatest" (Luke 9:46 Moffatt). Here was a clash of the intimate followers of Christ between themselves, because they had surrendered everything to follow Christ except themselves. Peter said: "Lord, we have left everything to follow Thee. What do we get?" That last question, "What do we get?" showed they had not given up themselves. This dispute revealed the un-surrendered selves. This un-surrendered self is at the basis of all our inability to get along with people. In the Open Heart session of the Ashram, one man said, "Everywhere I go, I go too, and I spoil everything." A woman said, "I have come here to get myself off my back." Another woman added, "I have come to get myself out from under my feet. I'm constantly tripping over myself." A pastor confessed, "I'm a self-holic " —addicted to himself. We laugh at these words, but it is no laughing matter, and it was no laughing matter among the Twelve. The un-surrendered self blocked the Kingdom's operation. Everything turned sour.

Then John spoke up and said: "We saw a man casting out demons in your name and we forbade him, because he does not follow with us" (Luke 9:49 RSV). Here was the second clash — the clash of a group of workers with a group of workers: "he does not follow with us." Jesus' reply: "Do not forbid him; for he that is not against you is for you." (In Luke 11:23 RSV, he said: "He who is not with me is against me." Why the change? Obviously this: In the one, following them was the issue. And he said, following you is not the issue, so if they are not against you they are for you. But I am the issue and following me is the issue, so if you are not with me you are against me.) So, because John and the rest were still un-surrendered in themselves they wanted their group to be first. They were ready to have the devils stay in if their group could not get them out. This was the group

> *This un-surrendered self is at the basis of all our inability to get along with people.*

or denominational clash. Self-clash can be with the self, it can also be with the group.

Then the third clash came — a bigger one. The Samaritans refused to receive the disciples who came to prepare for Jesus' coming to their village "because his face was set toward Jerusalem" (Luke 9:53 RSV). The Samaritans showed race prejudice and so did the disciples. They showed it with teeth bared: "Lord, do you want us to bid fire to come down from heaven and consume

135

them?" (Luke 9:54 RSV). They made it religious — fire from heaven, but down underneath it was the racial self against racial self. Jesus rebuked them. The race clash and the group clash were rooted in the un-surrendered individual selves. That was the root, the others were fruit. To change the figure — the un-surrendered was the key log in the jam. Until that log was pulled out at Pentecost by the coming of the Holy Spirit, the river of redemption could not flow to the entire world.

To sum up: The disciples had hold of the greatest knowledge ever imparted to man: Jesus was the Son of the living God. But that knowledge did not help them one bit and it solved none of their problems; all the old clashes were there in intensified form. So the basis on which modern psychiatry is founded — give man knowledge of what is the matter with him and he will be cured — is false. It doesn't cure him. Unless the un-surrendered self is surrendered to something beyond itself, the Kingdom, nothing is cured. The central loyalty of the Twelve was to themselves. They wanted the Kingdom to come at Jerusalem for what they could get out of it — front row seats. They would be on top in that coming.

10. IN ENTERING THE KINGDOM — WHY DO WE BALK AT THE SURRENDER OF THE SELF?

The answer is simple: We feel that in surrendering the self, we have nothing left. For the self is the one thing we brought into the world, the one thing we will take out of the world, and the one thing we live with intimately day by day. Let go that—then we have lost all. That is the basic fear. But it is a false fear. For the opposite happens. If we save ourselves, become centered in ourselves, we lose ourselves automatically.

Every self-centered person is an unhappy person—no exception. Center yourself on yourself and you won't like yourself and nobody else will like you. As one psychiatrist said, "It's a million chances to one that the self-centered are unpopular." With whom? First of all, with themselves. They do as they like, and then they don't like what they do. They have their way, and then they don't like their way. They express themselves, and then they don't like the selves they are expressing. Why? Because

> *Every self-centered person is an unhappy person— no exception. Center yourself on yourself and you won't like yourself and nobody else will like you.*

we were never intended to be the center of the universe— to be God. If you try to be God, organize life around yourself as God, you run against the grain of the universe. The universe won't back your being God. So you are frustrated. You are made to belong—to belong to the Kingdom. Seek that first and all these will be added to you; seek yourself first and everything, including yourself, will be subtracted from you. Said a banker to me one day, "I was afraid to surrender myself, but when I did I was promoted." He lost the old self-centered self and found a God-centered self, a "promoted" self, and a self he and others could live with. He fulfilled the deepest law of the kingdom of God: "Whoever would save his life will lose it, and whoever loses his life for my sake [in a higher cause, [i.e., the Kingdom] will find it" (Matt. 16:25 RSV).

It is the same surrender that ink makes to an author. Mere coloring matter taken up into the purpose of the author becomes words that burn and bless and transform. The same surrender that a wire makes to a dynamo—alone and not attached to anything except itself it has no light, no power, but surrendered to the dynamo it throbs with light and power. When you surrender to the Unshakable Kingdom and the Unchanging Person, you surrender to creative love and all you say, do, and are is heightened by that impact. You think thoughts you couldn't think, you do things you couldn't do, and you are a person you could not otherwise be. You are a surprise to yourself and to others.

And now you can love yourself because you love something (the Kingdom) and someone (Christ) more than yourself. You in your own hands is a problem and a pain; you in the hands of Christ is a possibility and a power. A Swedish lady said in the Ashram's *Open Heart*, "I don't like myself and yet I have to live with myself." A few days later she surrendered to Christ, and she came down in the morning and said: "I love everybody this

AND THE UNCHANGING PERSON

morning and strangely enough I love myself." So when you seek the Kingdom first, then all self-loathing, self-rejection drops away. How can you hate what he loves? How can you reject what he accepts? A man came down the steps one morning and said to his friend, "John, I do thank God for you." And John replied, "Well, I thank God for myself," —rightly so and beautifully so. You will be able to say, "Blessed are my eyes for they have seen him and do see him, my hands for they have clasped his, my feet for they walk in his way, my heart for it belongs to him, now and forever— blessed am I, for I am his."

You in your own hands is a problem and a pain; you in the hands of Christ is a possibility and a power.

There was a man, a top psychiatrist in Puerto Rico, who had everything —and nothing. He was a nominal Catholic, but inwardly empty. He got hold of the Spanish version of my book, *Victory Through Surrender*, dipped into it, was intrigued, took it to his summer home—the only book he took— determined to spend a week with it. He read it twenty times. At the end of the week he was convinced that this was it—he had to surrender, not this, or that, but himself. He came to our Ashram and when he heard me speak on self-surrender and use the phrase, "If you surrender to Christ, you surrender to creative love," it triggered something in his mind. He got up while I was speaking and came to the altar of prayer, though I had given no invitation, and he stayed there the whole time I was speaking. When I gave the invitation for others to come, he remained with them until they all got up together. He said to the group, "I knew this was what I had to do. Now I've done it. I have surrendered myself." I saw him three years later and when I asked him what had happened in the meantime, he replied, "I am the happiest man in Puerto Rico." And no wonder! For this was his story: "I found I could support myself and family by practicing four hours of psychiatry, from eight in the morning to twelve noon each day. Then the hours from one to nine at night, I give to persons who are alcoholic and drug addicted without charge. I have set up twelve rehabilitation centers in San Juan in which five hundred patients a day receive treatment. I have put half a million dollars of my own money into these centers and others have helped me as well. I work with patients to put up their own centers, so they learn carpentry, masonry, cooking, etc., while they are in treatment. I have five thousand persons on the waiting list to get into care. Among the drug addicts in treatment, by the grace of God, sixty-five percent are cured within a year. The alcoholics are a little more difficult, for the person who is an alcoholic is accepted in society, but the drug addict is not, so he has an added incentive to get well. I had four cars, but my wife and I only needed two, so we sold the other two." At an Ashram meeting in his enthusiasm for telling his story, he ran over into the next speaker's time. The next day he asked for permission to apologize to the group for doing so. We were all moved by the story of a self-surrender turning into community redemption, but personally the simple apology by one of Puerto Rico's leading citizens moved me as much as his amazing story. When he volunteered to go to San Domingo Island to start an Ashram there, or to go to India to take over the psychiatric center at Lucknow, India, we said, "No, in three years you have made yourself indispensable to Puerto Rico and beyond!" For when I told that story in the United States a doctor said to me, "Why can't I do that, instead of retiring? I'll do it." That psychiatrist in Puerto Rico has set a pattern: Surrender yourself to the Kingdom, seek that first, and instead of piling up money beyond your needs when it becomes a burden and a stumbling block, hold your income to your needs and give the rest of your time (and money) to meet the needs of others. And you will say with that devoted doctor: "I'm the happiest man in..." and you can fill in the name of your city or town. It works! (Forgive this personal reference: In over half a century of evangelism at home and abroad, I have never taken a penny for my work, — I turn all donations back into mission projects and live on a portion of the royalties from my books.)

The biggest payoff was in the person of the psychiatrist. Before he surrendered himself, he was a problem dealing with problems, and "getting by" somehow, perhaps because of his medical and psychiatric knowledge. He was the word of healing become word; now he is the word of healing become flesh. He is no longer a part of the disease — he is an example of the cure. He is a witness. The biggest payoff in self-surrender is in the self that is surrendered. "It is so comfortable to get yourself off your own hands," said a woman. She too was a witness. A psychiatrist has written a book entitled, *The Therapeutic Value of Self-surrender*. He concludes that it is not only comfortable to get yourself off your own hands — it is healthy. A sick mind and soul makes for a sick body. A self-surrendered to the Kingdom is a self at home. A self that says, like the prodigal son, "Father, give me" will soon be saying with the prodigal, "I perish with hunger." But when he says, "Father, make me," he will soon be in the Father's house — his homeland, and with plenty.

11. THE KINGDOM — SOME SIDE EFFECTS OF SELF-SURRENDER

"Therefore, my brothers, I implore you by God's mercy to offer your very selves to him: a living sacrifice, dedicated and fit for his acceptance, the worship offered by mind and heart. Adapt yourselves no longer to the pattern of this present world, but let your minds be remade, and your whole nature thus transformed. Then you will be able to discern the will of God, and to know what is good, acceptable and perfect" (Rom. 12:12 NEB). A doubt remains for many about self-surrender. The doubt was expressed by a Finnish newspaper reporter: "Why is God so cruel? Why does he demand so much of us?" God was asking for the only thing she possessed — herself — so she was in rebellion. This woman was a bundle of concentrated misery, and she said in protest, when I suggested that she surrender herself to God, "Why, if I did that I would be at God's mercy." She felt that God was looking for a chance to make her even more miserable, and that God's will lay in the direction of making her unhappy. Nothing, absolutely nothing, could be further from the truth. God's will is always and everywhere in our highest interest. He couldn't be God and will anything other than our highest interest. He would violate his own nature in doing so. For God never asks us to do anything that he himself is not doing.

Take this matter of self-surrender. God asks us to do that: "I implore you, therefore, to offer your very selves to him." (Rom 12:1). Does God do what he is asking us to do? Does he offer his very self? Yes. Note the word "therefore" — it points back to what Paul was saying in the previous chapters. And what was he saying? He was saying nothing less than that God gave himself as a living sacrifice. "He did not spare his own Son, but gave him up for us all" (Rom. 8:32 NEB). "God was in Christ reconciling the world unto himself" (II Cor. 5:19 NEB). God gave his Son, but he also gave himself in his Son. The outer cross lights up the inner cross upon the heart of God. So if God asks us to surrender ourselves, this is not cruelty, but an invitation to share with him the deepest joy that this universe knows — the joy of saving others at a cost to one's self. The happiest people in this world are the people who deliberately take on themselves sorrow and pain to help others. Their hearts sing with a deep, wild joy. And the most miserable people in this world are the people who won't do a thing for anybody but themselves. They are automatically centers of misery. So the God of the kingdom of God is a God who will and does do everything he asks his subjects in the Kingdom to do. I can love a God like that.

A maharajah in India made a law that every man in his kingdom should not have more than one wife, but he himself took another wife. When objection was raised his reply was: "I make laws; I don't obey them." The people arose and deposed the maharajah. If God would ask us to obey laws he himself did not obey, then that God would be dismissed as God, and ought to be. But the God who not only obeys his own laws, but who would go the second mile and take on himself the consequences of disobedience of those who break the laws and would bear them in his own body on a tree — that God can have my heart without reservation and without qualification. The self-giving was good for God — it is also good for us. So when he asks us to offer our very selves as sacrifice, he calls it a living sacrifice. When you offer yourself as sacrifice, you become a living sacrifice; you are alive to your fingertips, alive with life, with love, with God. "All that came to be was alive with his life" (John 1:4 NEB). When put into him by self-surrender, every created thing became life in his life. In itself— un-surrendered—it became death, and decay set in. Every self-surrendered person is a living sacrifice. Like the Sea of Galilee it loses its life. Then it shares what it gets and is alive and makes everything alive that touches it. The un-surrendered self is like the Dead Sea, it gets everything and gives nothing, and so it is dead and spreads deadness.

There is a wonderful side effect to this self-surrender: You become dedicated and fit for God's acceptance. A Roman Catholic nun in an Open Heart session said: "I, as a nun, am supposed to be dedicated. I am—to myself." The dedication to self made her unhappy and frustrated and ineffective in spite of vows, dress, and renunciation of so many things. Self was at the center, and unhappiness reigned. She surrendered herself and joy reigned. It was as simple as that— and just as profound. Then, here is another side effect: you will be fit for his acceptance. What produced acceptance? Not joining the order, not vows, not different dress, not renunciation of this or that, not believing in Jesus, but just one thing: self-surrender. *You don't have to be good before you are accepted— you have to be*

> *So the God of the Kingdom of God is a God who will and does, do everything he asks his subjects in the Kingdom to do. I can love a God like that.*

his. If the citadel holds out against him all else is irrelevant. When the citadel, the un-surrendered self, capitulates, then the fortress goes with it; it is all his, and fit for his acceptance, and for your own acceptance. You can accept yourself; it is a self that is acceptable, for it is under redemption. You love him supremely, now you can love yourself subordinately.

Here is another side effect: "the worship offered by mind and heart." The worship is now from the heart. Your lips are not merely saying it — you are saying it from the heart. He has the center. It's real. A pastor's wife said: "Whenever the church bells begin to ring, I feel like throwing things." Why? Because for her, church bells stood for unreality. For the self wanted its self, not to kneel in devotion, but to throw things in protest. Now you want to throw yourself at His feet — with joy.

Yet another important side effect: "worship offered by the mind." Is self-surrender and obedience to an absolute cause (the Kingdom) whimsical or wisdom? This is important for that which doesn't hold the mind will soon not hold the emotion and the will. Is this sentiment or sense? Jesus in summing up the Sermon on the Mount — which many people have thought to be idealistic, but not very wise and practicable — used the word "wise" in describing the man who built his house upon the rock of what Jesus was saying; and "foolish" in describing the man who built his house in some other way — on sand.

Self-surrender is written into the very basis of life. The male cell has forty-six chromosomes. The female has the same number. To unite in forming a new life, each has to reduce the forty-six to twenty-three, so that the new life will have forty-six. Self-surrender is at the basis of life in its inception and in its continuance. There are three basic urges in human nature—self, sex, and the herd. The self is obviously self-regarding; the herd urge is obviously others-regarding; and the sex urge is partly self-regarding and partly others-regarding. So there are just two basic driving urges in human nature—the self-regarding and the others-regarding. If you build your life on the self-regarding alone, you will be unhappy, for the others-regarding urge—the herd-urge—is unfulfilled. Both of these urges must be fulfilled simultaneously. To love your neighbor (the herd urge) as you love yourself (the self-urge) is sense. To do anything else is foolish. To live in the kingdom-way is sense, and the more you try it, you have to call it, sense. It is not by chance that it is said of him: "Whom God has made our 'Wisdom'" (I Cor. 1:30 Moffatt). A daughter said to her mother, recently surrendered to God: "Mother, I did not know that anyone could be as good and as wise as you are." But the good, the really good, are wise, and the wise are good. The good is not only good, it is good for us. The bad is bad for us.

The next great discovery of the Christian mind, and the scientific mind, will be in the realm of seeing that the Christian way is not only the good way, but also the wise way to live. Let the Christian mind go to work on that, and it will be the richest vein of ore it has ever explored. A famous swami in India said to his followers: "Kill the mind and then you can meditate." When the swami said that, he wrote the epitaph of his movement. Jesus said the opposite: "Thou shalt love the Lord thy God with all thy mind." The mind was not to be killed, but consecrated. It was a yes to the human mind, not a no! That set the kingdom of God right down at the center of an intellectually inquiring age. It was at home there—its native land. It has been said of the early Christians that they conquered that ancient world because they outlived the pagans. That was true. And they also out-loved the pagans, they out-thought the pagans, and they out-died the pagans. That can happen again for we have the soundest starting point for our thinking—the Unshakable Kingdom and the Unchanging Person, the absolute order and the absolute Person. Assumption? No, verified knowledge—verified to the degree it is tried, anywhere and everywhere.

So when you surrender yourself to the Kingdom, a side effect will be the worship offered by mind and heart. The emotions will be kindled and the mind quickened, for they will both be on the exploration of the richest and most exciting vein that mankind in his long quest has ever explored. The Christian way is the Way—unqualified. The way to do everything—to think, to act, to feel, to be—everything for God and man, in the individual and in the collective—it is the Way.

And then there is this side effect of self-surrender:"Adapt yourself no longer to the pattern of this present world." To surrender yourself to the Unchanging

Person and to the Unshakable Kingdom brings emancipation from the herd urge and its patterns in this present world. We stepped out of the bondages of slavery and feudalism and *dastur* (custom) into the modern bondage of fashion. The devotees of fashion can be counted by the hundreds of millions and they offer upon the altars of fashion hundreds of billions of dollars. "Everybody does it" — that settles it for a while for somebody behind the scenes cracks the whip, and everybody stands at attention and hears the command — "change." And everybody changes whether it is good, bad, or indifferent. So society creates robots — not persons. And this goes over into our thinking and acting, not merely into fashions. So we produce a generation of copiers, out of character. If you don't surrender to God, you will fall for anything.

So self-surrender is the greatest emancipation that ever comes to a human being. Seek first the kingdom of God and all things will be added to you, including yourself. You will no longer be an echo — you will be a voice. You will no longer merely copy, you will create. The freest man in those early centuries was a man in chains — in chains because of his allegiance to the kingdom of God. Standing before the religious and political leaders and the gentry of the city, Paul could say to King Agrippa: "I wish to God that not only you, but all those also who are listening to me today, might become what I am, apart from these chains" (Acts 26:29 NEB). And the point was that nobody laughed. For it was a fact. He was free to be, to contribute, and to create. The men around him, whose chains he wore, would never have been heard of again, had they not been in contact with the deathless life of Paul. In his commission he had heard, "I will deliver thee from the people to whom I send thee." He was free to serve the people to whom he was sent because he was delivered from them. No man can serve the people unless he is delivered from them by a higher allegiance, the kingdom of God.

Another side effect of self-surrender: "But let your minds be remade and your whole nature thus transformed" (Rom. 12: 2 NEB). This reverses the usual procedure, which is change your mind and then you will change your nature. This procedure says surrender yourself and that will remake your mind and transform your whole nature. Which is correct? I believe this latter is profoundly and importantly correct. The mind gathers reasons to justify the emotions and the will. The center of your loyalty will determine your thinking. This verse is luminous: "Those who live on the level of our lower nature have their outlook formed by it, and that spells death" (Rom. 8:5 NEB). Your outlook is formed by your life decisions and your life loyalties. So to change your outlook, your thinking, you have to change your central loyalties. Self-surrender is the profoundest change of loyalty that one can make. Christ, not you, is the central loyalty. He determines your life. From that moment your outlook, your thinking, is changed. Before the surrender, you and your desires were the starting point of your thinking. Now Christ is the starting point. You love differently, therefore, you think differently, and therefore you are different. It is the explosive power of a new affection. But it must be an affection that the mind can respect and revere. I can respect and revere with the consent of all my being, especially my mind, the Unshakable Kingdom and the Unchanging Person. My whole nature is being thus transformed. I am under a process of redemption. Goethe says, "Be the Whole, belong to the Whole." I can't be, nor do I want to be, the whole. But I can belong to the whole—that fully satisfies me body, mind, and spirit. It has got me, and I have it—him.

The climactic side effect of self-surrender is this last side effect: Then you will be able to discern the will of God and to know what is good, acceptable, and perfect. You will discern that when you surrender to the will of God, that will is your highest good and your deepest freedom. When you try it, you discover the will of God is good—not only good in itself, it is good for you. I try it further and I discern that the will of God is acceptable—I can accept it for my body, my mind, and spirit. It is acceptable to my whole being. I try it further and I find it is perfect. I wouldn't change a thing about the Kingdom nor about the Person. In the words of Rufus Moseley, "He is Perfect everything." He is everything and he is perfect everything.

12. THE SELF-SURRENDER OF JESUS
TO THE KINGDOM OF GOD

In our study of the necessity, the first necessity, of entrance into the kingdom of God, namely, is self-surrender. And we said that God obeyed this law of self-surrender. He gave himself for us. And Jesus, in the uncovering of the nature of God and the nature of the kingdom of God, also obeyed the law of self-surrender. This fact of the self-surrender of Jesus needs further emphasis. For if this law of self-surrender is a universal law applying to God and man, then this is important. And if it is true, it is undebatable—we do it and live, we refuse to do it and we decay and perish.

Fortunately, we have a vivid account of Jesus' inner debate when he was confronted with an alternative to self-surrender. He was confronted with self-serving. When the Greeks came to Jesus and asked to see him, it was more than an interview regarding some spiritual or doctrinal question. It precipitated one of the most profound crises in the life of Jesus—why? From the content of the crisis, something like this possibly happened: The Greeks saw that if Jesus should go on to Jerusalem, the Jewish leaders would put him to death, would crucify him. These Greeks felt they should head that off by inviting him to come to Athens instead of going to Jerusalem—come to Athens and be their honored and beloved teacher; put this teaching concerning the Kingdom through the philosophical thinking of the

152

Greeks and it would spread throughout the whole world. So the issue was Athens or Jerusalem—Athens, with honor, and respect, and success with his Kingdom and a long life; or Jerusalem, with its crucifixion and death. It was a real issue and one that confronts every man: shall I save my life or shall I fling it away for a cause; shall I teach the Kingdom or shall I illustrate it, incarnate it with all the consequences? Listen: "The hour has come for the Son of man to be glorified. Truly, truly, I tell you, unless a grain of wheat falls into the earth and dies, it remains a single grain; but if it dies, it bears rich fruit. He who loves his life loses it, and he who cares not for his life in this world will preserve it for life eternal.... My soul is now disquieted. What am I to say? 'Father, save me from this hour'? Nay, it is something else that has brought me to this hour: I will say, 'Father, glorify thy name.' [Father, I give you a blank check—if you fill in Jerusalem then I go.] Then came a voice from heaven: 'I have glorified it, and I will glorify it again.'" It was settled. What was the result? "Now is this world to be judged; [judged from a cross, the center of power shall be the Cross;] now shall the Prince of this world be expelled. [I shall conquer all evil with good, all hate by love, all men by a cross—the weapons of the Kingdom will be self-giving love.] But I, when I am lifted up from the earth, will draw all men unto myself" (John 12:23-25, 27-29, 31-32 Moffatt). The heart of Jesus was to be the capital of the Kingdom. No, the heart of Jesus is *now* the capital of the Kingdom. Not Rome, not Athens, not Washington D.C., not London, not

Paris, not Moscow, not Peking, not Tokyo, not Jerusalem, but the heart of Jesus is the capital of the Kingdom: "I will draw all men unto myself." The kingdom of God would not be a philosophical concept taught by a philosophical rabbi. It would be something to live for and to die for; Jesus would not be a teacher—he would be a redeemer, heading the greatest movement that ever struck our planet, the kingdom of God.

13. THE THEOLOGICAL ACCOUNT OF THE SELF-SURRENDER OF JESUS TO THE KINGDOM OF GOD

We have seen the inner account of Jesus' surrender of himself obeying the deepest law of the Kingdom. We now see the theological account through the devoted eyes of Paul: "Treat one another with the same spirit as you experience in Christ Jesus. Though he was divine by nature, he did not set store upon equality with God, but emptied himself by taking the nature of a servant; born in human guise and appearing in human form, he humbly stooped in his obedience even to die, and to die upon the cross. Therefore, God raised him high and conferred a Name above all names, so that before the Name of Jesus, every knee should bend in heaven, on earth, and underneath the earth, and every tongue confess that 'Jesus Christ is Lord' to the glory of God the Father" (Phil. 2:5-10 Moffatt). Never was anything of greater importance than this penned: Self-surrender was not merely something for the creatures to do—it is something for the Creator to do, a universal principle and a universal attitude for God and man. So morality is not based on the will of God. It is based on the character of God. Everything God asks us to do—he does. He is not a fingerpost pointing the way. He is the loving Shepherd saying, "Come, and follow me." So morality is not something imposed, but something exposed, something exposed out of the very character of God. So morality is not something verbal—it is vital, out of life, God's life.

Self-surrender was not merely something for the creatures to do—it is something for the Creator to do, a universal principle and a universal attitude for God and man.

If Jesus is the human life of God, God available, God lovable, then this description of how Jesus surrendered himself, going even to a cross for us, is a revelation to us that if we want to go up we must first go down. Jesus took seven steps down: (1) he was divine by nature; (2) he did not set store upon equality with God; (3) he emptied himself; (4) taking the nature of a servant; (5) appearing in human form; (6) he humbly stooped even to die; (7) to die upon a cross. He hit bottom. Then he went to the heights, and there are also seven steps up: (1) God raised him high; (2) conferred a Name above all names; (3) before the Name of Jesus every knee should bow; (4) in heaven; (5) on earth; (6) underneath the earth; (7) every tongue confess that Jesus Christ is Lord. He went from the highest to the lowest and from the lowest to the highest. This is not a paper narrative but was done in person.

14. THE CORE OF THE MORALITY OF THE KINGDOM REVEALED

"Treat one another with the same spirit as you experience in Christ Jesus." This new morality of the Kingdom is the high-water mark of morality of the universe. I say universe for it includes all worlds and is the same for time and eternity, for God and for man. Beyond it, the human race will not progress. It is more thoroughgoing than love your neighbor as you love yourself, for the standard in that statement was self-love; here the standard is Christ-love. Do unto others as you would they should do unto you—here the standard is what you desire for you, but this new morality of the Kingdom sets the standard of what Jesus Christ would do for you. The standard set in the Sermon on the Mount of loving your neighbor as you love yourself was the highest until Jesus amended it upward in the light of his own unfolding, then it became, "Treat others as I treat you." This is the ultimate—the kingdom-ultimate.

This clarifies the mystery of the Kingdom—the open secret of the kingdom of God. The mystery, open secret of the kingdom of God, is the fact that Jesus himself is the secret, the open secret of the Kingdom. He is the Word of the Kingdom become flesh. When you see Jesus, you see what the Kingdom is like. The Kingdom is the spirit of Jesus universalized. There isn't a situation, individual or collective, in heaven or on earth, which would not be resolved if the spirit and attitudes of Jesus were applied to that situation.

The objection is raised: "Yes, that it true, provided both sides in a situation to be resolved were willing to apply the spirit and attitudes of Jesus. But suppose one side was not willing —what then?" Even so, the Kingdom wins. Jesus said: "Let your first words be, 'Peace be on this house.' If there is a man of peace there, your peace will rest upon him; if not, it will return and rest upon you" (Luke 10:6 NEB). If they receive your peace— good; if they refuse to receive it—still good; your peace has come back to you. You are more peaceful for having given the peace. You always win if you take the kingdom-attitude. You are better whether the person accepts or rejects your peace. The payoff is in the person. And the payoff is also in the person who rejects it. He deteriorates, decays. The Kingdom works, in that case, as silent, automatic penalty. Break its laws and you are broken. Fulfill its laws and you are fulfilled. It works with a mathematical precision, and there are no exceptions.

This morality of treating one another with the same spirit which you experience in Christ, supersedes and revokes all other lesser or contradictory attitudes. Take the Old Testament dictum of an eye for an eye and a tooth for a tooth. Israel publicly announces that this is her national attitude. She publicly appeals to other nations for armaments to maintain it. She is tense, anxious, and insecure. She maintains insecurity by a threat, an unworkable attitude. Take the modern psychological dictum: "Accept yourself as you are." This asks you to accept an unacceptable self," which is impossible. Jesus treats us differently. He says: "I will accept you as you are, but I will make you into a self whom you can accept, for it will be acceptable. It will be under redemption, therefore acceptable." But psychology's dictum of accepting yourself as you are is false, morally and psychologically. It leaves the person frustrated. You can't accept an unacceptable self.

How does Jesus treat us? Hopefully, but not permissively. Paul says: "The life I now live I live by the faith in the Son of God." Not merely by faith in the Son of God, but also by his faith in me—faith of the Son of God. He believes in me when I can't believe in myself. So I respond to his belief when I can't believe in my own. Jesus believes belief from the belief-less, faiths faith from the faithless, loves love from the loveless. He creates the thing he believes in. He is the great believer in man. But he is not permissive. He is redemptive. He holds us to the highest. An American soldier adopted a German boy during World War II. The boy uttered profane and vulgar language in the presence of his adoptive father and looked guilty because of it. The soldier said: "That's all right. Say all of that you want to." The boy replied: "If you were my father, you wouldn't tell me that." A pastor told me that when he went to a psychiatrist about his sexual problems, the psychiatrist said: "If you want to do it, then why don't you do it?" The pastor was inwardly revolted. Later, as he sat in a bus reading my book on conversion, he surrendered himself and his problem to Christ, then and there, and walked out of his problem — free, happy and creative. The advice of the psychiatrist would have fulfilled the words of the prophet: "This guilt of yours shall split you" (Isa. 30:13 Moffatt); would have created problems and solved none.

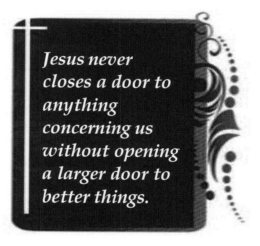

Jesus never closes a door to anything concerning us without opening a larger door to better things.

So the psychiatrist's advice illustrated bad psychology as well as bad morality.

Jesus knew the truth of this statement of Dr. Richard Cabot: "The great moral imperatives are laid down in the biological and psychological structure of human beings and in the structure of the world in which we live." So his statements have the sum total of reality behind them. A woman told me she went to a pagan psychiatrist about her sexual desires. He told her: "You're too heavily loaded in that area, I suggest that you take up drinking and smoking to distribute the load." Bankruptcy! She did it and became worse. Now she was fighting on three fronts instead of one. She turned to Christ, surrendered herself and all of her urges, and walked out of all her problems into the arms of the Redeeming Christ and the Unshakable Kingdom and was free!

Jesus never closes a door to anything concerning us without opening a larger door to better things. "Treat one another with the same spirit which you experience in Christ Jesus." Parents take note in the treatment of your children. Never say no, unless you can say yes to something higher.

Jesus' treatment of us always adds up to sense. I picked up my newspaper and the headlines tell of three people shot in a quarrel over putting up a fence between neighbors. That is the non-kingdom way of living and resolving differences. Take the Kingdom way: A man started to build a fence between himself and his neighbor. The neighbor came and said: "When you bought that lot you bought a court case along with it. That fence is going to be five feet on my land." The man replied: "I knew I would always have a nice neighbor next to me. I'll tell you what I suggest: You put up the fence where you think it should go, send me the bill and I'll pay for it." The fence was never put up — no need, friendship was their security. To treat people in the same spirit that you experience in Christ is not only the highest, it is the best, and it is sense. All else is nonsense.

15. SOME "NOES" AND SOME "YESES" IN BRINGING IN THE KINGDOM—THE WAY JESUS CHOSE TO BRING IN THE KINGDOM

This amazing background is recorded to give the setting for a simple statement: "The word of God came to John ... in the desert." "Now in the fifteenth year of the reign of Tiberius Caesar, when Pontius Pilate was governor of Judea, Herod being tetrarch of Galilee, Philip his brother tetrarch of the country Iturea and Trachonitis, and Lysias tetrarch of Abila, during the high priesthood of Annas and Caiaphas, the word of God came to John ... in the desert" (Luke 3:13, Moffatt). This array of the top leaders in government and religion were only a background, a setting for the most important event of that age, or any age—the word of the Lord coming to John. That word turned out to be the Word, and that Word turned out to be the Word become Flesh, and that Word become Flesh became the Word of God become flesh, and the Word of the kingdom of God became flesh. That impressive background of human power and pomp has turned out to belong to the shakable kingdoms. They have all been shaken to the dust; one Unshakable Kingdom remains: "Thy Kingdom is an everlasting Kingdom." One Person remains: "the same yesterday, today and forever." Never did any kingdom have such lowly beginnings: The man who announced its coming lived on locusts and wild honey; the Babe who was destined to hold the scepter of the universe was born in a stable. He began his ministry

161

by taking a baptism of repentance along with repenting people.

This was not only a menial beginning. It was a low moral beginning. He took his place in that line of repenting people, a thief in front of him, and a prostitute behind him — took his place, but this wasn't his place! He who wore a stainless conscience was taking a baptism among the stained. Was this deliberate? He was the Son of God, the voice at baptism said so, now he would choose to be the Son of man, the Son of man at man's lowest place, the place of sinful man. This was a key attitude. He would be a savior by identification. He had been baptized into the world's toil as a carpenter; now he would be baptized into the world's sin, as one with sinful men. "During a general baptism of the people, when Jesus too had been baptized . . ." (Luke 3:21 NEB). He would be a savior from within — not from above, apart from, separated, but from within. Here he was baptized between sinners and this identification would be culminated at a cross where he would be crucified between two thieves — as one of them. He would cry the cry of dereliction, which you and I cry when we sin: "My God, My God why hast Thou forsaken me?" He would be hungry in our hunger and would become sinful in our sin. This was unthinkable. No savior ever becomes a part of the sinful: no redeemer ever begins by becoming one with those needing redemption. The reaction must have been thoroughgoing and deep. So he went into the wilderness to think it through and fight it out. Was this the way to bring in the

Kingdom by becoming one with his subjects — and the lowest of his subjects? Was he to become sin for us? For forty days he fasted and prayed and was hungry. Then the devil saw his opening: "If you must go back, don't go back the way you began. This identification business is all wrong. You're the Son of God, so be the Son of God. Let the Son-of-man business go. Command these stones to be made bread, feed yourself apart, live on miracle, be the Son of God alone, aloof, superior."

This is the temptation of the ascetic — the temptation to be apart. The Church has often tried the method of bringing in the Kingdom by escape, escape within the within. The monasteries and convents and the retreats witness to the pull — the pull apart. Jesus' reply: "Man cannot live on bread alone; he lives on every word that God utters" (Matt. 4:4 NEB). "And the Word from God for me is that being the Son of God, I must also be the Son of man by identification. So no trying to be alone with the Alone, no escapism."

Then the Tempter tried another approach: "If you must go back, don't go back the way you began: Don't stand with the people as one of them, stand above them, on the pinnacle of the temple as the symbol and sign of religion. Let the people look up to you and bow down to you. Even if you throw yourself from that pinnacle to be one with the people again, God will not allow it. He will put you back on the pinnacle by miracle. You are his beloved. He will take special care of you." This is the temptation of ecclesiasticism — to stand on the pinnacle of the temples, different in dress and position and be looked up to and reverenced, and even be called "the Reverend."

This is the temptation to live above and be looked up to as we stand on our pinnacles of position and privilege. The answer of Jesus was decisive: "You are not to put the Lord your God to the test" (Matt. 4:7 NEB). You must not tempt God by attempting to play God, by taking things that belong to God alone."

Then comes the last and final temptation, on a high mountain: "See all these kingdoms of the world. They are mine. I can give them to anyone I choose. All these I will give you, if you will fall down and do me homage." This temptation was not to live apart, nor to live above, but to live as—accept my spirit and methods—do me homage. This is the temptation to use worldly methods to get the world—be a politician, wrangle people, be one of them to get them, be secular to win the secular. To get the devil's result, take the devious ways of the devil. This means: Come to the level of people in spirit and action and language in order to get the people. To live *as*.

Jesus' word was decisive again: "You shall do homage to the Lord your God and worship him alone" (Matt. 4:10 NEB). When he uttered "him alone," the devil left him. He couldn't stand this "him alone," no foothold for the devil to stand in. God's kingdom was to be brought in by God's methods and the method of God was the method of Jesus. He would be the Son of man, but there would be an inner core of difference. It was clear—and it was powerful.

He went into the wilderness full of the Holy Spirit, He returned in "the power of the Spirit" (Luke 4:1 NEB). He went in full of the spirit and he came back in the power of the Spirit—mere fullness turned to power under temptation. So if you know how to use the devil, not just bear him, but use him, then you are victorious! The devil defeats himself, for his way is anti-nature, anti-life, anti-universe, anti-everything.

It was all clear now. Jesus wouldn't live apart from men— or above men on pinnacles, or as men, like them in character and life. He would live with men as the Son of man, with them but redemptively with them.

16. HIS PROGRAM FOR THE BRINGING IN OF THE KINGDOM—SOME YESES

It was crystal clear, so he went to the little synagogue at Nazareth and announced his program. One would have thought that the Christian Church would have fastened on this synagogue at Nazareth as one of the greatest shrines in Christendom, for here the greatest program for the reconstruction of the world was announced. But today it is left unadorned and practically unremembered. Shrines are built around his birthplace, the places of his crucifixion and his resurrection, but no notice of the place where he launched his kingdom with its program. This is a striking reminder of how the Christian faith has lost the kingdom of God as its central program and emphasis — the good news of the kingdom of God.

Here at Nazareth he gave the kingdom manifesto — the content of what the Kingdom would bring to men. We hold our breaths as we listen to see what the coming of the Kingdom would mean. The destiny of a new world is in these words: "The Spirit of the Lord is upon me." Here he gave five important changes, regenerative changes, that would come as a result of the coming of the Spirit of the Lord upon him (Luke 4:18-19 NEB).

(1) "Good news to the poor," the economically disinherited. We usually make this mean the spiritually poor. It does, but it doesn't say so. It says the poor — the poor. Some are rich in things and poor, totally poor, in spirit. Some are rich in spirit and poor in things. This would apply to both — he has come to abolish poverty of both kinds. To those in our churches who are comfortably off it has seemed to mean the spiritually poor. That relieves the conscience of the necessity for the abolition of physical poverty. Two classes think too much about money — those who have too much and those who have too little. I want just enough money so I can forget it and think about the Kingdom. The problem children in our schools come from two classes — those above the privilege level and those below. Too much and too little produce challenges for children. The "normally" adjusted children come, for the most part, from the middle class homes. We worked this out as a working principle in our Ashram movement: Every person has a right to as much of the

material things as will make him mentally and spiritually and physically fit for the purposes of the kingdom of God. The rest belongs to the needs of others. Give your child a good education, but no more. To leave him a legacy so he doesn't have to work is to put him on the road to decay. Good news to the poor would mean that poverty should be abolished, that there should be no poor. We could abolish poverty in one generation if we had the will to do it. We have the means and the pressing necessity. What we lack is the will. Kingdom allegiance should create that will — and does when followed.

> *Good news to the poor would mean that poverty should be abolished, that there should be no poor.*

(2) "Release to the captives" — the socially and politically disinherited. There are those in our society who are means to other people's ends. They are exploited because of race, class, social standing, and lack of education. There is a simple remedy — profit sharing. That would give an incentive to the worker, for the more everybody worked, the more everybody would receive. It also distributes wealth. Wealth is like manure; put it in one pile it stinks, distributed across the fields it results in golden grain. The largest industrialist in London, Ontario, Canada, came up to me at the close of a meeting and said,

"You're right. My business was a feud. I was giving as little as possible and my employees were doing as little as possible. We were tied in knots and getting nowhere fast. I called in the men one day and said to them: 'We are functioning on a pagan basis. I am on it, you are on it. Let's change it to, Love your neighbor as you love yourself. Hitherto, I've had the right of hiring and firing. I now give it to you. You decide who comes in and who stays in. And we will set aside 23 $\frac{1}{3}$ percent of the profits for labor, above wages. My factory turned from a feud to a family overnight." One method, the first, was anti-kingdom, and the second pro-kingdom. Nothing was behind the first and everything was behind the second. They worked with the grain of the Kingdom, so all the kingdom-powers were behind them, they were free to create and contribute.

While any man is captive, we are to that degree bound in his captivity, we are poor in his bondage. We are down in his down-ness. We go up in his rising. We are free in his freedom.

A labor organizer said to me at the close of a chamber of commerce meeting when I talked on profit sharing: "What are you trying to do? Trying to put the labor unions out of business?" The labor unions were geared for conflict, not for cooperation. So organized labor and organized capital function on a pagan basis: "Thou shalt love thyself," hence, sand is in the machinery of industry, creaking at half its capacity because it is calling on the self-interest motive alone. The others-interest motive is inoperative. To put industry on a kingdom basis, "love thy neighbor

168

as thyself," would put both the motives self-interest and others-interest — to work, and industry would have one hundred percent backing instead of the present fifty percent. It would hum — it would sing with the music of the spheres.

(3) "Recovery of sight for the blind" — the physically disinherited. The healing of sickness and infirmities was an integral part of the coming of the Kingdom. "He went round the whole of Galilee, teaching in their synagogues, preaching the gospel of the Kingdom, and curing whatever illness or infirmity there was among the people" (Matt. 4:23 NEB). The preaching of the gospel of the Kingdom included the healing of physical sicknesses and infirmities. Sickness is not the will of God. The New Testament nowhere says God sends disease. The evil of the mind is error, the evil of the emotion is suffering, the evil of the will is sin, and the evil of the body is disease. God is out to banish all evil up and down the line, including disease. But some diseases must await the coming of the healing of the resurrected body. This is a mortal world, and we were never expected to be immortal in a mortal world. So sometime or other the body breaks down. But God

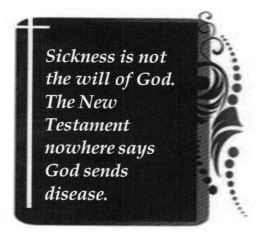

Sickness is not the will of God. The New Testament nowhere says God sends disease.

will heal the disease or give you power, not merely to bear the disease, but to use it until the final cure in the resurrection. Cure it, or give you power to use it; in both cases, it is an answer. When General Booth, the head of the Salvation Army, went blind, his son broke the final news to him. The old warrior replied: "You mean to say, Bramwell, that I will never see your face again?" Then he passed his hand over his son's face and said: "Bramwell, I've served God and the people with my eyes, now I will serve God and the people with my blindness." And he did. That was victory. He belonged to the Unshakable Kingdom.

(4) "To let the broken victims go free," or as the Aramaic version says: "To strengthen with forgiveness them that are bruised." If that is the correct translation, then the bruises are moral and spiritual for they can only be lifted by divine forgiveness. Running against the laws of the Kingdom bruises the inner life. The bruises are guilt complexes, a sense of inferiority, of missing the mark, of being out of harmony with God and oneself, a sense of wrongness. Divine forgiveness wipes out all that sense of inner hurt and condemnation. Divine forgiveness brings a sense of at-home-ness — at home with God and oneself and with life. The universe opens its arms and takes one in. God accepts you — by yourself, and by life. All self-loathing, self-rejection, all inferiorities drop away. You are a child of God; now born from above, you walk the earth, a conqueror, afraid of nothing. Without this new birth from above, life has a central lack. Give life

everything, except this birth from above, and a central dissatisfaction will eat like a cancer. But healed at the heart, you can say to life: "Come on, I'm ready for anything and everything."

(5) To proclaim the year of the Lord's favor, or as one translation puts it: "to proclaim the Lord's year of Jubilee." If that translation is correct, then this refers back to the Jewish celebration when every fifty years a year of jubilee was proclaimed during which all debts were cancelled, all slaves freed, all land redistributed, and the nation began on a closer approximation to equality. Note it was a year of jubilation—

Any plan for riches for the few, to the ruin of the many, has the seeds of its own ruin upon it.

of jubilee. Not because one person had fallen heir to immense riches, but because the nations, the people as a whole, were richer, everybody being a part of the jubilee. That was a healthy jubilation, a healthy jubilee. Jesus here proclaimed "the Lord's year of jubilee;" the Jewish year of jubilee was national and racial, this year of jubilee was the Lord's year of jubilee, extending to man as man and not to man as Jew. This was the Lord's year of jubilee as a phase of the coming of the kingdom of God—it belonged to man as man. Any plan for riches for the few, to the ruin of the many, has the seeds of its own ruin upon it. To be rich in a world of poverty is sin — sin against the many and against yourself and your own happiness for it is anti-kingdom. If your riches are dedicated to the opening of opportunities for others to share the goods intended for all, then that is consecrated riches, hence, rich riches; but if they are dedicated to your own so-called enjoyment, then it is poor riches, making others poor and making you poor, inwardly, in the process. If you dedicate your riches, you have your riches; if you don't, they have you. You are their slave. You slave to get and to keep them, and in the process you lose the one thing you own — yourself. "What shall it profit a man if he gain the whole world and lose his own soul?" That question has been asked for two thousand years, and no one has as yet come up with a balance sheet showing a profit. It always shows a loss — it always will.

The choice before us is: the Lord's year of jubilee, the Kingdom, or man's year of confusion and misery. Now let us go back and summarize up the program, which Jesus enunciated as the content of the good news of the kingdom of God:

(a) Good news to the poor — the economically disinherited.

(b) Release to the captives — the socially and politically disinherited.

(c) Opening of the eyes of the blind — the physically disinherited.

(d) The strengthening with forgiveness those who are bruised — the morally and spiritually disinherited.

(e) The Lord's year of jubilee—a new world beginning on the basis of a closer approximation to equality of opportunity for all.

Now note the redemptions to be brought with the coming of the Kingdom. Did redemption ever go into more important and more creative channels? God's revolution which is God's kingdom, brought redemption into: (a) the economic—good news to the poor, (b) the social and political—release to the captives, (c) the physical—recovery of sight to the blind, (d) the moral and spiritual—to strengthen with forgiveness those who are bruised, and (e) a fresh world beginning on the basis of equality of opportunity for all—the Lord's year of jubilee. Here was a revolution that is to remake the economic, the social and political, the physical, the moral and spiritual, in effect the total structure of life. Could anything be more inclusive, more thoroughgoing, more constructive, more needed, and more possible? Take out one item of the five and you have disruptions; put them together and you have the Kingdom—now on earth.

17. THIS KINGDOM-OF-GOD REVOLUTION IS ROOTED IN THE DEEPEST SPIRITUAL EXPERIENCE OF LIFE

"The Spirit of the Lord is upon me," therefore, this revolution. This is important for it roots the outer in the inner. You don't have to cut your roots in God to put your roots in man. They are parts of one soil—the Incarnation, the Word become flesh. This gives the movement resources. God is behind the movement, in the movement, and guiding the movement. It has stability with progress with God at the center. A non-Christian was asked by a YMCA official to become a member of the board of governors of a student hostel in London. He replied: "You Christians began this hostel, didn't you? Well, you had better run it. Whatever you begin you continue. You have staying power. We soon drop things we begin." You have inner resources—God. Those allied to the kingdom of God have cosmic backing. They have the patience of God, and the persistence of God. I saw in London the original page of the constitution of the Young Man's Christian Association (YMCA) drawn up in the handwriting of George Williams, the founder. Up at the top was originally written Young Men's *Religious* Association." A line had been drawn through the word "religious" and the word "Christian" inserted above. That was perhaps the most important short line drawn in history, for it meant that the YMCA would not be vaguely religious, but it would be definitely Christian—its roots would be in Jesus Christ and it would have its sustenance from him. The movement has been vital to the degree that it has been Christian.

When Jesus said, "The Spirit of the Lord is upon me," the five fruits of the Spirit, which issued from that impact of the Spirit upon him, make some of the supposed signs set forth in the modern day as signs of the Holy Spirit within look sick. These five things are as up-to-date as tomorrow morning and as vital as the air we breathe and the food we eat, and more so. For these five things touch the total person and his total environment. And if the Church would embody them, then the question of the relevancy of the Church would never be raised, for it would become relevancy itself.

18. THIS FIVE-POINTED STAR IS THE MORNINGSTAR OF THE NEW WORLD

"I will grant him to see the Morningstar" (Rev. 2:28 Moffatt). When Jesus announced his manifesto of the Kingdom the eyes of all in the synagogue were fixed on him (as the eyes of the peoples of the world are now being fixed on him— the Morningstar has arisen!) and he said: "Today, ... in your very hearing this text has come true. There was a general stir of admiration; they were all surprised that words of such grace should fall from his lips" (Luke 4:21, 22 NEB). "This text has come true. The Word of the Kingdom has become flesh—in me! The Kingdom has broken through in realization —in me! You have heard about it, now you see it. I am not only the Son of God (you heard about that at the baptism on Jordan's banks), you now see that I am the kingdom of God standing in your synagogue. I am not only revealing God's nature, I am revealing the nature of God's reign—his Kingdom." (The greatest memorial ever built should have been put up at that spot, for this was the blueprint of a new world, interpreted and personalized in Jesus).

But while Jesus was revealing the Kingdom in himself, he would not go on with a basic misunderstanding unclarified. They had the picture of a Jewish Messiah who would set up a Jewish messianic kingdom at Jerusalem. When he rode into Jerusalem in the triumphal entry did not the people cry: "Blessings on the coming kingdom of our father David" (Mark 11:10 NEB)? They tried to turn the kingdom of God into a Jewish kingdom, the kingdom of "our father David." Had not every Jew there prayed that very morning his daily prayer: "God, I thank thee that I was not born a woman, a leper, or a Gentile"? He let them see how far he meant to go with the new order — the kingdom of God. "There were many widows in Israel . . . and Elijah was sent to none of them, but only to Zarephath, in the land of Sidon, to a woman who was a widow." She was a Gentile woman. "There were many lepers in Israel at the time of the prophet Elisha; and none of them was cleansed, but only Naaman, the Syrian," a Gentile (Luke 4:25-27 RSV). What was he saying: that God cared especially for lepers, women, and Gentiles — thus cancelling their prayer? Their reaction was immediate. Their administration became antagonism: "When they heard this, all in the synagogue were filled with rage; they rose up, put him out of the town, and brought him to the brow of the hill on which their own town was built, in order to hurl him down" (Luke 4:28-29 Moffatt).

They stumbled over a tiny word *all*. This new Kingdom embodied in Jesus was for all. They wanted it for some. The struggle in the world is over just two words, some or all. When Nathuram Godse shot Mahatma Gandhi those same two words came together: Godse wanted an India for Hindus; Gandhi wanted an India for Hindus, Muslims, and Christians — for *all*. The "some" shot the "all," but the all goes marching on. In America the same two words are in a deadly struggle: an America for some — the white man — or an America for all, — all men, with liberty and justice for all.

The "some" people did then what they are doing now — more polite, more hidden, more cultured, but the same: They "took him to the brow of the hill on which it [their town] was built, meaning to hurl him over the edge" (Luke 4:29, 30 NEB). What happened then is happening now. The some, wanting to throw the all over the brow of the hill, only succeeded in overthrowing themselves. They who rejected the "all," became the rejected people: "Behold your house is left unto you desolate." . . . "The kingdom shall be taken away from you and given to a nation that shall bring forth the fruits thereof." "A nation" meaning any nation. The future belongs to the people who stand with and for the all.

And how does the Nazareth episode end? "But he passing through the midst of them went his way" (Luke 4:30). He glanced this way and that way — they fell back at the awful majesty of the Incarnate All, and "he went straight through them all" (NEB), and "went his way" —

his way, not theirs. Those who want "some" will get the some, but it will be a dwindling some, until finally the some will become me—and that will become the payoff. The some become "so-me." S-o dropped off and left the m-e—the hell I wanted and got!

The next paragraph gives a postscript to the story: He taught the people of Capharnahum; "they were astounded at his teaching, for his word came with authority" (Luke 4:31, 32 Moffatt). The center of authority for the future lies with One who stands for the all, who embodies the all in himself as the Son of man, and who lets people know at once where he stands and for what he stands and who is willing to take the consequence of rejection. But the rejection is a rejection—into universality. "With authority" grows through the years and as the half-answers break down, as they are breaking down, his authority will have to be listened to, or we perish—literally.

19. WE BECOME DISCIPLES OF THE KINGDOM OF GOD

"Every scribe who has become a disciple of the Realm [kingdom] of heaven is like a householder who produces what is new and what is old from his stores" (Matt. 13:52 Moffatt). Herein Matthew, Jesus devoted a whole chapter to the kingdom of God, and in the midst of it he used a phrase, a disciple of the kingdom of God. This was illuminating and revealing. He had called them to be his disciples, and he was to call them to make all nations his disciples, but here he went further and called his disciples to be "disciples of the Kingdom of God." Here he put together these two things and made them one— to be his disciple was to be a disciple of the Kingdom of God. To be his disciple was to be a disciple of his message, the Kingdom. He taught them many things, but he never asked his disciples to be disciples to anything except himself —nothing else, except the

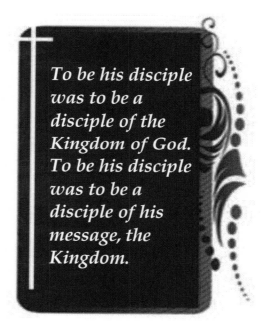

To be his disciple was to be a disciple of the Kingdom of God. To be his disciple was to be a disciple of his message, the Kingdom.

Kingdom. He identified himself and the Kingdom so completely that to be a disciple of one was to be a disciple of the other. But here what God has joined together man has put asunder. We have called men to be disciples of Jesus, but not disciples of the kingdom of God—to take the King but not his kingdom. This has weakened the impact of Jesus upon the world. It is a personal relationship of a person to a Person, but not a relationship with the order embodied in that Person. This was a vital loss, for the order was to be the life program of the disciple. Nothing can be compared with that loss, and nothing can be compared to the gain when we become disciples to the Kingdom.

20. THE DISCIPLES OF THE KINGDOM ARE THE SONS OF THE KINGDOM WHO ARE CALLED "THE GOOD SEED ... THE SONS OF THE KINGDOM"

Note in what world-encompassing terms he speaks: "He who sows the good seed is the Son of man; the field is the world; the good seed means the sons of the Realm (Matt. 13:38-39, Moffatt). Did a Galilean carpenter speak in such World-encompassing terms as a carpenter, or as the architect of a new world? He either had illusions of grandeur or he held the ground plan of the universe.

Now note the good seed sown was the sons of the Kingdom. This is important. The seed sown was called the word: "When anyone hears the word of the Realm" (Matt. 13:19 Moffatt). Here the seed was the word of the Kingdom, but later the sons of the Kingdom were called the seed. So the sons of the Kingdom is the word sown in the world by the Son of man. So the seed of the Kingdom was not an abstract word of the Kingdom but a concrete, embodied word "the sons of the Kingdom." This puts it in the line of the succession to the Son of man—he was the word become flesh, and we as sons of the Kingdom are to be the word become flesh, sown in the furrows of the world and bringing fruit in all the worlds—feeding the world, serving the world, sustaining the world and the new order, the Kingdom. This personalizes the Kingdom; the Kingdom is to come in us! The phrase "son of" was important in those days. A man was referred to as the son of the dominant quality in him. Barnabas, after he gave his all to Christ, became Barnabas, "the son of encouragement." Judas was called "the son of perdition," "the son of waste," that "wasted son." You were the son of your dominant quality. The kingdom of God was to be the dominant quality in the followers of Jesus, and hence, they were called sons of the Kingdom. Never was a more significant name given. But if any group of the followers of Jesus were ever called the sons of the Kingdom, I have never heard of them anywhere in the world. This reveals again the loss of the kingdom of God in Christendom. Within Christendom, the kingdom of God was lost as the dominant quality, so the phrase, the sons of the Kingdom, was never adopted.

But I've seen sons and daughters of the Kingdom around the world. When Amy Wilson Carmichael was the head of a school, mostly for girls, three hundred of them rescued from prostitution, she was wracked with pain of arthritis for eighteen years. She said, "I may be in Nero's prison, but I'm not Nero's prisoner." She was a daughter of the Kingdom, the Unshakable Kingdom.

The disciple to the kingdom of God produces from his stores. He has stores. These stores could refer both to the conscious and to the subconscious mind. We keep storing up in the subconscious mind, daily, hourly, momentarily, a good store if we are in the Kingdom and the Kingdom is in us. That good store becomes a reserve upon which we can call when in the hour of testing and temptation. We get through a crisis with surprising ease and power. We wonder why and how? The good store threw reserves into the battle and you come through with flags flying. The spiritual life is no longer precarious. It has reserves of power. The area of the work of the Holy Spirit is largely, if not entirely, in the subconscious mind. So the reserves are under the control of the Holy Spirit and are available when you most need them. So you belong to the Unshakable Kingdom.

21. "THE KINGDOM OF GOD IS WITHIN YOU"

"The kingdom of God is within you," but not only within you. The kingdom of heaven is at your doors. And the kingdom of God is coming. All three — not one exclusively, but all three inclusively. The kingdom of God is within you, was not spoken to disciples or converted people — it was spoken to the Pharisees (Luke 17:20). Is the kingdom of heaven within everybody — good, bad, indifferent? Yes. Because the laws of your being are the laws of the kingdom of God. This Kingdom is built from the foundation of the world — built in, within the structure of your being. You are built to obey the laws of the Kingdom. If we obey the laws written within us, we are fulfilled; if we go against those laws, we are frustrated and if we persist, we are broken. All is Love and all is Law. God doesn't have to punish you if you break his laws written in you. Sin and its punishment are one and the same thing. You don't have to punish the eye for having sand in it, nor the body for having a cancer in it, nor the soul for having sin in it. As Augustine said, sin and its punishment are one and the same thing. You take one and you get the other. In a procession to agitate against polygamy, African women carried banners saying, "He who brings another woman in the house, brings poison." They knew that sin is not nectar — it is poison, poisoning relationships and the person who brings it in. Another banner: "Let the men bring in other women they will only

God doesn't have to punish you if you break his laws written in you. Sin and its punishment is one and the same thing.

hurt themselves." These women knew that sin and its punishment are one and the same thing. A modern woman of the West wrote to a newspaper: "They say to have an affair with another woman's husband is heaven. I can tell you it is ten percent heaven and ninety percent hell." A Christian woman was asked by a doctor, "Are you allergic to anything?" "Yes," she replied: "I am allergic to sin."

Note the great imperative laid down in the Bible, "getting in their own persons the due recompense of their perversity" (Rom. 1:27 Moffatt). A man came up to Sam Jones, the evangelist, and said: "I only know one verse of Scripture and I know that one is true: 'The way of transgressors is hard'" (Prov. 13:15). The Christian way is not the hard way—it is working with the universe: evil is the hard way—it is working against the universe. Evil is perverse, an attempt at the impossible, and the result is that those who try it, get in their own persons the due recompense—their persons deteriorate, break down, and perish. This passage puts it more vividly: "that nature which crumbles to ruin under the passions of moral deceit" (Eph. 4:22, 23 Moffatt). The Apostle saw that when we are deceitful, we deceive no one except ourselves. The result of the deceit is that our own natures crumble to ruin.

These words sum it up: "the fruitless enterprises of darkness" (Eph. 5:11, Moffatt). Evil blossoms and blooms and gives promise of fruit, but then decay sets in, and we have rottenness on our hands. The great moral imperatives laid down in the biological and psychological structure of human beings guarantees the ultimate triumph of the good. The good is stable; evil is unstable. "This guilt of yours shall split you." Everyone who sins is a split personality, a civil war. The great moral imperatives versus the impulses, "Your fury shall consume yourselves" (Isa. 33:11 Moffatt). The fury against others by its very nature recoils upon oneself and consumes the consumer.

Sin is no laughing matter, but this story makes it laughable: A boy was seen crying disconso-lately. Someone asked what the matter was. He replied: "I've been playing hooky all day, and I just found out this is Saturday." When we play hooky against our best interests, we play hooky against ourselves.

When we play hooky against our best interests, we play hooky against ourselves.

The kingdom of heaven is within you — in our very makeup, in the laws of our being, and in the nature of the universe in which we live. So when we revolt against God, we revolt against ourselves and against the universe. The prodigal son returning to his father said: "I have sinned against heaven, and before thee, and am no more worthy to be called the son" (Luke 15:18-19). He saw he had been sinning in three directions: against heaven — the impersonal moral universe, the moral imperative written in the nature of things; against the personal love of his father — before thee — we don't merely sin against an impersonal moral universe, we sin against the personal love of our heavenly Father, we sin against law (heaven), we sin against love (the Father); then we sin against ourselves—I "am no more worthy to be called thy son." So sin is not only an allergy, it is an alienation—from the moral universe, from God, and from ourselves.

The kingdom of God is our homeland. But this kingdom within, within everybody, is not a chosen kingdom; it is inherited from the Creator. He made us that way. Now comes the second phase of the coming of the Kingdom—it is come upon you. "But if it is by the finger of God that I drive out devils, then be sure the kingdom of God has already come upon you" (Luke 11:20 NEB; or "reached you already" Moffatt). The kingdom of God is within you, now it is come upon you in the person of Jesus—come upon you for a choice. Having vaguely felt that the Kingdom is within me, I now see it personalized and I now choose it as my kingdom. That introduces us to the second phase: The Kingdom stands at my door, is upon me as a deliberate choice resulting in a new birth. "Except a man be born-again [or from above], he cannot see the kingdom of God" (John 3:3). "Except ye be converted, ... ye shall not enter the kingdom of heaven" (Matt. 18:3). Now Everyman —I spell it with a capital E— feels vaguely that he is made in his personal structure for the kingdom of God, and the nature of the universe is made for the kingdom of God. So Everyman is caught between the pincers of a personal destiny and a universal destiny, both of them pressing on him and urging him to take the next great step to be born-again, to take this next great step and accept the kingdom of God as his personal choice and his way of life, his total way of life. This kingdom is at his door — at his door in the most wonderful Person that ever broke into the plane of human existence and he makes us an offer, the offer of the Kingdom, the Unshakable Kingdom, as our very own.

This new birth from above puts us on top of the world. There are five kingdoms, each representing a stage in life: (1) the mineral kingdom, (2) the vegetable kingdom, (3) the animal kingdom, (4) the kingdom of man, or human kingdom, (5) the kingdom of God. Members of each of these kingdoms might imagine that life ends with their particular kingdom with nothing higher. The mineral kingdom might imagine that there is nothing higher than the mineral. But the plant kingdom knows that plant life is higher than the mineral. When we come to the kingdom of man, the humanists say that life stops with men — "know thyself" and you know all there is to be known. But in all ages, among all men, there is the pressure from above which awakens men to prayer, to aspirations, to God. We hear about this kingdom and we know it is our real destiny, but we also know that we have spoiled that destiny by responding to our past evil inheritance, to our present "evil world," and to our own choices. So we feel the chances are loaded against us. But the Good News of the kingdom of God arouses our hope and expectation: We can be born from above. The best Man who ever lived and the most powerful Man that ever lived and the most trustable, offers me a birth from above, leaving out all I've accumulated since my biological birth. It seems too good to be true, but I'll try it; I'll give up all my earthborn attempts to be worthy, to be good enough, to earn it, and I'll trust his offer of the Unshakable Kingdom.

I get my clue from the lowest kingdom: Here is foul, impure mud, and it looks up and sees the purity of the lotus flower in the purity of the plant kingdom. How can the mud become the lotus flower? It can't except in one way — the lotus flower comes down amid the foul mud and says: "Be willing to cease to be mud, surrender yourself to me." It does. It knows not how, but it is taken hold of by the lotus flower and transformed and transfigured — it is born from above.

Jesus seems to be heaven's lotus flower coming down into our mud — pure amid our impurity, generous amid our selfishness, and loving amid our hate. He asks me no questions as he flings open the door of the Kingdom and says, "Enter." Hesitatingly I do, but I do. I belong to the Unshakable Kingdom, and, wonder of wonders, I, too, am pure in his purity, generous in his generosity, and loving in his love. I'm in.

Is this a pipe dream? No, it is solid reality. I spoke one night in a meeting presided over by a man who heard a group talk about the Unshakable Kingdom and their experience in it. He reacted violently against it. He jumped in his car to run away from it, drove one hundred miles at ninety miles per hour, ended up in a ditch — a physical and emotional and spiritual wreck, hovered between life and death for many weeks, consented to take two drops of communion wine by an eyedropper, symbol that he was willing to come back home. He did and now he is a transformed, radiant person, leading others — multitudes of them — to come back home.

Another, calmer and composed, but basically empty example: A businessman spent $65,000 to be psychoanalyzed. (I believe in Christian psychiatry and have established a Christian Psychiatric Center in India, the first of its kind and it is very successful.) The psychiatrist analyzed twelve hundred of the man's dreams, but was long on analysis and short on synthesis and he did not know how to put the man back together again. The patient grew worse. Sadly he left the office of the psychiatrist, now a defeated, disillusioned man. He heard a voice speak to him as he went down the steps, "Look this way." He felt it was the voice of Christ. But didn't know how to find him. He heard that I was to speak in the National Christian Mission in St. Louis and so drove the hundred miles from his home in Quincy, Illinois. He

> *Jesus seems to be heaven's lotus flower coming down into our mud — pure amid our impurity, generous amid our selfishness, and loving amid our hate.*

was in the Kerr Auditorium with twenty thousand others and listened while I spoke on the kingdom of God. He did not react violently against it, but instead quietly said to himself: "This is it. My quest is over." Quietly, but decisively, he entered the Unshakable Kingdom. He became one of the most spiritually integrated men I ever knew. He wrote to me in India and said: "If you will transplant the Christian Ashram movement to America, I'll pay the bills." (The Christian Ashram movement has become a worldwide movement with over a hundred centers around the world.) This man left a Laymen's Trust for Evangelism with several million dollars in it to be spent in twenty-five years. All he had to do to turn from defeat to victory was to say: "This is it. My quest is over." His quest was off, but his life had just begun!

So the Kingdom is present in two phases: The kingdom of God is within you. You are built for the Kingdom. It has been built into the structure of your being from the foundation of the world. The second phase is this: The kingdom of God is at your door. It is your structural destiny, but without your decision to make it your own, it would be coercion—coercion, not conversion. So the Kingdom is not a kingdom of puppets, but a kingdom of persons. The Divine Patience waits: "Behold, I stand at the door and knock: if any man hears my voice, and opens the door, I will come in to him and eat with him, and he with me" (Rev. 3:20). The absolute order stands in the absolute Person at our door to await the fateful decision. What lowliness: "I stand at the door and knock." And what sovereignty: "And he with me." He becomes our guest—"I will eat with him"—in the beginning, but note in the end—"he with me," we are his guests and He is Lord. He begins with the lowly, but he always ends with the lofty—on the throne.

The third phase is the consummation phase. Jesus depicts that phase when he gave the parable of the nobleman who went into a far country to receive a kingdom and return. This depicts Jesus going to the Father to receive the Kingdom and returning to earth to set it up universally. Here I repeat for emphasis: concerning that third phase, we know little, and he said we would know

The kingdom of God is within you. You are built for the Kingdom. It has been built into the structure of your being from the foundation of the world.

little or nothing. He said it is not for us to know: "It is not for you to know about dates or times, which the Father has set within his own control" (Acts 1:7 NEB). That was wise, for if he had given us timetables and maps about his coming, we would have concentrated upon times and seasons instead of making the Kingdom our total program for our total life now. So he hid the future that we might concentrate on the Unshakable Kingdom and the

Unchanging Person now. He said he was coming again. I believe he will. He came once. He will come again. That once is so wonderful and so all sufficient, that I feel I have only touched the fringes of the wonder of it all. I am so intrigued and excited about the unfolding of the open secret of the kingdom of God, that this is all I can stand for the present. I put up my question marks about the future coming of the King and the Kingdom. I simply don't know, nor does anybody else know, only the Father, but I have no question marks about this first coming, this present Unshakable Kingdom, and nothing but exclamation marks about it. It works to the degree that we work it. A man who has spent his life on the second coming of Christ said at the end of his life: "I wasted my life in fruitless guesses at the meaning of 'times and seasons.' I should have given my attention to the gospel of the First Coming."

The human personality has as its goal perfection, but perfection in love, as God is perfect, but never becoming God. The finite will infinitely approach the Infinite, but never becoming that Infinite. Our joy will be to infinitely approach the Infinite. That growth into his likeness will be our joy—our eternal joy.

22. THE GOAL OF THE KINGDOM: SHARING HIS THRONE

"To him who is victorious I will grant a place on my throne, as I myself was victorious and sat down with my Father on his throne" (Rev. 3:21 NEB). If our last item in the Kingdom's program and plan was amazing, namely, that we should be perfect in love as the Father is perfect in love, then this item is just as amazing, for it says that we shall share not only in his character, but in his authority and power. We shall sit on his throne as he sits on the Father's throne. Here is a kingdom, which demands total obedience and then offers us a share in total power. This cleanses the center of power in the universe from the charge of autocratic power. He even invites us, provided we are victorious, to a place on the throne of Christ as he is on the throne with the Father. But note, there are three on that throne: the Father, Jesus Christ, and man. Many who on earth were used to producing on earth (activists) would welcome being made in the

> *We shall sit on his throne as he sits on the Father's throne. Here is a kingdom, which demands total obedience and then offers us a share in total power.*

likeness of a loving God; but a life now of loving and an eternity of loving would not quite fulfill their nature. They want to create. This promise offers us a share in creation — at the center!

"Power corrupts and absolute power corrupts absolutely," says Lord Acton. Then how would we be saved from that corruption if given a place in ultimate power?

This 'power' is free from that egotism which corrupts men in every other realm. A self-giving God is at the center, and His self-giving Christ reveals the self-giving God and his self-giving kingdom divided against itself, scatters his relationships and that self-giving kingdom. The ultimate Power on the throne has lost its life and has found it again. I can bow to that kind of power, not because I have to, but because I can't help it. If there isn't power like that in the universe, there ought to be. If there is — it has me, has me with the consent of all my being.

A kingdom, which has a God like that, will ultimately hold our allegiance, or we will ultimately perish, perish by our self-born impossibilities. Jesus said: "He that gathers not with me, scatters." Scatters his own personality — he becomes a kingdom divided against itself, scatters his relationships, his society, his world. But if we gather with Jesus, we gather, we are unified within, we produce unified relationships, a unified society, and a unified final power. If man with such a spirit were on the throne, he would gather with Christ and God and the Kingdom. All is love, and all is law — the Kingdom rules all, frees all, redeems all, and creates all.

In the kingdom of God, man is in the place of final power. God moves over and gives a place on the throne to the God-man, and the God-man moves over and gives a place for man. That reveals the nature of the Creator — the Creator creates creatures that will share in the government of the creation. When God moves over, does God move down, or does he move up? Obviously, it is up. By becoming the servant of all, he becomes the greatest of all. He not only obeys his own laws — he embodies his own laws. His laws are a transcript of his own character.

A kingdom, which has a God like that, will ultimately hold our allegiance, or we will ultimately perish, perish by our self-born impossibilities.

We will leave for the time being the Kingdom in heaven and return to the Kingdom on earth. We will leave it with this comment: We see that the sons of the Kingdom are to be made into the Father's perfection, perfection in love. And we are to share the creative ruler-ship, share it with the Father and the Son. What that means I do not know. But it will be better than I think. And that is breathtaking. And yet I see that now this process is taking place. Those who obey the laws of the kingdom of

God do belong to an Unshakable Kingdom now and an Unchanging Person; they do become the salt of every situation they are in and do become the light of every situation they are in. They become dominant, not because they want to be dominant, but because every situation they are in demands the very things they stand for and embody. That is the wave of the future. Former Assistant Secretary of State, A. A. Berle, Jr., put it in these words: "No group of human beings, however implemented, has been able to challenge the great design." The great design is the Unshakable Kingdom of God.[1] Align yourself to the great design and you have the sum total of reality behind you.

We now turn to the qualities of character and life, which characterize the sons and daughters of the Kingdom, the persons who are the wave of the future, the light and salt of the present.

---

[1] Adolf Augustus Berle, Jr. was a lawyer, educator, author, and U.S. diplomat. He was the author of *The Modern Corporation and Private Property*, a groundbreaking work on corporate governance, and an important member of U.S. President Franklin Roosevelt's "Brain Trust. (http://www.bing.com/search? q=A. +A.+ Berle, +Jr& src=IE-Search Box&FORM= IENTTR &conversationid=). Accessed 7/23/2017

23. THE SONS OF THE KINGDOM OF GOD — THEIR OUTLOOK AND SPIRIT

So Jesus said: "You know that in the world, rulers lord it over their subjects, and their great men make them feel the weight of authority; but it shall not be so with you. Among you, whoever wants to be great must be your servant, and whoever would be first must be the willing slave of all — like the Son of Man; he did not come to be served, but to serve, and to give up his life as a ransom for many" (Matt. 20:25-28 NEB). This sets the central pattern of character in the Kingdom. They are to be servant-minded rulers. Note he expected them to rule. He set his lowly followers and his kingdom in the framework of rulers, contrasting their rule with the rulers of the Gentiles. He expected them to rule the world in the name of, in the spirit of this new order, the kingdom of God. It was a reversal of the prevailing spirit of rulers: Among the prevailing rulers, those were the greatest who had the greatest number of servants; in the new order, the Kingdom, those were greatest who served the greatest number. Then if you wanted to be first, you were to be the slave of all. Then the highest of all, the Son of man, came not to be served, but to serve and surrender his life as a ransom for many. So there are degrees of greatness: Great — servant of all; first — slave of all; highest — the Son of man who surrenders his life as a ransom for all. So the way up is the way down for man and God. Never was there such a method of greatness revealed. And never

197

was there such a method of greatness that made it beneficent to all concerned. Those who are served go up through that service; those who serve go up through that lowly serving. Naked desire for greatness corrupts the aspirant and corrupts those upon whom the naked desire for greatness is exercised — they resent it. But the desire for greatness in the Kingdom — the self-interest — is linked with the desire to serve others, the others-interest; so everyone is benefitted and fulfilled. Only a divine mind could put those two things into such a living blend.

So there is a place for ambitious men in the Kingdom — if you want to be great be the servant of all. If you want to be first, be the slave of all. If you want to be like the Son of man, give your life as a ransom for all. For that is the way he went to firstness. But the desire to excel is linked with a desire to renounce for the sake of others.

Here I must pause for a moment to comment on two movements, one in economics and the other in religion, which are very popular. One has as its slogan, "Dare to be great," and the other has "Self-love, the secret of success." Both of these have a truth in the slogan and in the outlook. You must cease all self-hate, self-distrust, and self-depreciation — affirm yourself. This truth gives a positive attitude toward you and toward life. As such, it is to the good. But it is a half-truth and, as such, it gives an initial boost, but ends in a final bust. Its fatal flaw is that it leaves you at the center, and anything that leaves you at the center is off-center. You are not God and to act as though you were is to invite disillusionment. The central slogan in the kingdom of God is: "Seek first the kingdom of God, and all these things [including yourself], will be added unto you." That puts God in his place, you in your place, and your neighbor in his place. God is first, then the rest of us are second. Then what happens?

When you seek first the kingdom of God, then you fulfill the three basic needs of humanity according to psychology. First, the need to belong — you belong to the highest order, the Unshakable Kingdom and to the Unchanging Person, Jesus Christ. You belong! When you belong you can no longer look down on yourself. You belong to the Ultimate. Therefore, all self-hate, self-loathing, and self-depreciation drop away. How can you hate what God loves, loathe what God accepts, and depreciate what the God-man died for.

Second, the need for significance. If I make self-love or the desire to be great the secret of success, then all the significance I have is the significance of me — nothing behind me except me.

Third, reasonable security. If I make self-love and desire to be great first then I have this security behind me: I am taking an affirmative attitude toward myself — I turn from fear to faith, I'm a yes, instead of a no. That helps and helps greatly, but what happens when failures, sickness, old age, death come — then do the securities hold? Professor Royce of Harvard said, "No man is safe unless he can stand anything that can happen to him." Then the one who belongs to the Kingdom is safe, for not only can he bear failure, sickness, old age, and death — he can use them. He is the only safe man in the universe. He has the significance of the ultimate order.

So I would agree with the self-acceptance and the self-affirmation attitude, provided the Kingdom is first and the self-affirmation second. But if you make the self-affirmation first and the Kingdom second, then the self will be sticking out all down the line, and instead of self-affirmation it will turn into self-credit. But if you take the kingdom-first attitude, it puts humble gratitude at the center. All you say and do and are is colored by humble gratitude.

24. THE SONS AND DAUGHTERS OF THE KINGDOM — FURTHER SIGNS OF THEIR SPIRIT AND ATTITUDE

"Besides, all they do [scribes and Pharisees] is done to catch the notice of men; they make their phylacteries broad, and they wear large tassels. They are fond of the best places at banquets and the front seats in the synagogue, they like to be saluted in the marketplaces and to be called 'rabbi' by men. But you are not to be called 'rabbi,' for One is your teacher, and you are all brothers. You are not to call anyone 'father' on earth, for One is your heavenly Father. Nor must you be called 'leaders,' for One is your leader even the Christ. . . . Whoever uplifts himself will be humbled, and whoever humbles himself will be uplifted" (Matt. 23:5-12 Moffatt).

Here, the sons of the Kingdom were to be differentiated from the rest of the world by a difference in the outward and a difference in the inward. The scribes and Pharisees were devotees of the outward; outwardism was their religion. Jesus has been criticized for the woes against the Pharisees and scribes. Did not his love grow thin or nonexistent? On the contrary, never was love more manifest than when he lanced this suppurating boil of outwardism and hypocrisy in religion on the body of a nation. Had the leaders reacted in repentance and regeneration, the nation might have been the instrument of the coming of the kingdom of God. Instead, they crucified the "Surgeon" and committed spiritual suicide themselves. India has never had a prophet who dared perform that operation on the soul of India. Instead, the religious leaders of India have taken in the good, bad, and indifferent—"all roads lead to the same goal" —and that has poisoned the good. For the good has not been used very often for a cleansing, but for justifying the unjustifiable. India has needed a loving "woe unto you." And America needs the same moral cleansing, for toleration has become so tolerant that evil is included in that tolerance. We are in danger of becoming "moral cows in our plump comfortableness."

So, Jesus in the new order, the Kingdom, told us to beware of certain titles, which carry with them certain un-kingdom attitudes. He named four things we were not to be called:

First, "Be ye not called 'fathers.' " The attitude of the fathers is: "Because of my age, I know and you don't—listen, wisdom is now speaking." Its litany: "As it was in the beginning, is now and ever shall be, world without end, Amen." The fathers' attitude is the attitude that Jesus condemned when he said: "He that puts his hand to the plow and looks back is not fit for the kingdom of God." It could be translated, "cannot fit into the kingdom of God." For the Kingdom stands for the new. An aging saint who seemed to get younger and younger as the years came and went said: "You must take out your brains periodically and jump on them to keep them from hardening." For while many people die from hardening of the arteries, others die mentally and spiritually from "hardening of the categories." So don't be identified with yesterday alone, but to the today, to the tomorrow, and to the forever. One of the best compliments I've ever had came from a little girl who asked her mother: "Mother, how old is Stanley Jones?" And when told that I was eighty, she said, "How can that be, he acts as though he is just beginning." I am just beginning, for I belong to the ageless kingdom, to the bright and Morning Star; He was never called the evening star—there is always a dawn in every happening in him. Be ye not called, "fathers."

Second, "Be ye not called 'teachers,'" for the attitude of the teacher is "I know and you don't know—listen, for wisdom is now speaking." This attitude is self-assertive. The attitude of the Kingdom is to become as a little child—not childish, but childlike, open, receptive, eager to learn;

never like the young man who when he graduated from college sent a telegram of one word to his parents: "Educated."

Third, "Be ye not called leaders'" — for the attitude of the leader is: "I'm your leader, fall in behind me." But we have classes for leadership in our churches, which is a mistake. This does not produce leaders — it only produces fussy managers of other people. A young man who found within himself a tendency to try to manage other people said in one of our Ashrams: "I have resigned as general manager of the universe." A woman came to the Ashram and said: "I have come here to learn how to manage my family." Our first advice was, "Don't try to manage your family; learn to love and serve them, then leadership in the family will come as a byproduct of the loving and serving."

That leads to the one attitude that fitted into the Kingdom, the one attitude with which he could trust them: "He who is greatest among you must be your servant." The title of servant was the only title he could trust them to use, for it was the only attitude that fitted the kingdom — greatness through service. If there were no other unique things in the Kingdom than this one thing — greatness through service — would stand out as unique and vitally unique. For where you have this quality of greatness through service, you have real greatness; where you have any other quality, you have tinseled greatness which proves to be a ridiculous attempt at greatness. I saw this in India where a row of women was seated on the platform. One of them was to be chosen as chairman. One woman nudged her chair out of line, a little in front of the rest. When the others saw it, they nudged their chairs in line with the first woman. She forged ahead again, pushing her chair farther forward. The others followed suit. The audience saw what was happening and began politely smiling, but when it went on till the woman reached the edge of the platform, the audience broke out in laughter. They were never as small as when they tried to be big.

A daughter of two prominent people said, "My father's name is printed in the newspapers, my mother's name is written in our hearts!" The father tried to be great by advertising himself. The mother was great by her humble service to everybody. One tried hard to be great, the other was great by her lowly service to all.

I saw on a platform in India two men who represented two attitudes toward life—one was a religious politician, who pulled strings to gain greatness; he was successful, outwardly. On the platform, he performed, shook himself, but nobody else. Inwardly we said, "Oh yeah?" The other man on the platform was Sadhu Sundar Singh. He had no signs of greatness and wanted none, none except a great Lord and a great single-hearted devotion to that Lord. When Sundar Singh spoke, we were all shaken to our depths. He had no outer authority and wanted none, but when he spoke in a subdued voice, we were shaken as reeds in a wind—the wind of the Holy Spirit.

When Jesus said, "The servant of all shall be the greatest of all," the emphasis was on all. Many are willing to be the servants of some — my family, my class, my race, my country, my religion, but that doesn't make us great, except a great snob. Jesus gave his life for — all, all classes, all races, and all sinners — all. Therefore, he is the greatest of all.

25. THE KINGDOM OF GOD —
UNREAL AND REAL FOR HIM AND FOR US

"Whereupon Jesus perceived that they meant to come and seize him to make a king of him; so he withdrew by himself to the hill again" (John 6:15 Moffatt). Twice in his life they tried to make him a king — once a secular king and once a political king. He refused them both. He would be a king on his own terms or not at all. After he fed the five thousand — they came to make him a king by force — he must be our king, for he can supply

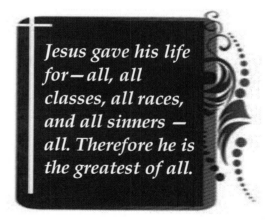

Jesus gave his life for — all, all classes, all races, and all sinners — all. Therefore he is the greatest of all.

our physical needs, and support our economic motive and drive. He left them and went upto a mountain to pray. Prayer would keep his eyes focused and his vision clear.

The other time, was after his resurrection when he spoke to them for forty days on the Kingdom. The disciples asked him: "Wilt thou restore at this time the kingdom to Israel?" They took his universal kingdom and tried to jam it into a nationalistic mold. They didn't reject the Kingdom, but they reduced it into their own mold; they tried to capture the Kingdom for nationalistic purposes. He refused to be either a bread king or a Jewish nationalistic king. In both cases, it meant that Jesus would do everything and they, his followers, would do nothing except to receive the benefits of his kingship. In both cases, it would be a handout and the prayer would be "gimme." They would have withered into being noncreative. His bringing in of the Kingdom would be a joint product of God and man and the Son of man taking the heavier part of the load. It would be a program for God and man and the Son of man — a total program for the total life for total humanity and the total divinity.

Note the modern attempts to reduce the Kingdom and make it innocuous: (1) to reduce the Kingdom and make it synonymous with the Church, to make the Church the Kingdom. The Roman Catholics have done this frankly and openly. To keep infallibility they had to make the Church infallible. A Roman Catholic bishop has written a book entitled: *The Infallibility of the Pope, Scripturally Examined*. He shows that there is no scriptural basis for the infallibility of the pope. There has been no infallibility in the Roman Catholic Church except that it has been infallibly fallible like the rest of us. So with the crumbling of the infallibility of the Church, there is no infallibility of the Kingdom, for it was identified with a fallible church. The Church is a relativism, related to something higher than itself, the kingdom of God. The Church is built up, the Kingdom is built in, built from the foundation of the world, built into its very structure. The Church is the subject of redemption: "Christ loved the church and gave himself up for her to consecrate her" (Eph. 5:25, 26 Moffatt). If the Church is the subject of redemption, how can it offer it? If the Church takes you beyond itself to the feet of Christ and his Kingdom, it is beautiful. But if it stops you and makes itself the issue, then it is not beautiful. It is idolatrous.

> *The Church is built up, the Kingdom is built in, built from the foundation of the world, built into its very structure.*

(2) The Protestant Church has made the Church and the Kingdom one, not overtly, but covertly. It puts the idea in its hymnology in a hidden way, for instance: "I love thy kingdom, Lord, . . . The Church our blest Redeemer saved." You don't save the Kingdom. The Kingdom saves you. The Church holds the best life of the Kingdom, but it is not the Kingdom. You get into the Church by joining it; you get into the Kingdom by being born-again, or from above.

(3) The third way we render the Kingdom inoperative is by identifying the coming of the Kingdom with the second coming of Christ: "The Kingdom will not come until Jesus Christ comes." So we can do nothing now except save individuals; an individual answer now, but not a total way of life. That can only come with the coming of Jesus. That cuts the nerve of the Kingdom by postponing it until the coming of Jesus. It is not a total way and program for life now. But Jesus taught the Kingdom as a present issue and a present program for life now. He went out preaching the gospel of the Kingdom, now; it is within you, it is at your doors, you are to seek first the Kingdom and then all these things will be added to you. So the Kingdom as presented by Jesus was an issue and a total issue and total program for the total life now. So to make the Kingdom a refuge into which you run and are safe — a kind of fort into which we run for security — is to cut the nerve of the gospel of the Kingdom. You set it off into a millennial reign and not a market reign now, and hence, you render it innocuous now. But you have the security of the Kingdom now when you believe in and practice it now. You may do it imperfectly but you commit yourself and surrender your life to the seeking first of the Kingdom now. Then grace covers what you do imperfectly. But grace does not cover your imperfections if you have a life commitment, which is other than seeking first the Kingdom. If you seek yourself first, then you have the security of yourself only — not the kingdom-security.

26. THE SERMON ON THE MOUNT —
AN EPITOME OF THE ETHICS OF THE KINGDOM
OF GOD — ARE THESE ETHICS PRACTICABLE?

The answer to this question about the practicability of the kingdom of God as an imposed ethical system can be answered straight off — no. If it is a system imposed, no. But if it is a system not imposed, but exposed — exposed out of the nature of the kingdom of God and exposed out of our human nature, then the answer is yes. Anything else is impracticable. As I see it, the basis of human nature is in the statement that God made man in his own image. The full statement in Genesis is: "So God created man in his own image, in the image of God created he him; male and female created he them" (Gen.1:27). Note that the statement is repeated for emphasis: "So God created man in his own image, in the image of God created he him." Whatever you may believe about the Genesis account of creation, the emphatic portion is that God and man have a kinship — they are not alien, they are affinities; the same laws of character are in God and man; the kingdom of God is man's native land; man is built to obey and enjoy that kinship; it is man's native land; it is man's natural way to live.

And this includes the fact of humankind's being male and female — it includes the fact of the sexual: "male and female created he them." So sexuality is a built-in fact of creation and comes to its own in the kingdom of God. All the other drives in human nature, when they obey the laws of the kingdom of God, come into their own—are fulfilled. Human nature itself is fulfilled when it obeys the laws of the kingdom of God. When we obey the laws of the kingdom of God, we are obeying the laws of our own being. It is the natural way to live.

Now man fell—he sinned against the kingdom of God and sinned against the laws of his own being. We call that the "Fall." But the Fall does not mean the obliteration of the image of God. The laws of the kingdom of God are still the laws of the being of fallen man. Persons may live against those laws. If so, that is the basic reason of the fact of the unhappiness of fallen persons. He is living against the laws of God written in his own being, but he is still made by God and for God, and hence, he feels divided, at war with himself, when he is living a life of sin. He feels estranged from God and from himself.

When Jesus said, "The Kingdom of God is within you" (Luke 17:21), he said it to the Pharisees, not to his disciples. The Scriptures speak of a man tortured by evil spirits—if evil spirits torture a man by their very presence within him, how can evil be natural? If evil were natural, then one should blossom and bloom under evil. It is the opposite. Evil is disruptive. It is an attempt to live against life and it cannot be done. We say, "as ugly as sin." Why? Because sin is ugly—literally. But if sin were natural, why should it be ugly? Goodness is beautiful and good to look at. It is natural. Evil is an unnatural intrusion, a foreign body, in God's creation, and therefore, suppuration, an inflammation sets in, an attempt of nature to throw it off.

Even the swine, when evil spirits entered into them, couldn't live with themselves and rushed down the slope to put an end to themselves. Sin is slow or fast suicide, but it is suicide. Every man of sin hates himself. A mechanic said to the owner of a car: "Your car is beginning to self-destruct." When you take sin into your life you begin to self-destruct. When a person begins a life of sin, we say of him that he is going to pieces. That is literally true. *Hamartia*, the Greek word for iniquity, is literally "missing the mark." So sin is un-natural, a missing of the mark, an attempt to live against life.

The Christian way is the natural way, super-naturally natural. Sin is the accustomed way, but it is not natural. When the people came to see the demonic of the tombs after Jesus had healed him, they found him "clothed and in his right mind, . . and they were afraid" (Mark 5:15 RSV). Afraid of sanity! We have become so accustomed to the insane un-kingdom ways of life that we are afraid of the sanity of the Kingdom. This is particularly true of the

> *The only thing that holds this civilization together is the leaven of people who, within the Church and outside the Church, are living in Kingdom ways. They hold the world together.*

Sermon on the Mount, which contains many, if not most of the laws, the principles, and the attitudes of the kingdom of God. As we unfold the laws, principles, and attitudes of the kingdom of God as seen in the Sermon on the Mount, I believe we will be astonished at the sheer sanity of the kingdom of God. Alongside of it, the life lived in un-kingdom ways seems bedlam; "life's music jangled out of tune" — "the tale told by an idiot, full of sound and fury, signifying nothing." The only thing that holds this civilization together is the leaven of people who, within the Church and outside the Church, are living in Kingdom ways. They hold the world together.

The Epistle to Diognetus, written in the third century, says this: "What the soul is to the body, the Christians are to the world. ... the Christians hold the world together." They do — the real ones. The rest pull it apart by their unkingdom ways. Is this the partisan view of a partisan? Well, I am a partisan, a convinced partisan, driven to this partisanship by observing how life is lived in East and West, North and South, for over half a century — lived in un-kingdom ways and in kingdom ways. The difference is a difference between darkness and light, between insanity and sanity.

27. THE KINGDOM OF GOD AND
THE SERMON ON THE MOUNT

The Sermon on the Mount has as its context the kingdom of God: "Then he made a tour through the whole of Galilee, teaching in their synagogues, preaching the gospel of the Reign....Great crowds followed him.... So when he saw the crowds, he went up the hill and sat down; his disciples came up to him and opening his lips he began to teach them. He said: 'Blessed are —'" (Matt. 4:23, 25; 5:13 Moffatt). Then follows the Sermon on the Mount, which was an extension of the gospel of the Kingdom, which he was preaching. In fact, the sermon is an expounding of the laws, principles, and attitudes of the kingdom of God. His first sentence shows that. "How blest are those who know their need of God; the kingdom of Heaven is theirs" (Matt. 5:3 NEB). However, it was more than an expounding of the laws, principles, and attitudes of the kingdom of God. It was an exposure of his own soul, a photograph of his own inner and outer life, and thus, an exposure of life in the Kingdom. For he was the Kingdom embodied. This sermon is vascular. Cut it anywhere and it will bleed.

It is divine realism, a revelation of what God is, what the Kingdom is, as seen in Jesus, and what we can be like if we embody the Kingdom. It is a life sketch of God, the Son of God, the kingdom of God, and the sons of the kingdom of God. It is, therefore, realism — no, Realism — for God and man. It is an exposure of what reality is like

213

and what we can be like. Instead of its being an imposed idealism, it is stark realism. Take every item of the sermon on the mount and do the opposite of what it inculcates. You will be wrong—dead wrong. Take any item in the sermon and embody it and you will be right—absolutely right. Embody the opposite of any item and you will be at loggerheads with reality. You will be up against it, frustrated, at war with reality. There are no exceptions.

So we approach this reality, not as an impossible idealism, but as the only possible realism. Take it, embody it, and you live now and hereafter. Resist it, embody the opposite, and you perish, now and hereafter. Dogmatism? No, verified fact. The most universally verified fact on this planet. Threat? No, thread—a dark thread running through human history, everywhere.

But as we approach the sermon, it is not with a bludgeon hanging over our heads, but with a beckoning, a divine beckoning, and an offer to us to partake in the most wonderful life imaginable, one beyond our fondest dreams.

The first note is a ringing standard note: it sets the tone of the whole, "How blest are." This is no funeral dirge. This is wedding bells. But how weak that sounds. It is more like when at creation "the morning stars sang together, and all the sons of God shouted for joy." For this is the new creation. So instead of a dark thread of doom running through it, a scarlet thread of redemption sends new life and hope through the withered veins of humanity: We can be different, redeemed, and belong to the Unshakable Kingdom and the Unchanging Person.

Since the sermon is a revelation of the character and conduct of the most beautiful character who ever lived, it means nothing less than that we are being invited — being offered the opportunity of being made into that likeness. So we come to it not with the tense whipping-up of the will, but with the eager surrender of the will.

28. THE KINGDOM AND THE BEATITUDES

The first prayer in the Lord's Prayer is for the coming of the kingdom of God: "May Thy Kingdom come and thy will be done on earth as it is in heaven." And the first beatitude is for the receiving of the Kingdom: "How blest are they who know their need of God; the kingdom of Heaven is theirs" (Matt. 5:3 NEB). The two most important things Jesus ever spoke, the Lord's Prayer and the Beatitudes, both began with the kingdom of God. And the most important thing he said in the Sermon on the Mount was: "Seek first ye the kingdom of God,... and all these things shall be added unto you" (Matt. 6:33). And the last thing he spoke to them was about the kingdom of God: "revealing himself to them for forty days, and discussing the affairs of God's Realm" (Acts 1:3 Moffatt). So first and last and between times the emphasis is upon the kingdom of God. And it is not a marginal emphasis, but the organizing emphasis upon which everything revolved and from which everything gets its meaning.

Now look at present-day Christianity. What is its central organizing principle and power? It is almost everything, varying from period to period, *except* the kingdom of God. And when it is the kingdom of God, it is almost always a coming kingdom, identified with the second coming of Christ. But Jesus preached the Kingdom as a mode of life now, a mode on which the total life, individual and the collective, is to be organized, now. It was a possession and a program for the total life, now. Listen to how he opens that Sermon on the Mount: "How blest are they who know their need of God, the kingdom of heaven is theirs." The need for God and the kingdom of heaven belongs to them now, not in heaven, not when Jesus comes again, but here and now. Moreover, it is not idealism, incapable of being practiced now, but it is stark realism. The opposite of the sermon is an impossible illusion — life in any other way is a muddled, maddening, and an impossible way to live. This was a supernatural naturalism. It seems at first sight that it is an unnatural idealism, but only so because we have been naturalized for so long in the unnatural.

29. SOME SNAGS REGARDING THE KINGDOM

There are three places in the sermon where many become 'hung up'. Before we take up the whole sermon let us look at those places:

(1) Love your enemies, turn the other cheek, and go the second mile when compelled to go one. Impossible

idealism— you would be everybody's doormat, everyone would walk on you. Would they? The aim of a quarrel is to get rid of your enemy. Suppose you strike back and give blow for blow. Do you get rid of your enemy? You fix the enmity by every blow you give. By turning the other cheek, you disarm your enemy. He hits you on the cheek and you, by your moral audacity, hit him on the heart by turning the other cheek. His enmity is dissolved. Your enemy is gone. You get rid of your enemy by getting rid of your enmity. "Why didn't Jesus strike back when he was struck by the attendants at the judgment hall; didn't he have a legal right to do so?" a Hindu asked me one day. My reply: "Yes, I suppose he did, but suppose he had struck back. I wouldn't be talking about him tonight. If he had struck back, I would never have looked at him again. 'He is like me,' I would have said to myself. And I would never have looked again." Nor would anybody in the entire world have looked again. But he turned that other cheek and the blow falls on your heart and mine. The world is at the feet of the Man who had power to strike back, but who had power not to strike back. That is power—the ultimate power.

There are three levels of life: (a) The demonic level where we return evil for good, hate for love, (b) The human or legal level, where we return good for good and evil for evil tit for tat, you did this to me and I will do that to you, (c) The Christian level where we return good for evil, love for hate— the only level of real power. The other two are levels of weakness. For suppose the other person doesn't accept your love? Are you a loser? No, Jesus said: "If you go into a city, let your peace rest upon it." If they receive it—well and good; if they do not receive it, "let your peace return to you again." You are the more peaceful for having given the peace. The Christian always "wins" if he remains a Christian. The payoff is in the person. So the Christian way is sense— the opposite is nonsense.

(2) "Give to him that asketh thee, and from him who would borrow of thee turn not thou away" (Matt. 5:42). This seems impossible. But is it? Note, it doesn't say to give him *what* he asks. It says, "Give to him" — it may be what he asks, or it may be something better than he asks. It may be you will give to him the desire and impulse to earn what he asks. But give to him. The Samaritan woman asked: "Give me this water, that I thirst not, neither come hither to draw" (John 4:15). And Jesus gave her a spring of living water welling up to eternal life within her heart. Be so full that everyone who comes in contact with you will get either what he wants or what he needs.

(3) "Be ye, therefore, perfect, even as your Father which is in heaven is perfect" (Matt. 5:48). Isn't that an attempt at perfectionism, which is being classed by psychology as a sign of mental imbalance? No, this is as healthy as Jesus was healthy — the most balanced character that ever moved through the pages of human history. He was not only infinite sanctity, he was infinite sanity — every virtue balanced by its opposite virtue and all held in a living blend. This is the kind of man who said, "Be

ye, therefore, perfect." What did he mean by it? "Therefore" is the key word. It points back. He was talking about loving your enemies. The word points back to this kind of perfection, perfection in love. It is possible to be perfect in love without being perfect in character or service. The word "as" could be translated "since" — since your heavenly Father is perfect as God, you can be perfect as a child of God.

Tagore, the Indian poet, said: "Everything in nature lifts up strong hands after perfection." So in the Christian faith, the perfection is patterned after the most beautiful and the strongest character who ever lived — Jesus Christ. So the perfection offered saves us from perfectionism by making it a byproduct of loyalty to Jesus Christ, so that it is not a self-conscious striving after perfection, but a perfection after the pattern of the most balanced character who ever lived, infinite sanity blended with infinite sanctity and motivated by love — infinite love. Perfectionism is self-centered, therefore, self-defeating. Perfection in love is others-regarding, therefore, self-dedicating, therefore, self-fulfilling and self-releasing.

30. THE SERMON ON THE MOUNT AND THE BEATITUDES

After this diversion in looking at the three places where people get hung up in regard to the Sermon on the Mount and never get to its real meaning, we return to the Beatitudes and to the rest of the sermon. The Sermon on the Mount is life lived as illustrated in the life of Jesus and in a lesser way in the lives of those shaped and guided by the Kingdom. So this is not an exhortation to live by the Kingdom, but an exhibition of life lived in and by the Kingdom. So this sermon is not written in the subjunctive or the imperative mode. It is in the indicative mode. "How blest are" — not how blest ought to be, or must be, but how blest *are*. This is a description of how the universe in the individual and in society works. And it is given by the most authoritative Person in that universe — Jesus Christ. In the language of today: "Jesus is telling it like it is."

"How blest are they who know their need of God; the kingdom of Heaven is theirs." This is the keynote of the Kingdom. It strikes a dart straight at the heart of self-sufficiency, the ego. Be poor enough to receive and everything is open to you, above all the very kingdom of heaven belongs to you. Not that you belong to the kingdom of heaven — you do — but more astonishing still, the kingdom of heaven belongs to you — all its resources, all its forgiveness, all its power, all its everything belong to you if you are poor enough to receive it. This is a universal principle of the Kingdom relevant from the baby to the scientist. The baby has the kingdom of food provided in the mother's breast — if it is poor enough to receive it. The growing youth has the kingdom of education — it is all his, provided he is poor enough to receive it. But if he refuses to receive it, he becomes a dropout, empty amid plenty. Then the highest set of facts and the most valuable — the Kingdom of God — is open to the receptive. This means that the highest is open, not to the good, the deserving, the worthy, but to the receptive. That opens the gates of grace to all regardless — regard-less except for one thing. Are they poor enough to receive? The highest, the Kingdom, is open to the lowest, those poor enough to receive.

This reverses the modern idea of *building* the kingdom of God. The New Testament nowhere tells us to build the kingdom of God. It is a kingdom built from the foundation of the world. It is built into the structure of reality — it is ultimate reality. We build the Church. "On this rock I will build my church." For the Church

> *The Kingdom of God — is open to the receptive. This means that the highest is open, not to the good, the deserving, the worthy, but to the receptive.*

is a relative, not an absolute. The Kingdom is the absolute, and the Church being a relative obeys that absolute. And when it obeys that absolute, it has all these things added to it. The Church is under redemption: "Christ loved the church and gave himself up for her, that he might sanctify her." The Kingdom is not under redemption. It offers redemption. Obey it and you are redeemed.

Then we are redeemed by an *it*? No, we are redeemed by a *him*. But the *it* and the *him* are one. Jesus used interchangeably for my sake and the Kingdom's sake. He was conscious of being the embodied Kingdom. That saved religion from being a personalism, a person attached to a person with no corporate obligations or interest. A devotee of Ram, a Hindu god, came to our Ashram in Sat Tal, and when I asked his name, he replied, "Ram, Ram." When I asked him where he had come from, he replied, "Ram, Ram." Where was he going? "Ram, Ram." He had vowed that he would say nothing except the name of his god. He was "Ramized," with no interest beyond his god. His face showed the devastation of this single-pointedness. It was blank. I saw this same devastation in the faces of Hindu widows who would repeat the name of Ram continuously for six solid hours. Their faces were as blank as paper. They were depersonalized in concentrating on a person.

On the other hand, I've seen people attached to impersonal organizations and causes until they, too, were impersonalized, machines attending to machines. But the kingdom-person is personal and social at one and the same time; by its very nature the Kingdom is both. To be attached to Christ without the Kingdom is religion without social change and redemption. To have the Kingdom without Christ is to have religion without spiritual content and without cosmic backing. To have them together is to have a gospel of total meaning and total field and total goal. It is relevant everywhere, in every field, and for everybody.

Moreover, the King-dom is offered to every-one, everywhere on equal terms — to those who are inwardly poor enough to receive it. We are not to achieve it, but receive it. But it is not a cheap receiving. It means the Kingdom is received as sovereign and determinative. You abdicate as lord and become subject. But in that subjection you become free. For you become subject to that for which you are made. You, therefore, are blest — supremely happy. You are not the recipient of happiness; you are blest, happy in yourself as a person.

Then comes the corrective of that happiness, and you are among those who mourn. "Blessed are they that mourn" (Matt. 5:4). That seems a contradiction; You are supremely happy to belong to a kingdom, a happiness that may drive you to inwardness, to self-centered enjoyment. So the second beatitude: the beatitude of those who mourn, of those who care, care that many, yea, that most people, do not know this kingdom and are unhappy and frustrated. So we

> *To be attached to Christ without the Kingdom is religion without social change and redemption. To have the Kingdom without Christ is to have religion without spiritual content and without cosmic backing.*

223

mourn for them, a redemptive mourning, and a mourning that does something about it beyond mourning!

These blessed mourners become the meek, which inherit the earth. So the thesis: those who are blest in being poor enough to receive, creates the antithesis: those who vicariously mourn because many are missing this blessedness of the Kingdom. Then out of the thesis and antithesis arises the synthesis: the meek who inherit the earth.

Is this fantasy or fact? Do the meek prove themselves to be the fittest to survive and to inherit the earth? Yes, for they embody in a living blend the two most valuable qualities of character — the quality of being poor enough to receive so that the kingdom of heaven belongs to them, and the quality of sensitivity in that they mourn vicariously for those who are outside of, and hence, do not belong to, the kingdom of God. They combine certainty in themselves and sensitivity for others, the meek who inherit the earth. The meek are not the weak. They are the strong in that they combine the strength of certainty in themselves and the strength of sympathy for others. They combine the self-regarding and the others-regarding, the two basic urges, and will, therefore, prove the fittest to survive and inherit the earth. You are weak if you rejoice in the belonging to the Kingdom and care little or nothing for those who do not belong to the kingdom of God. And you are weak if you do not mourn for those not in the Kingdom, but who themselves cannot rejoice in that kingdom. You are strong and inherit the earth if you combine both.

The second group of these qualities which combine thesis, antithesis, and synthesis is this: "How blest are those who hunger and thirst to see right prevail; they shall be satisfied. How blest are those who show mercy; mercy shall be shown to them. How blest are those whose hearts are pure; they shall see God" (Matt. 5:6-8 NEB). Here is a new and important set of three qualities. First, "How blest are they who hunger and thirst to see right prevail." The old version puts it: "hunger and thirst after righteousness" — personal righteousness; but the New English Bible says, "hunger and thirst to see right prevail" — in human relationships. This is the center of human concern today: Is the right destined by the nature of reality to prevail? Those who are humanists are bound to say that it is a question mark. It depends solely on the choices of men — and men are unpredictable. Those who are Christian and believe in the message and fact of the kingdom of God believe it is the purpose and plan that the Kingdom will come; and that purpose and plan is built into the structure of reality, that those who live according to the Kingdom live, that those who live against the Kingdom perish.

So those who hunger and thirst that righteousness prevail will be satisfied. It will happen. The nature of reality decrees it. "Whom ... he also predestined to be conformed to the image of his Son" (Rom. 5:29 RSV). We can live against that destiny written in our blood, our tissues, our organs, our relationships, for we are still free; but if we do, we get hurt automatically. This is the most verified fact in history. "He shall see of the travail of his soul, and shall be satisfied" (Isa. 53:11). So God and man who hunger and thirst to see that right prevail will be satisfied. Everyone who hungers and thirsts that something other than right shall prevail will be dissatisfied, now and forever.

Now comes in the second element — the antithesis — the thesis is that those who hunger and thirst to see right prevail shall be satisfied. The antithesis is: "How blest are they who show mercy; mercy shall be shown to them" (Matt. 5:7 NEB). To be satisfied that right will prevail is fraught with a subtle danger, a danger that this may produce a smug satisfaction, or worse, may produce intolerance, an unmerciful attitude toward those who are not of the right. Instead of hating evil, they end in hating evildoers. They become hard, bitter, and censorious. Lilies that fester smell worse than weeds. A soured righteousness is close to unrighteousness. So we need the antithesis of the thesis. We need to be merciful toward the unrighteous. We must spread the Kingdom in kingdom ways, merciful to the unmerciful, overcoming evil with good, hate by love.

The combination of thesis and antithesis produces the most wonderful thing in the world—the pure in heart, the person who sees God. The pure in heart are the undivided in heart, the persons who want to see right prevail and who using right means to bring that prevailing of right into being. They are not divided between means and ends. They are pure in their ends and pure in their means to get to those ends.

That kind of person sees God, not in a vision, but sees God working with him and in him and backing him. He sees God at work everywhere. The universe becomes alive with God — every bush aflame with him, every event full of destiny. And life is an exciting adventure with God. You see him at work in you, in events, in the universe. He talks with you, guides you. You work in the same business, in the same

We must spread the Kingdom in kingdom ways, merciful to the unmerciful, overcoming evil with good, hate by love.

occupation — the Kingdom. And it is the most thrilling, exciting business and occupation in the world. All else is tame and inane — dull. Here you are working at the biggest job, on the biggest scale, at the most worthwhile task, for the greatest outcome — the kingdom of God on earth.

The third element in the Beatitudes: "How blest are the peacemakers" — not only those who find peace, but those who make peace, who are so full of peace that they produce it in others. On the other hand, it is possible to advocate peace in such a warlike manner that war is produced out of the spirit and methods. The means and ends must be the same. The Kingdom can never be brought in by un-kingdom means. So the peacemakers bring peace by methods that produce peace. Here we run into Jesus Christ and his kingdom, and in a lesser way into Gandhi. I once said to Gandhi while he was in jail at Yerwada: "Isn't your fasting unto death to get the Hindus to abolish untouchability a sort of coercion?" "Yes," he replied, "the same kind of coercion that Jesus exercises upon you from the Cross." I was silent with an acquiescent silence. Gandhi's method was this: "I won't hate you when you are wrong, nor will I obey you. Do what you like. I will match my capacity to suffer against your capacity to inflict that suffering, my soul force against your physical force, and I will wear you down with good will." This is nonviolent non-cooperation, and it is power. This kind of power matched against the greatest empire of that day — Rome — conquered Rome; and matched against the greatest empire of this age — Britain — it brought Britain to an agreement with India and brought about the freedom of 340 million people (1946 data) and began the dissolution of the British Empire. The spirit of this movement was seen in this illustration: A leading non-cooperator was in a tea party and he said to us: "I must eat as many of these sandwiches as possible, for I will soon have His Majesty's jail fare. We can thank our lucky stars that we were fighting people like the British. They have something in them to which we can appeal. We as masters will send them out, but before the boat has gone out of the harbor, we will call them back as friends." A new kind of warfare! You see some good in your enemies and then appeal to that goodness.

This power of non-violence steps into the world situation where it seems that we have no alternative between going to war and knuck-ling under wrong doing, and gives an alternative. You don't have to go to war and you don't have to submit to wrong doing. You can be a peacemaker with new weapons to bring in the new order, the kingdom of God. The peacemakers shall be called the sons of God, for in those days men were called sons of the quality dominant in that person. James and John were called sons of thunder for they were tumultuous, like thunder. The peace-makers are called the sons of God because they do what God does. He overcomes evil with good, hate by love, and the world by a cross. You become like God by overcoming evil with good, hate by love, and the world by a cross — so you are sons of God.

You don't have to go to war and you don't have to submit to wrong. You can be a peacemaker with new weapons to bring in the new order, the kingdom of God.

That is the thesis, now comes the antithesis: "How blest are those who have suffered persecution for the cause of right" (Matt. 5:10 NEB). The peacemakers become the persecuted, for peacemaking is a judgment on the warring of society. Society demands conformity: If you fall beneath its standards, it will punish you; if you rise above its standards, it will persecute you. If your head is lifted above the multitude, it will get whacked. So the peacemakers must get used to the sight of their own blood. "Woe unto you," said Jesus, "when all men speak well of you." You are like them—you have taken on protective resemblance; you're not a person; you are an echo. The peacemaker breaks with society on one level to meet with society on a higher level. The end is not a break, but a higher fellowship, when the lower wrong is righted and a higher fellowship comes into being.

So the peacemaker moves into the synthesis—he rejoices and is exceeding glad for he rejoices in his present rightness and in an anticipated higher rightness and a higher fellowship. He is a happy warrior. So the Beatitudes are shot through with joy. They are not a dour striving to be good, but a dancing surrender to goodness, which produces joy either on account of or in spite of. You don't try to be happy. You are constitutionally and incorrigibly happy.

The secret of this basic happiness is found in the first and last beatitude: "The kingdom of Heaven is theirs" (Matt. 5:10 NEB). To whom? To those who know they are poor, poor enough to receive it. This shuts off the kingdom of God to the self-centered, to the proud, to the self-sufficient, to the smug and the self-complacent. It opens the Kingdom to the self-surrendered, the meek, and the receptive. Only Divine Love could make such a wise and beneficent condition of entrance into the Kingdom.

The second group to whom the Kingdom belongs is the peacemakers — the peacemakers who are positive enough to provoke persecution. In other words, the Kingdom belongs to those who are receptive and to the lovers of others, to the caring, to the in-taking, and to the out-going, to the receptive and to the responsive. Could the Kingdom belong to a more character-worthy group? And could conditions for entrance and belonging be more beneficent for the individual and for society? Only a Divine Mind and a Divine Love could lay down such conditions for such a society as the Kingdom. This fits in with the two commandments of loving your neighbor as you love yourself. Loving yourself is the intake and loving your neighbor is the output. This exactly fits human nature.

How blest are those who belong to that Kingdom because belonging to that Kingdom, the Kingdom belongs to you.

So there are just two urges in human nature: the self-regarding and the others-regarding. So the two basic commandments and the Beatitudes fit human nature. They have been made for each other — the mind and love, which structured the Kingdom, also structured us to obey that kingdom. So there is no war between the Kingdom and basic human nature. Between a corrupted human nature and the Kingdom there is a conflict. But corrupted human nature is not natural human nature. The accustomed may be regarded as the natural, but the corrupted unnatural nature put under the stress of life will not work. The Kingdom is the only workable way to live. You do not have to manufacture ways to be happy; you just are happy when you obey the Kingdom. You don't try to have a good time — you just have a good time. How blest are those who belong to that Kingdom because belonging to that Kingdom, the Kingdom belongs to you. Everything in that Kingdom, its eternal rightness, its resultant rhythm, its self-fulfillment; its situational usefulness, its sense of working with the Way, its surety about past, present, and the future, its capacity to use whatever happens, its attitude to love everybody, everywhere, its healing forgiveness — its very everything is all yours.

So no wonder the Beatitudes begin by saying: "The kingdom of heaven belongs to you" (to those who know they are poor) and ends by saying, "The kingdom of Heaven belongs to you" (the peacemakers). So first and last the thing that matters is that the kingdom of heaven belongs to you. When you have that, you have everything. Without that you have nothing.

Someone has said that all great discoveries are a reduction from complexity to simplicity. "The answer when found will be simple." "Seek first the kingdom of

God and all these things will be added unto you." In having the Kingdom you have everything, everything you need. Your needs are guaranteed. Some young people asked me for an interview for their school paper and they asked this question: "Is there anything in life which you haven't got or need?" I replied: "No, not a thing, except more of what I have." Christ and the Kingdom was all I needed — I wanted nothing different, only more of what I had. So the Beatitudes open and close with the same proposition; the kingdom of heaven belongs to those who know how to receive and know how to give — the in-takers and the out-goers, the receptive, and the re-givers. Then life becomes as natural as breathing. You breathe in and you breathe out — you breathe in God's kingdom and you breathe out God's peace.

But note these words: "How blest are" — the first emphasis is on what you are, not on what you do. For what you do comes out of what you are. Your characteristics come out of your character. The kingdom of God is concerned primarily with what you are. The kingdoms of this world are concerned with what you do. Their laws concern themselves with your actions. The kingdom of God begins with you and works out to your actions. "You must be born-again." "Except ye be converted" — it begins with the root and works out to the fruit. It begins with you and works out to what you do.

31. THE KINGDOM OF GOD BEGINS WITH THE INWARD BUT DOESN'T STOP THERE — IT GOES FROM WHAT YOU ARE TO WHAT YOU DO

The humanistic ethical systems working from the outward to the inward, end in futility; the heaven-born system, the kingdom of God, working from the inward to the outer ends in fruitfulness, and fruitfulness on a universal scale. The Beatitudes are followed by this: "You are the salt to the world... You are light for all the world" (Matt. 5:13, 14 NEB). The idea of a homeless man telling a group of fishermen that they were to be salt to the earth and light to the world is either grandiose vaporing, or else it is the unfolding of the grand design — the kingdom of God on earth. It was either cosmic or comic. The ages say that it is cosmic. Wherever the principles and attitudes entrusted to this little group have been put into operation in society it has gone up. Wherever those principles and attitudes have been rejected or neglected, society has decayed and, if the rejection and neglect continued, society has been destroyed. If the world today is in a mess it is for one reason, and for one reason only: the neglect or the rejection of the principles and attitudes of the kingdom of God proclaimed and embodied in these emissaries of the new order. Jesus said they were to affect human society in two ways — as salt and as light. Salt was to save from putrefaction and give taste to life.

The sons of the Kingdom are the soul of any situation in which they are found. They keep that situation from decay. A Hindu said at the height of the conflict with Britain: "If God allows the British Empire to live it is because of men like Colonel _____. He holds it together." A Muslim prime minister of a Hindu state, said to an audience: "If bribery and corruption have been wiped out of the upper brackets of this state it has been because of the example and influence of two Christians, Mathan and Chandy." They worked with the Kingdom; others were working against it. A penetrating passage from Paul speaks of "the dethroned Powers, who rule this world" (I Cor. 2:6 Moffatt). They still rule, but they are dethroned, and doomed to decay. Every power — personal, economic, social, and political — not aligned to the kingdom of God, the great design, has the word dethroned written on it, perhaps in invisible ink, but the heat of God's judgment upon it will bring it out. "There is nothing covered that shall not be revealed." The sons of the Kingdom are the saving salt of every situation, individual and collective. Take them out and that situation will rot.

If the world today is in a mess it is for one reason, and for one reason only: the neglect or the rejection of the principles and attitudes of the kingdom of God...

235

But the sons of the Kingdom are salt in another way: they put taste into life. Food without salt is tasteless. The aborigines of Australia, living a thousand miles from the coast, would go in search of salt, and by a strange instinct would carry items the coastal tribe would need. The two groups would meet half way and exchange items, and the people from the interior of the country received their desired salt. Men want something to put taste into life. The kingdom of God puts taste into life— makes you feel there is total meaning in the total life. Life begins to pop with novelty. There is a surprise around every corner. There is never a dull moment. An American engineer who won the top prize in gliding had the world of gliding at his feet. He had defeated the experts in gliding—Russian, German, and French. He had won everything. But he found he had nothing within. He then came across the kingdom of God. This was a discovery. His life began to click into meaning—total meaning. His first words when I met him were: "This business of being a Christian is so exciting. I am tingling with realization and expectancy. Life is alive. Winning a world competition is tame alongside of this." I was excited about a man who was so excited about the Kingdom. His most exciting moments are not gliding high, but introducing jaded people to the Unshakable Kingdom and to the Unchanging Person and then seeing the jaded become the joyous, seeing the un-joyous become the joyous.

A scriptwriter called me up and the first thing she said to me was: "I have run smack into God. I'm all excited about it." She soon began to be a much called for public speaker and witness. Now she is writing books—good books, one of which is entitled *Never a Dull Moment*. Evil is under the law of decreasing returns. You have to put more into it to get the same return. You have to invent ways to keep life tolerable. It begins with a flare, then a flicker, then a sputter, and then an ash.

There is more joy to the square inch in being a Christian than there is to the square mile outside. Recently I had a birthday. It is a joy to be eighty-seven years of age and a Christian. And it is getting more enjoyable all the time. For when you don't know what else to laugh at, you can always laugh at yourself. So the sons of the Kingdom are the expert tasters. They have tasted life without the Kingdom and the life in the Kingdom, and there is just no comparison. An alternative lifestyle is as Bertrand Russell described it: "Life is a bottle of very nasty wine." The sons of the Kingdom know nothing of such nasty wine or modern "futilitarianism" — where men have fled to hell where they were

> Gratified to gain
> That positive eternity of pain
> Instead of this insufferable inane.

Life in the Kingdom is not this "insufferable inane," but a dancing joy, if not on account of, then always in spite of. Life has taste and the taste is good, acceptable and perfect. The sons of the Kingdom are salt to the earth.

But the sons of the Kingdom are also light to the world: "You are light for all the world." The salt works silently and unobtrusively, light is open and outward. So the Kingdom works inwardly and silently and outwardly and openly. There is nothing of the esoteric in the Kingdom. It is inward, but also it is outward. And the sweep of the outward is breathtaking: "light for all the world." Is the kingdom of God light for the entire world and to the entire world — the personal, the social, the economic, the political, and the total life? We can answer a flatfooted yes to that question. And I know of nothing else that is light to the entire world. Wherever the kingdom way is applied to any situation, it is light to that situation and everything else is darkness. So wherever the Kingdom comes, and it comes everywhere, it is light to that situation. Work that situation in the kingdom way and it will work well. Work it some other way and it will gum up the works.

A management engineer friend, who works with problem businesses to put them on their feet again, told me that ninety five percent of the difficulties in business are not in the business, but in the persons working in the companies. They get tangled up within themselves; then they project those tangles out into their relationships; cooperation dies and the business turns "sick." "This friend told me that he couldn't straighten out the business until he straightens out the people. So he sits until midnight with executives and heads of departments and they say, "Yes, we are tangled up, but how do you get untangled?" Then he begins to talk to them about God — some point of reference beyond themselves so they can break the tyranny of self-preoccupation. "Yes, but how do you find God?" they ask. Then he has to talk to them about conversion, a new birth. "Yes, but how do you find a conversion, a new birth?" Then he tells them about *Abundant Living.* (It happens to be a book of mine, a book about which a doctor said: "I've given a thousand copies to my patients. I give it instead of a cathartic.") Here are groups of hardheaded businessmen wanting to straighten out a business, but running into the Kingdom as the way out, running into God, the new birth, and finding that the Kingdom way will work. The Kingdom was light to their situation and its opposite was darkness.

This example was from a seasoned businessman, a man of seventy-two years of age. However, consider this example from a college student, a youth of twenty-two. As a summer employee he was given the job of managing relationships between Bethlehem Steel and its employees. He chose two approaches for two separate groups: To one group he went in as an overseer dressed in a coat and tie and represented the company's viewpoint and position. He did his best to represent the company. To the second group he went in worker's clothes to listen to the human needs of the workers. He listened to their grievances and immediately attended to them. Soon a spirit of comradeship grew up and the friendship and cooperation took possession of the workers. When the work output of the two groups was examined they found that the output of the second group had increased by ten percent. The first group's output stayed the same. The question of wages did not arise. When the president of the company heard about the approach taken by the college student, he was granted a brief interview. However, the company president kept the young man for an hour and a half. Here was a youth who knew nothing of the technique of running a steel mill and yet increased the output by ten percent by applying the laws of the kingdom of God to a complicated situation. He was offered a lucrative job with the steel company, but chose instead a job in *Young Life*,[2] a movement that works with high school students. So the management engineer at seventy-two and the college student at twenty-two were "light" to their respective situations and got the same results.

In any situation the Kingdom is relevant, everything else is darkness. So if the Church wants to be relevant, let the Church take the Kingdom as its position, its program, and its procedure and it will always be light. But if it makes itself or something else its position, its program, and its procedure its light will become darkness. "If then

---

[2] Since 1941, *Young Life* has been reaching kids with the simple and profound truth of the Gospel. Over that time, we have learned the importance of investing in personal relationships and "earning the right to be heard." We have learned how to create a fun, safe place for kids to gather. And we have learned how to do outreach camping like no one else in the world. In short, we have learned and refined methods that make a difference in the lives of kids around the world every day. https://www.younglife.org/Jobs/Pages/default.aspx (Accessed July 25, 2017).

the light in you is darkness, how great is that darkness!" (Matt. 6:23 RSV.) The search for relevancy is the search for revelation and the search for revelation ends in a twofold revelation – the search for God's personal character and the search for the character of God's rule or kingdom, and Jesus is the revelation of both. In him we see what God is like. He is Christ-like, and in him we see what the nature of his kingdom is like. It is Christlikeness universalized. This is light – and if we miss this, we stumble in the dark.

32. THE KINGDOM AND ITS RELATIONSHIP TO THE PAST, THE PRESENT, AND THE FUTURE

"Do not suppose I have come to abolish the Law and the prophets; I did not come to abolish, but to complete" (Matt. 5:17 NEB). This is breathtaking: A lone man sat on a hillside and said that in this Kingdom he was inaugurating he was not destroying the Law or the prophets – the cultural and religious background of a great people, the Jews – but completing it. Here ultimate authority was speaking, or consummate madness. Jesus was announcing something more than the relationship to the Jews – he was announcing something universal. The term, "I did not come to abolish, but to complete," is a generic term, locally applied to the Jews and their law and prophets, but capable of being applied to other nations and other religions and cultures. Here then is a universal attitude: Jesus came not to destroy or abolish any good, any truth, any reality found anywhere, but to complete it or fulfill it. This could be applied to scientific or philosophical or political truth found anywhere. As the Son of man he completes any good or truth found among the sons of men. He is not only the desire of the ages—he is the fulfillment of any good or truth in the desire of the ages.

But while this statement seems all encompassing and accommodating, it is destructive by its very nature. Jesus fulfills the good and the truth in any nation, so having taken the kernel up in his fulfillment, the people on their own accord throw away the shell as useless. What Jesus gives is not a syncretism, it is a fulfillment. Eclecticisms pick and choose, synthecisms combine, but only life assimilates. Christ is life and he assimilates any good or truth, but the husks drop away by the very assimilation.

So the Kingdom is radical and conservative by its very nature. It cannot be identified with radicalism or conservatism for by its very nature it is both. So when a book entitled, *The New Left and Christian Radicalism*, uses those terms, it uses terms that will soon be outgrown. The New Left will become the Old Right, and Christian Radicalism will soon become Christian Conservatism. Whereas the kingdom of God, as Jesus interpreted it, is radically conservative and conservatively radical, it is never outgrown or outmoded, or outdated—it is historical, contemporaneous, and futuristic. It is all three in one. So why should the Christian align himself with passing groups which soon fade out with the passing of time when he has a term of his own, the kingdom of God, which like his master is the same yesterday and forever, the same yet unfolding. For the more you see, the more you see there is to be seen. The kingdom of God is static and dynamic, fixed and unfolding. Christians, real Christians, shy at being called left or radical and rightly so, for all persuasions are included in these terms. But when we use the terms Jesus used — sons of the Kingdom, a disciple to the Kingdom, the Kingdom —we need not shy at these terms, but live up to them for they represent an attachment to the absolute order — the kingdom of God.

> *Jesus is the human life of God, God approachable, God simplified, God at hand, and God within. Jesus puts a face on God—a human face.*

However, the Kingdom — the absolute order — on our way to that absoluteness gathers up in itself all the good in the relativisms found anywhere and everywhere. "I came not to destroy, but to fulfill." Jesus came to fulfill the innate desire for God found in some degree, in some form, in all men, everywhere. Jesus is the human life of God, God approachable, God simplified, God at hand, and God within. Jesus puts a face on God—

243

a human face. "That one Face, far from vanish, rather grows — Become my universe that feels and knows!" He fulfills the truth in idolatry—men want God near. Jesus fulfills that desire for he is the express image of God. But in fulfilling idolatry, he destroys it, for idolatry misrepresents God and Jesus represents God. God is near in him, "closer than breathing, nearer than hands and feet." The Hindus say there are three *margs* or ways to God — the Gyana *Marg*, the way of knowledge; the *Bhakti Marg*, the way of devotion; the *Karma Marg*, the way of works—the mind, the emotion, and the will. Jesus said: "I am the way" — the *Karma Marg*, the way of action; "I am the truth" — the *Gyana Marg*, the way of the mind; "I am the life" — the *Bhakti Marg*, the way of devotion or emotion (John 14:6). Jesus is all three in one. For he told us to love God "with all thy mind" — the intelligence; "with all thy heart" — the emotions; "all thy soul" — the will. The total person loving God. And he adds: "With all thy strength" (Mark 12:30) — that may refer to physical strength, but it may mean the strength of the mind, the strength of the emotion, the strength of the will. Some love him with the strength of the mind and the weakness of the emotion. That makes for the intellectualist in religion. Some love with the strength of the emotion and the weakness of the will — the emotionalist in religion; some love with strength of the will and the weakness of the emotion—the man of iron morality, but forbidding and unappealing. But if the content of the Kingdom is in the obedience to Christ, then it is loving God with the strength of the mind, the will, and the emotion— a complete loving with your total being with no reservations. But when it comes to loving your neighbor, you are not to love him all-out, but love him as you love yourself. You love yourself redemptively, not all-out as you love God. Your mind sees you are an imperfect being, but loves the self redemptively, believing you can change; the emotion loves the self redemptively feeling that you will change; the will loves the self redemptively in that you decide to change. So you love yourself and your neighbor subordinately and qualifiedly under an all-out and unqualified love to God, Christ, and the Kingdom. You then save your self-love and your self-respect and your neighbor love and neighbor-respect, while not always agreeing with or approving of yourself or your neighbor.

To sum up this section on fulfillment: We will appreciate and be grateful for any truth and insight found anywhere and where useful will assimilate it, but Paul puts this passage as the final attitude and result: "When the Old Testament is read aloud the same veil hangs. Veiled from them the fact that the glory fades in Christ" (II Cor. 3:14 Moffatt). The glory fades in Christ. We do not try to make of any halfway house a home. Our home is Christ and the Kingdom! We do not stop at truths, if we are true to the absolute order and the absolute Person, but go on to the truth, not as a way, but the way, not as a life, but the life.

33. THE KINGDOM OF GOD AND WHAT CONSTITUTES DEPARTURE FROM THAT KINGDOM—WHAT IS SIN?

Jesus defines sin as departure from the Kingdom in act and in thought. The old law said murder not, but Jesus moved sin back from the act (murder) to the thought (anger). Adultery, the act, he moved back to the lustful look, from divorce for any reason, to one reason only— physical death or adultery (moral death); from failure to fulfill oaths to abolition of all swearing of oaths; from limitation of revenge (one eye for one eye, one tooth for one tooth) to the abolition of revenge. The passages involved are these: "You have learned that our forefathers were told, 'Do not commit murder,' . . . but . . . anyone who nurses anger against his brother ("without a cause") must be brought to judgment.... You have learned that they were told, 'Do not commit adultery.' But what I tell you is this: If a man looks on a woman with a lustful eye, he has already committed adultery with her in his heart. . . . They were told 'A man who divorces his wife must give her a note of dismissal.' But what I tell you is this: If a man divorces his wife for any cause other than unchastity, he involves her in adultery; and anyone who marries a divorced woman commits adultery. . . . Again, you have learned that our forefathers were told 'Do not break your oath.' . . . But what I tell you is this: You are not to swear at all— You have learned that they were told, 'an Eye for an eye, a tooth for tooth.' But what I tell you is this: Do not set yourself against the man who wrongs you... You have learned that they were told, 'Love your neighbor, and hate your enemy.' But what I tell you is this, Love your enemies" (Matt. 5:21-22, 27, 31-34, 38-39, NEB).

Here Jesus was not drawing up a code for people in general. He was describing life in the Kingdom and the kind of life they should live if they are to stay in the Kingdom. Otherwise, people would point to the murders in war, hatred, the loose divorce laws, the adulteries of modern life, the disregard of truth, the giving of an eye for an eye, and the fighting of enemies instead of loving them.

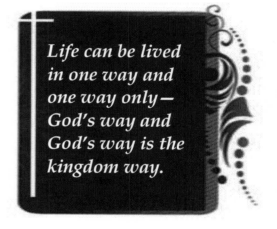

Life can be lived in one way and one way only— God's way and God's way is the kingdom way.

People would point to all these things and say Jesus and his kingdom are impracticable idealism. It won't work. It is impossible. But the point is that every departure from these laws, principles, and attitudes of the kingdom of God has turned out badly, is turning out badly, and will forever turn out badly. The mess of the modern world, the worldwide mess in which we are living, is directly caused by breaking the laws, principles, and attitudes of the kingdom of God. Life is rendering a verdict, and it is an adverse verdict on the rejection of the kingdom of God.

Life can be lived in one way and one way only—God's way and God's way is the kingdom way. So Jesus is telling it like it is, leaving it to man to find out by trial and error, to see that Jesus is right. Jesus was not proscribing a set of laws, but describing how life is and how it works. The punishment for not heeding God's way is not imposed but exposed. Break these laws, principles, and attitudes and you get broken. You don't break these laws, you break yourself on them. That is inherent and immediate. Sin against God and you sin against yourself. If you won't live with God, you can't live with yourself. That is the payoff—the payoff is in the person.

Take the six things Jesus mentions: Jesus sets murder back from the deed to the attitude—hate. Does murder murder the murderer? Yes, it murders his peace, his liberty, his very self. Does hate make the hater hateful—to himself and others? Yes. Does adultery show itself in the adulterer? Does divorce produce more evil than it cures? Has divorce not struck a blow, perhaps a fatal blow to the most sacred institution on earth—the home? Does oath-taking produce more lies than it prevents? A truthful man does not need an oath, an untruthful man will not heed an oath. Does revenge mean avenge? Do two wrongs produce a right? Can Satan cast out Satan—can you, by acting like the devil, get the devil out of people? Is there any way to get rid of evil except to overcome it with good? Or to get rid of hate except to overcome it by love?

If the way of the Kingdom is difficult, the way of the opposite is impossible. If you nurse hate in your heart, you nurse a cobra. Instead of divorce, the Christian has another alternative—more than merely bearing the unhappiness of an unhappy married life, he can use it. The pearl is made out of an irritated grain of sand. If you cannot experience joy and satisfaction with your spouse, you do not have to take to divorce. You can always receive joy and satisfaction out of your home, your children. Or if there are none, then you can draw joy and satisfaction from your own inner well. There is always a way out—it is the way up.

> *God has two hands—the hand of grace and the hand of judgment. If you won't take it from the hand of grace, you have to take it from the hand of judgment.*

About an oath: It violates your integrity, meaning, if you don't take an oath, you will not tell the truth. It downgrades you.

"An eye for an eye and a tooth for a tooth." Before this law was given, revenge was unlimited. If an enemy knocked out one eye, you did not knock out as many of his eyes as possible. This at least limited the revenge—one eye for one eye. It was higher. However, it had the fatal flaw—it allowed the other man to determine your conduct; he did this, you do that. You must work out from your own principles regardless of what the other man does. Then you are not in the control of your enemy.

You slip out of his control and slip into God's control. You are free to love, to overcome hate by love. You are free from the descending spiral of hate producing hate.

The Christian always wins if he remains a Christian, for being a Christian is the victory. He is in the Unshakable Kingdom and that is the victory.

God has two hands—the hand of grace and the hand of judgment. If you won't take it from the hand of grace, you have to take it from the hand of judgment. You may wriggle, twist, try to evade, swear, and rebel, but the hand of judgment takes over when the hand of grace is refused. I write that and I'm fallible, but I believe—and the experience of humanity corroborates it—that I transcribe what is written in the nature of reality. The universe decrees it. You can't buck the universe. You will get hurt. When you sin against the Kingdom, you sin against yourself. That is a losing game.

34. THE CLIMAX OF THE SERMON AND THE CLIMAX OF THE KINGDOM – WHAT ABOUT WAR AND PEACE? IS WORLD GOVERNMENT AN ANSWER?

The climax of the Sermon on the Mount and the climax of the kingdom of God is in these words: "Be ye therefore perfect, even as your Father which is in heaven is perfect" (Matt. 5:48). When I wrote the book *The Christ of the Mount* in 1931, I said perfection, personal perfection, was the key word of the sermon. All revolved around it, all else was commentary. The years have taught me that I was wrong. That would leave our perfection and us at the center. We were never intended to be the center of the universe — individually or collectively. God is the center and loyalty to him and His Kingdom should be the center of our loyalty. But perfection is a byproduct of that loyalty. You lose your life and find it again. This verse is to the point: "He died for all, that those who live might live no longer for themselves" (II Cor. 5:15 RSV). His dying was to break the tyranny of self-centeredness. That is the center of redemption — to be redeemed from trying to be God, from organizing life around yourself as God.

When you seek first the kingdom of God all these things will be added — among these things is yourself and its perfection. If you seek first yourself and its perfection, it will elude you; seek first the Kingdom

God is the center and loyalty to him and His Kingdom should be the center of our loyalty. But perfection is a byproduct of that loyalty.

and its perfection and it will include you. The kind of perfection Jesus is talking about is a kind of perfection that saves you from perfectionism — self-regarding perfection. The key is in that phrase: "Be ye therefore perfect." The "therefore" points back to what Jesus had been talking about, namely, perfection in love toward others—going the second mile, turning the other cheek, and loving your enemies. This makes the viewpoint different and it makes the person who takes that viewpoint different. We will never be perfect in character—that will be an infinite pursuit. But you can be perfect in love now, though imperfect in character.

A father came home after a long absence and was joyously received by the family. The little boy came up to him and asked, "Daddy, can't I do something for you?" The father replies, "Yes, son, bring me a drink of water." The little fellow in his eagerness came with a stream of water from the glass. He took out his finger from the glass and a trickle of muddy water ran down the side of the glass. The father turned it around and drank it all. The boy with glistening eyes said, "Daddy, can't I do something else for you?" That was perfect love, but not perfect service. But in the presence of the imperfect service, the little boy was being perfect. He wanted to do more.

A girl came to one of our Ashrams bent on her own perfection. But it was a self-centered perfection, including obtaining a husband. However, the prospective husband saw that she was using him as a means to her own perfection and he called off the marriage. The human personality has as its goal perfection in love, but never perfection in character and never identity with God. The finite will forever approach the Infinite, and in that approaching the Infinite finds its infinite joy, but never become the Infinite. He will be God, forever the Creator, and we will be forever sons of God, the created; otherwise, if we were merged into God, then God would be loving himself alone, and we would be loving ourselves alone as God, which wouldn't be Christian love, but a self-centered love.

Christian love is the most beautiful fact in the universe. Even non-Christians recognize it as such. A Hindu said to me: "I hope I took the Christian attitude toward that Muslim." During the *Moplah* (Muslim) uprising Mahatma Gandhi sent a telegram to C. F. Andrews: "Pray do please get the *Moplahs* to take a Christian attitude toward the Hindus."

However, the word love has been bantered back and forth in this modern world — "I love her, therefore, I have a right to commit adultery with her." So love in modern life often is not expressed as real love, except where people have consciously or unconsciously come in contact with the Kingdom; there the word is purified and redeemed. In that ancient world where the Gospel was born, love meant *eros* — sexual love. Jesus converted *eros* into *agape*.

This *agape* love was between person and person, group and group, race and race, nation and nation. A little boy of six and a little girl of five came across the dining hall hand-in-hand at a Canadian Ashram, came up to me and said: "Brother Stanley, may we ask a question: What is the Christian attitude?" I thought maybe I didn't understand, so I asked them, "What did you say?" So they repeated it and then I was on the spot and replied: "Well, I suppose the Christian attitude is to love everybody, everywhere." The little boy thoughtfully nodded his head and they went back hand in hand. When I asked his father, a minister, where the boy got that, he replied: "He didn't get it from me." He got it because it is written in everyone's mind, especially children. That is the way we are structured to live.

Then obviously war is impossible for one who is in the Kingdom or wants to be in the Kingdom. "Couldn't I kill lovingly?" said a perplexed youth. "Kill lovingly?" I slowly said, "That is a contradiction in terms and attitudes. It can't be done." And the facts are now saying the same thing: War is now becoming impossible. Russia and America both have enough armaments, which if used in an atomic war would destroy both countries, some say in four hours and some say in twenty-four hours. Each side has, according to Swedish investigators, the equivalent of fifteen tons of explosive power for every man, woman, and child in the world. War is bankrupt as a means of settling international disputes: Use what armaments we have and both sides are ruined. Does war defend the innocent and the weak? No, it does the opposite. War is bankrupt. We must find a new way and that way is the one Jesus indicated: "Put up again your sword, into its place: for all they that take the sword shall perish with the sword" (Matt. 26:52). "And he touched his ear, and healed him" (Luke 22:51). That is the attitude of the sons of the Kingdom. They prevent war—"put up your sword"

—and they heal the results of war—"healed him"—prevention and cure. Out of sheer necessity we are being driven to the Kingdom. God has us now with our backs to the wall and he is saying, "Cooperate or perish." And this time it really is to perish. To add armaments to armaments is futile—and madness. For the more armaments we have, the less security we have. We have never had so many armaments and so little security. That is the descending spiral.

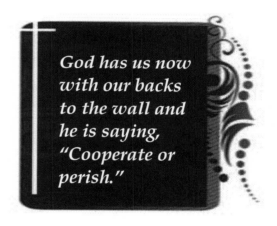

God has us now with our backs to the wall and he is saying, "Cooperate or perish."

However, those who believe that the kingdom is God's total answer to man's total need would not ignore the world situation and say, "you may stew in your own juice, but we belong to the Unshakable Kingdom whatever happens." We think we can see a way out of this impasse and it is world government. There are two great proposals for peace: leagues, pacts, treaties, and charters between sovereign nations; or, world government. The method of leagues, pacts, treaties, and charters function simply as truces between wars. There were 4,800 treaties in operation when this last war broke out. We broke the treaties without compunction and without hesitation. Over the course of human history, peace treaties have lasted an average of two and a half years. They were supposed to last forever. The peace treaties lack a very vital element— they lack government oversight. The United Nations is the best thing we have on the horizon, but it is not government. The veto power of the members of the United Nations demonstrates that we have surrendered no sovereignty to a government. When what is known in America as the *Wild West*, now seen only in the movies, was first opened to white men, they went around armed. When a dispute arose they would simply shoot it out. Why? Because they had no "government" over them. When government was established, men argued their disputes before courts instead of shooting it out inter-personally. It was the coming of government that made the private arming of persons unnecessary. In our world we do not have a government over all of us, so nations must arm themselves to the teeth. Until world government is established, this arming of countries will continue. Until world government takes over security, nations will take care of their own security to the bankruptcy of everybody.

I strongly recommend world federal union. For example, under world federal union, Russia will be able to carry out her way of life under collective security— within Russia. America, under collective security, will be able to carry out her way in life—within America. It will be the same for the rest of the world's nations. Whichever countries produce a better way of life will win—win morally. I am not afraid of that test, for I believe we can produce a higher way of life out of free people rather than by systems that take away freedoms.

What about a world police force under world government? Would that be allowed under world government? Why not? The world police force would be different from an army trained in warfare. The police force would use just enough force to bring a culprit before a tribunal of right. In war, men are not brought before a tribunal of right, but a tribunal of might. The stronger wins. That is an immoral use of force. However, to bring a culprit before the tribunal of right by just enough force is a moral use of force.

Will we come to world government before catastrophe strikes us? I believe we will and should. Is it wishful thinking? Of course it is wishful thinking, but it is a wishful thinking based on the character of God. He has brought us a long way on the road upward, and I believe he will not now allow us to destroy ourselves with the atomic bomb. He has invested deeply in humanity. His stake is a cross. Love is pulling us and necessity is pushing us, so I believe we will make it. We will have to— or we could all perish. World government would not solve all our problems, but it would give us a structure under which we could solve our problems more easily. But even world government at its best would not be the total answer. Only the kingdom of God would be that answer, for the kingdom of God is the absolute. The Church, world government and all human or divine/human institutions are relative. The kingdom of God would judge and redeem all the relativisms that would be redeemed.

However, world government would be a step, a huge step, in the direction of cooperation, which would be a step in the direction of the Kingdom. For cooperation would mean that the nation state is not sovereign, which is at the root of many, if not all, of our conflicts and wars. The idolatry that the nation state is sovereign — my country, right or wrong — that idolatry would be smashed and the way paved for the ultimate sovereignty of the kingdom of God. For the idolatry of the sovereignty of the nation state is the cancer eating at the heart of human relationships, virtually everywhere. I love my country and will love my country, right or wrong, but I will not add to that country's wrong when it commits the sin of idolatry in making my country sovereign. It is not sovereign. We have put within the pledge of allegiance to the flag this: "one nation, under God." That "under God" saves the pledge from the idolatry of making the nation supreme and opens the gates to the next great step of saying the kingdom of God is the final order, and it and it alone is the final sovereignty. We have "under God" in the pledge of allegiance, but in our practice we often have everything else but... However, the words are there in our pledge and they remain a beacon for us.

Now back to the phrase: "Be ye, therefore, perfect, even as your Father which is in heaven is perfect" — perfection in love, in us, and God. The highest in God is to become the highest in man — love. God's character and our characters coincide. Twice the New Testament says, "God is love." When John wrote that, all heaven, leaning over the battlements, must have broken out in applause. "They've got it—at long last they've got it." For the first time in human history that phrase was used —"God is love." "God loves," has been said before, but never "God is love" for by his very nature, God is love. God couldn't do an unloving thing without violating his very nature.

Now philosophy had never arrived at that affirmation about God, not even in India where philosophy reached it's highest. In the Vedanta, which is looked on as the height of Indian philosophy *Brahm*, the highest, has three attributes: *sat*, truth—*chit*, intelligence—*anand*, bliss. *Brahm* is truth, intelligence, and bliss. But not love. For if there were love it would tie

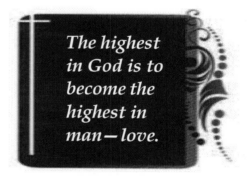

The highest in God is to become the highest in man—love.

him, or more correctly "it," to this *samara*, this world. So *Brahm* in the highest state is *nirguna*.[3] *Brahm* is without bonds, without relationships, and without love. Love is absent from the highest in Hinduism. But in the kingdom of God love is the highest in the Highest. And love is to be the highest in us. Is man in his long course upward

---

[3] The Absolute without qualities, is impersonal, without *guna* or attributes, *Nirakara* (formless), *Nirvisesha* (without special characteristics), immutable, eternal and *Akarta* (non-agent). It is above all needs and desires. https://www.yogapedia.com/definition/6162/nirguna, (Accessed July 25, 2017).

coming to that conclusion—and coming to it by trial and error? Yes. Listen to a skeptical modern philosopher, Bertrand Russell. When speaking at Harvard University, he said: "I am coming to a startling, simple conclusion, which sounds absurd, that love, Christian love, is the only way out of the world's problems." Even the "hippies" in their revolt from modern society could choose nothing better than what they saw the world needed: love and peace, both supreme characteristics of Jesus. When Smiley Blanton, a psychiatrist, wrote a book entitled, *Love or Perish*, he meant it and in writing the book wrote the epitaph for a loveless individual and a loveless society. They both perish.

It is not enough to be an individual — one must be an individual with a social program. Jesus is that individual and his social program is the Kingdom of God on earth. And its central characteristic must be love. The kingdom of God is Christ likeness universalized with love as the organizing and the driving force. So the highest in God is the deepest in man. The highest in God—love—is the deepest necessity in man.

If the philosophers, statesmen, moralists, revolutionaries, the men of good will everywhere can think of something better and produce something better than the good news of the kingdom of God on earth, let them now speak up or forever hold their peace. To me, there is nothing comparable on the field. It is the Kingdom—or chaos.

If we put ourselves in line with the Kingdom we would put ourselves in line with perfection in the individual and in society. We would work with the grain of the universe and the sum total of reality will be behind us. We would be on the Way — the way of the great design!

35. THE KINGDOM OF GOD — HINDRANCES ON THE WAY TO ITS REALIZATION

After laying down the absoluteness of the Kingdom and the perfectness that will come as a result of being completely committed to that absoluteness, Jesus then points out nine ways the Kingdom is blocked in our lives. Jesus shared nine beatitudes and now there are nine hindrances to the Kingdom expressed in those beatitudes showing an inner division in thought and life:

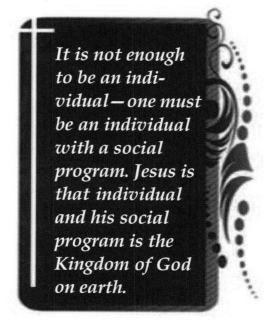

It is not enough to be an individual — one must be an individual with a social program. Jesus is that individual and his social program is the Kingdom of God on earth.

(1) You do your beautiful religious acts with divided motive — you give your alms to God, but also to be seen of men. (Matt. 6:14)

(2) You pray in two directions—to be heard of God and to be overheard of men (vss. 5-6).

(3) You fast with divided purpose—you do it before God, and you hope that men will give you credit for abstemiousness (vss. 16-18).

(4) You try to lay up treasures in two directions—on earth and in heaven (vss. 19-21).

(5) You see in two directions—your outlook is divided (vss. 22-23).

(6) You are trying to be loyal in two directions—trying to serve God and mammon (vs. 24).

(7) You are anxious in two directions—toward what you shall eat and drink and wear and also toward the kingdom of God (vss. 25-34).

(8) You are criticizing in two directions—toward your brother with rather heavy emphasis and toward yourself rather lightly (7:15).

(9) You are giving yourself in two directions—giving yourself to God and also giving that holy thing called personality to the dogs of appetite and the swine of desire (vs. 6).

The first nine beatitudes sound the note of victory; the second nine strike the note of dismal defeat. The second nine are all rooted in inner division—trying to walk on two sides of the road at the same time. Eucken says: "The greatest danger to religion is that the old self after being put out by repentance and renunciation comes back again and takes over the new forms in the service of the old self. It is the old self; the only difference is that it is now religious." Here is an illustration: A planter's servant brought him an egg in an eggcup. Breaking the top, he found the egg wasn't exactly fresh, and he ordered the servant to take it away and bring another. The servant did so and the planter ate the egg only to find that when he got to the bottom it was the same old egg, turned upside down. Often the old evil smelling self comes back, clothed now in the proprieties of religion. But it is the same old self.

The psychiatrists are putting their finger on this inward division as the cause of mental and emotional upset. I talked to a missionary who was about to be sent home from Africa. I said to her: "What do you think is wrong with you as you look at yourself?" She replied: "I'm sitting on a lid." "What's under the lid?" "Two persons—one who does not want to be a missionary and the other who is afraid if I'm not a missionary I will be lost." I replied: "Neither one is very beautiful. You had better surrender both and become a new creature." She went home—a failure, a divided person.

The saying, "United we stand, divided we fall," is axiomatic and true, but it is just as axiomatic and just as true put this way: "United I stand, divided I fall." Perhaps I may not fall outwardly, but inwardly I do fall. Step out of the Unshakable Kingdom, and to that degree you become shakable. There are no exceptions and no exemptions.

If inner division is the problem, let those who would stay in this Unshakable Kingdom and would belong to the sons of the Kingdom, let them take this list of the nine departures, and perhaps once a week go over this list and check up to see how many of these departures are being closed or narrowed. What progress are they making toward creating a united person? But that sounds piecemeal and human striving as if the Kingdom is an attainment. No, the Kingdom is not an attainment, but an obtainment through grace. So there must be a once and for all surrender of the self – a complete surrender. My all for his all: all I know and all I don't know is all his.

Now take this list and see, by his grace, where you can be wholly his. Yesterday I did something I ought not to have done. I was expecting the Father to treat me with a silence that was guilt producing. Instead he said: "We will do better next time." Note "we." He was in the guilt and he was in the promise of resources that there should be no next time of failure. So now with the *we*, let's go through the list:

(1) What am I doing in any area of my life to be seen of men? Where does the herd operate in my life instead of the Kingdom? Where am I an echo, instead of a voice? Where do I look around, instead of up? Where are my morals second hand ones – from society – instead of firsthand – from the Kingdom? Does the phrase "everybody does it" decide things for me, or does "seek first the Kingdom" decide things?

(2) When I pray, am I listening for the approval of men or am I listening for the approval of God? Once in a public gathe-ring in India the program read: "Speeches by way of prayers." Does that fit my public prayers? Am I seeking

man's reaction (through my prayer/preaching) instead of God's action? Is prayer a communion with God or a seeking of commendation from men?

(3) When we fast—or do we fast at all? To fast means to say no on a lower level to say yes on a higher level. Life depends upon elimination as well as upon assimilation. When a college president was asked, "What is the first qualification for a college president?" He replied, "A waste basket." When I was compelled by a tendency to diabetes to fast from sugar for the balance of my days, I first felt deprived; now I feel delighted, delighted that I am not carrying around surplus "baggage." Do I go around gloomy and with a woebegone face over what I can't have, such as processed sugar, or do I anoint my head with the oil of gladness and wash my face with smiles over what I do have? "Unhappiness (religious or otherwise) kills more people than any other cause, especially the elderly," said a doctor to me. "A flow of happy feeling is a greater tonic to the human organism than any other thing." A group went to the railway station to welcome the new rector whom they did not know and

> *No, the Kingdom is not an attainment, but an obtainment through grace. So there must be a once and for all surrender of the self—a complete surrender.*

265

went up to a man and asked: "Are you our new rector?" The man said sadly, "No, it's dyspepsia that makes me look this way." Does the sight of me make people look up or look down or away?

(4) Are your life endeavors to lay up treasure upon earth or treasure in heaven? Jesus said: "Lay not up for yourselves treasures upon earth. . . . But lay up for yourselves treasures in heaven" (Matt. 6:21). Does this mean that those who belong to the Kingdom can own no property or wealth, or is the emphasis of this verse on "for yourselves"? A group that was trying to live the kingdom life came to the conclusion that everyone has a right to as much of material assets as will make him mentally, emotionally, and spiritually fit for the purposes of the kingdom of God. This includes those dependent upon him, and it includes provision for sickness and for old age. We need enough of the material to meet our own needs. Any excess belongs to the needs of others. So "for yourselves" is the decisive factor. Each one must draw that line in the light of his or her conscience, the Spirit of God, his own needs, and the needs of others. Blessed is he who draws that line according to the kingdom of God. For wealth can be *well-th* only if it meets your needs and the needs of others, but wealth can be *ill-th* if it is used largely or only for yourself. It is no kindness to the next generation if they are so endowed that they do not have to work. They often become "playboys and play girls" — unhappy and useless parasites. They break the law of the Kingdom, "If a man does not work, neither shall he eat."

But these sybarites eat and often overeat without working and receive the results—in their own bodies. Is this a harsh judgment on my part? Perhaps, but the facts are harsher.

Material things in the hands of the dedicated are instruments of the Kingdom; in the hands of the undedicated they are instruments of the kingdom of darkness. The destiny of your money decides your destiny. Dedicated to the Kingdom, you live in that Unshakable Kingdom; dedicated to yourself, you won't like yourself. It is as simple as that and as profound. The kingdom way conquers money, lest money conquer you.

(5) "The eye is the lamp of the body; so, if your Eye is generous, the whole of your body is illumined, but if your Eye is selfish, the whole of your body will be darkened" (Matt. 6:22, 23 Moffatt). Here the Eye has a capital E—meaning your Eye is your viewpoint on life, your outlook. This means apparently that you are to take the kingdom viewpoint—that the kingdom of God must determine how you view life. This brings us to the central tragedy of the world: We have lost the kingdom of God as the master light of all our seeing. We have lost it as our guide—our absolute from which we work down to all life. The result is we are being pushed about debating relativisms, and acting on those uncertain relativisms. Hence, the central characteristic in the world of today is confusion. A Chinese father in Malaya sent an application to have his child admitted in a Christian school. And on the form was the question: "What is your religion?" He wrote: "Confusion." He meant "Confucian." The religion of the modern man

267

is confusion. This is true both inside and outside of the Church.

The main cause of all our confusion is that we have lost the Kingdom as the way to look at the world and life. We have lost our absolute and so we are vulnerable. We go the way of pressures from the herd, from advertising in newspapers, Television, and radio. There is a science, the science of impressing the vulnerable. We are putty in the hands of these exploiters—until we discover the kingdom of God. Then our Eye becomes focused and then our whole body of relationships becomes full of light. We do not become infallible in our decisions and choices when we work from the Kingdom down to life, but our starting point is the absolute and it is redemptive. This verse becomes experience: "But if we live and move within the light, as he is within the light, then we have fellowship one with another and the blood of Jesus his Son cleanses us from every sin" (I John 1:7, Moffatt). The Kingdom is redemptive. We are very fallible sons of the Kingdom, but we have hold of an infallible gospel—the gospel of the Kingdom, the Unshakable Kingdom. It doesn't shake, but it holds us steady when we shake. So we are humbly certain in this Unshakable Kingdom—certain of our starting point and certain of our goal. A motto in our Sat Tal Ashram: "Nothing above the Kingdom, nothing outside the Kingdom, nothing against the Kingdom—every-thing within the Kingdom."

However, when we lose the Kingdom, as Christendom has in large measure, then our very light turns to darkness.

The relativisms to which we turn don't relate; our half-answers don't answer; the props upon which we lean break and pierce our hands and our hearts with disappointment; our goals recede for we are not on the Way. Our light has turned to darkness. "If, therefore, the light that is in thee be darkness—how great is that darkness." Even the doctrine of the Kingdom can become darkness if it remains a doctrine. A leading theologian said: "I'm tired of the doctrine of the Kingdom," and it was to him largely a doctrine, a doctrine instead of a direction.

> *The main cause of all our confusion is that we have lost the Kingdom as the way to look at the world and life.*

When we bind up the Kingdom and the *Parousia*, the Second Coming, our light has turned to darkness, for Jesus when he was here, went about preaching the gospel of the Kingdom. It is at your doors, has come upon you, it is within you, you enter it now by being born-again—and now—by being converted—now. It was the program for life now. You seek it first and everything else will be added to you now. To tie up the kingdom of God with the second coming of Jesus is without scriptural warrant. To say we can do little or nothing until Jesus comes is to have our light turn to darkness. The kingdom of God is God's total answer to man's total need now. It is a total program for man's total life now.

(6) You are trying to be loyal in two directions: "You cannot serve God and mammon." You can serve God with mammon, but you cannot serve God and mammon. That perhaps is the world's greatest and most fateful choice: "Shall I serve God or mammon? I can't serve both." That is the choice. The Tamils of South India have a saying: "If you say *panam* (money), a *pinam* (corpse) will open its eyes."

(7) You are anxious in two directions—toward what you shall eat and drink and wear and also about the kingdom of God. And both of them are anxieties for you are anxious about both, and anxiety eats like a cancer. I asked a doctor: "Is worrying enemy no. 1?" and he replied: "It is enemy no. 1 and 2—it is the greatest killer." We worry about what we have done and what we did not do. We worry about how things are going in the world and about how things are not going. We worry about the young, about the old, and about the middle-aged—we just plain worry. Worry is poison. It poisons our joy, our capacities, and our lives. The antidote seems to be this: "and the government shall be upon his shoulders." If we belong to an Unshakable Kingdom, we should not be shaky members of an Unshakable Kingdom. We must learn to surrender our burdens and ourselves.

"Soapy" Williams, the Governor of Michigan, as chairman once of one of my meetings told this story: "A little boy was carrying a heavy rock across the yard and his father said, 'Son, why don't you put forth all your strength?' The boy, sweating, said: 'But, Dad, I am.' And the father replied, 'But you haven't asked me to help you.'" Our resources are God's resources, and not always my responsibility, but my response to his ability. "I'm a third class person, but I've got a first-class God," said a doctor who was doing what she couldn't do alone.

As I walked home from a theater after a public meeting for non-Christians in India, a lady missionary said to me, "I'm completely exhausted from that meeting tonight." When I asked her why, she replied: "I've been sitting up in the gallery holding on to my bench for two hours with all my might, for I didn't know what they 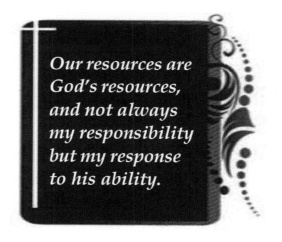 were going to ask you next, and I didn't know what you were going to answer." "Dear nervous saint," I replied: "I was having the time of my life for I knew that I belonged to an Unshakable Kingdom and to an Unchanging Person — the universe was at my back." My chief opponent, a leading lawyer, said afterward: "I believe I could answer his answers, but I didn't know what to do with his confidence that he really believed what he said."

Our resources are God's resources, and not always my responsibility but my response to his ability.

I did, for this is believable. I didn't hold my faith, my faith held me.

So just as there is no room for Jew or Greek, there is no room for slave or freeman; there is no room for male and female; and we may add, there is no room for worry or anxiety or fear in the Unshakable Kingdom and with this Unchanging Person: "Round my incompleteness flows His completeness, Round my restlessness His rest." So we bury that triumvirate of evil — anxiety, worry, fear — and write over their grave: "No resurrection," and go on our joyful way singing, *We shall overcome!* Not overcome here and there in the skirmishes, but in the total war. He shall reign, is reigning, and will forever reign. Jesus is Lord!

(8) You are criticizing in two directions — toward your brother with heavy emphasis, toward yourself lightly, or not at all. Center criticism on yourself- that is the demand of Jesus, and the very standard you set up in your own disciplined life will be the standard by which the other man judges himself. The only possible way of effective criticism is by a demonstration of the opposite in one's own moral life. The attitude of censoriousness is always the sign of a declining spiritual life.

When Christian people begin backsliding, they begin backbiting. For condemning others is a way of commending ourselves. When we say, "How bad he is," what we really mean is, "How good I am!" A man came to one of our Ashrams with a manuscript, almost a book, of what was wrong with his wife. He thought she would take it in that spiritual atmosphere. He soon found out what was wrong with his wife— he was her trouble! He sub-sequently surrendered himself and burned the manuscript. They both got their lives straight-ened out when he began with himself. The sons of the Kingdom live according to this motto on a Sat Tal Ashram wall: "Fellowship is based on confidence; secret criticism breaks that confidence; we will therefore renounce all secret criticism." So once a day, after the noon meal, we have a family meeting in which we bring up any criticism we may have, to make the fellowship better. If anyone doesn't bring it up there, he is not supposed to bring it up anywhere. The fellowship is relaxed. If there is no outer criticism, we know there is no inner criticism.

When Christian people begin backsliding they begin backbiting. For condemning others is a way of commending ourselves.

(9) You are giving yourself in two directions —you are giving yourself to God and giving that holy thing called personality to the dogs of appetite and to the swine of desire. Jesus said: Don't take your lighted personality and put it under a bushel—symbol of trade; under a vessel—symbol of housekeeping; under a bed — symbol of laziness or lust (Luke 8:16); in a cellar symbol of shut-in-ness, afraid to witness (Luke 11:33 RSV). The

following four examples illustrate how we take the lighted life and then render it innocuous or snuff it out.

(a) Under a bushel — symbol of trade. Your business can be a candlestick through which you witness where it counts. An architect who had been led to Christ through the life witness of a big businessman wrote to him thanking him and got back this profound and striking answer: "If there is anything good in me, put that down to Christ; if anything mean and low, put that down to me." His business did not snuff out the light — it scattered it. On the other hand, one's occupation or business can snuff it out: "Born a man and died a grocer, "appeared on a man's tombstone.

(b) Under a vessel — this may refer to a household vessel or a temple vessel. If a household vessel, it could refer to the work of some women, which can be housekeeping or homemaking. One may produce an orderly emptiness, the other a home that is orderly, inviting, and healing.

(c) Under a bed — a bed may be a place of recuperation and fellowship or it may be a place of laziness and lust. The bed may bring exhilaration or it may bring exhaustion; it is according to whether the bed is lighted by the kingdom life or whether the bed snuffs out the light. It is according to where the light is kept — on the lampstand or under the bed.

(d) In the cellar — this would seem to refer to the taking of the lighted life and putting it in the cellar for fear of the herd, because of timidity. A Roman Catholic bishop in the Open Heart session of an Ashram in a cathedral said: "I'm tied up, I can't communicate, and I can't give what I have inside me." At the close of the session of the Open Heart, I invited people to kneel at the three rows on the altar stairs to surrender themselves and their needs, which they had expressed to the Ashram participants. Now they would express them to God. The bishop was among them, and at the close said simply but joyously, "I'm free." His light was no longer in the cellar—it was on a lampstand to be seen by all. A missionary lady doctor told me she had come to India as a doctor, for as a doctor she needn't say anything about God; she could work for him with her hands. But she made a surrender of that timidity to God and she said with evident glee: "I'm really becoming vocal about God." Her light was out of the cellar on a candlestick. She was inwardly free and freely shining.

36. THE KINGDOM OF GOD—AFTER SHOWING THE WONDER OF THE KINGDOM AND THEN THE HINDRANCES TO ITS COMING, JESUS NOW OPENS THE RESOURCES OF GOD FOR ITS WORKABILITY THROUGH PRAYER

After going through these nine divisions that one finds within himself, you might inwardly throw up your hands and say, "It is impossible—it can't be accomplished." You are right if it is an "accomplishment," but suppose it is an acceptance? Here Jesus introduces among these seeming impossibilities this gloriously beautiful possibility: "Ask and the gift will be yours, seek and you will find, knock and the door will be open to you" (Matt. 7:7 Moffatt). Here Jesus offers the Kingdom as a gift of grace. That puts it in reach of all. So the attitude is not that of striving but of receiving. The opening beatitude is the key to the whole: How blest are they who know they are poor. The kingdom of heaven belongs to them — for they are "poor" enough to receive!

A High Churchman once said to me: "You talk about the living Christ within, and of knowing God, and of being immediately in fellowship with the living God. It all gets on my nerves. I don't like it. I go through my religious duties with care and regularity, but I know nothing of what you talk about. And I know Father W., also a High Churchman, and he talks the same language you do. He is a very High Churchman, and you are a very Low Churchman, and yet you talk the same language. You are both enigmas to me."We then went together to the High Church service, and as we came out he clutched my arm rather vigorously and said with a glow on his face: "I know it. It has happened. I am a new man." The Kingdom belonged to him — all its resources, all its power, and all its freedom. He had been poor enough to receive a ritualistic and theological training. Now he was poor enough to receive the kingdom of God, hence, his total lighting up in radiance.

The Church in large measure is like that High Churchman before his transformation that I previously described: "I go through my religious duties with care and regularity, but I have (and know) nothing of what Father W. and you talk about." Hence, the lost radiance of the Christian Church which has lost either Christ or his kingdom or both. When Jesus Christ is rediscovered and when his kingdom is rediscovered with him—then and then only will it be totally relevant and totally meaningful to us and to the world. For no other institution or movement on earth has any such person—Christ—and any such program—the Kingdom.. That is the uniqueness of the church!

The amazing thing is that all that I am describing is a gift, a gift of grace. Many think the Sermon on the Mount is a series of laws and prohibitions, but not of grace. Note that the "prohibitions and laws" are grace, too, hedges of grace put up on the edges of the "precipices" of life to keep us from hurting ourselves. They are preventive grace. They are conveying "no" on one level to say "yes" on a higher level. They serve as prohibitions on behalf of a larger possibility of grace, and what a possibility—the greatest ever presented to the mind and soul of man and presented to all men everywhere.

I once asked Kagawa, "What is prayer?" and he replied in a word, "Surrender." It is surrender to the person, Christ, and to his reign, the Kingdom. This means alignment to him and his kingdom. By that alignment, you are aligned to the Ultimate Person and to the ultimate order and to the ultimate power. The New Testament tells us what to ask for when we pray: "If a son asks for bread, will the father give him a stone?" "If you then, who are evil, know how to give good gifts to your children, how much more will the heavenly Father give the Holy Spirit to those who ask him" (Luke 11:13 RSV). (Matt. 7:11 RSV, reads, "good things.") It would seem that Luke is more in line with the mind of Christ. He didn't tell his disciples to tarry in the city of Jerusalem to be given good things, but to be given the Holy Spirit. And it doesn't say: They were all filled with good things, but that they were all filled with the Holy Spirit. Good things would not be an adequate endowment for a world movement and a world task, but the Holy Spirit is. It is the providing of divine energy, the Holy Spirit, for a divine entity, the Kingdom.

This perhaps explains why the Epistles talk about grace more than about the Kingdom. The writers of these epistles saw by experience that the problem of the Kingdom was the problem of the people who propagated that kingdom. So grace is introduced: "Ask and it shall be given," "give the Holy Spirit to those who ask him." This takes the Sermon on the Mount out of the realm of Law, to another sort of law, more spiritual, more inward, but still a law, a law of taking and trusting. The Sermon on the Mount is definitely redemptive—it is grace. If it demands the highest, it offers the highest, the Holy Spirit. The Holy Spirit is the applied edge of redemption, it is redemption applied where we need it most, applied to the sub-conscious mind, where the driving urges of life— self, sex, and the herd—reside. These driving urges push for their completion and fulfillment apart from any morality built up in the conscious mind. So there is a conflict between the conscious mind and the sub-conscious mind, between the flesh and the spirit, as Paul describes it. With this conflict going on inside of us, we cannot do the things we want to do.

However, with the coming of the Holy Spirit within us, we can do the things that we want to do. We become unified personalities. The Holy Spirit, with our consent and cooperation, takes over the *self*, cleanses it from selfishness, and dedicates it to the kingdom of God. You seek first the kingdom of God, and then all of these things are added to you. The Holy Spirit transforms the un-conscious *sexual* urge and cleanses it from raw sexuality and turns it into creative activity within the home as procreation and fellow-ship. Outside the home, it becomes creative

The Holy Spirit is the applied edge of redemption, it is redemption applied where we need it most, applied to the subconscious mind, where the driving urges of life—self, sex, and the herd—reside.

energy, creating new hopes, new movements, newborn souls; The Holy Spirit transforms the *herd* urge and unfastens its loyalties to the herd where you are merely an echo instead of a voice, and fastens it upon the kingdom of God; fastens it upon an ultimate, the Kingdom, instead of a relative, the herd; and gives you a sense of belonging, belonging to the Unshakable Kingdom and to the Unchanging Person; you belong! Until then you are a shaken soul in a shaken world. The Holy Spirit does not wipe out these urges. It doesn't depersonalize you, but cleanses, coordinates, and consecrates these urges and makes you a unified personality. The Holy Spirit is in charge of the conscious mind and the subconscious mind and has charge of you. And what he has charge of he empowers. He gives you no task which you cannot do. The Holy Spirit gives you the supreme task—the bringing in of the Kingdom of God, an impossible task, but this is the amazing point: The task turns out to be an offer, the offer of God within, the Holy Spirit. This is our calling and this is our offer: "Asking our God to make you worthy of his calling, and by his power, to fulfill every good resolve and every effort of faith, so that the name of our Lord Jesus may be glorified in you (and you glorified in Him) by the grace of our God and the Lord Jesus Christ" (II Thess. 1:11 Moffatt). Note, "worthy of his calling" (the Kingdom) and "by his power" (the calling is an enablement) to "fulfill every good resolve" (you resolve— he solves) and" every effort of faith" (you act in faith and he reacts in fulfillment), so that the name of our Lord Jesus may be glorified in you (you live for his glory, not yours), and you are glorified in him (you lose your life and you find it again). Your life is amazingly glorified in him! All self-loathing, all self-rejection is gone. He accepts

280

you, and now you can accept you. Are you made proud? No, you are made humble, for it is all by the grace of our God and the Lord Jesus Christ. You are low at his feet and you are raised in the highest heaven; you possess nothing and yet you possess everything.

However, a far greater loss of interest and emphasis about the Kingdom is the idea that we can do little or nothing major about the Kingdom as an issue now because we have to wait until Jesus returns to set up his kingdom. We can "rescue" individuals and get them into the Kingdom through the new birth and they will be safe as in a fort. That is all we can do. We often believe that there is nothing more that we can do except to focus on the individual and get him and her into a protective "fort" for safekeeping until Jesus returns. Let's look at what the Bible says. The New Testament does teach about the future coming of the Kingdom when Jesus comes again. Recall the parable of the nobleman who went into a far country to receive a kingdom and returned to set it up, depicting Jesus going to the Father to receive the Kingdom and returning to set

> *You are low at his feet and you are raised in the highest heaven; you possess nothing and yet you possess everything.*

it up. So there is to be a consummation of that kingdom with the return of Jesus. However, and this is significant, just as Jesus is alive now and is the issue, the world issue now, so the Kingdom is alive now and so is the world issue now as well. To tie up the Kingdom in heaven to await its coming when Jesus comes is to tie up Jesus now—he awaits his second coming to loose the powers of the Kingdom on the total life, while he exerts his personal powers on saving the individual now. That is a half-redemption—half applied; its nerve is cut or tied up. The New Testament picture is different. The Kingdom and the *Parousia*, the Second Coming, are not tied up together, not now. They may be connected some day when Jesus comes again. But when Jesus arose from the dead he stayed with the disciples for forty days, talking about what? He spoke about the kingdom of God. "He appeared to them and taught them about the kingdom of God" (Acts 1:3 NEB; or as Moffatt has it, "discussing the affairs of God's Realm"). The Kingdom was the chief emphasis after the Resurrection and before his second coming. His disciples tried to connect his kingdom and the Second Coming. He separated them: "Lord, wilt thou at this time restore the kingdom to Israel." His reply: "It is not for you to know the times and seasons, which the Father hath put in his own power. But ye shall receive power when the Holy Spirit is come upon you; and ye shall be witnesses unto me both in Jerusalem, and in all Judea, and in Samaria, and unto the uttermost part of the earth" (Acts 1:6-8). They tried to reduce this universal kingdom into a nationalism. "Do we at this time get back our self-government?" They didn't reject the Kingdom; they reduced it to nationalism.

That is what we have been doing ever since — reducing the Kingdom by putting it into narrow molds — a refuge now, a present security, a future hope. We have done anything but understand the Kingdom as Jesus preached it as God's total answer to man's total need now. "Be my witnesses," means to "witness to my witness," and his witness was the kingdom of God now. He went out preaching the gospel of the kingdom of God. So

We have done anything but understand the Kingdom as Jesus preached it as God's total answer to man's total need now.

to be his witness was to witness to what he witnessed to — the gospel of the kingdom of God. Did they go out to preach the gospel of the Kingdom to come? No, they preached the gospel of two things: "But when they believed Philip who preached the Gospel of the Reign of God and the name of Jesus..." (Acts 8:12 Moffatt) — the order and the Person, the kingdom of God, and the Person, the Son of God. They were the issues now. Paul had the same emphases: "From morning to evening he explained the Reign (Kingdom) of God to them from personal testimony, and tried to convince them about Jesus" (Acts 28:23 Moffatt). Two things again, he explained about the Kingdom and about Jesus—the order and the Person. And note: He explained the Kingdom from personal testimony—the Kingdom wasn't a hope to be fulfilled when Jesus came. Paul experienced the Kingdom as a total way of life now. Again: "He preached the Reign of God and taught about the Lord Jesus" (Acts 28:31 Moffatt)—the order and the Person, both of them available from personal experience. Paul also writes this luminous word, "Not one of you will ever see my face again—not one of you among whom I moved as I preached the Reign" (Acts 20:25 Moffatt). And he then adds this: "I never shrank from letting you know the entire purpose of God" (v. 27). The Kingdom of God was the entire purpose of God is now God's total answer to man's total need. Paul said, "Among whom I moved here as I preached the Reign."

Does the modern church preach the Kingdom as it moves among men? Fragmentarily, yes. As a total head-on and total answer—no. This is the center of the church's "weakness." We have no absolute from which to face all the relativisms of today. We face relativisms with relativisms and end up relatively confused and paralyzed and frustrated. Does the Church desire to be relevant? Then let it cease to give itself to outworn relativisms that die almost before they are born. And let her return to her absolute—the kingdom of God—and make the Kingdom the master light of all her seeing and seeking and acting, and almost overnight the Church will be relevant on all fronts, personal and social, individual and collective — totally relevant. Is it too good to be true? It is too good not to be true. Is there any alternative on the horizon — communism, capitalism, socialism, secularism, spiritualism, atheism, agnosticism, or nihilism? Eat, drink, and be merry? Every man for himself and the devil take the hindmost? What about the status quo? Should we be stoic and accept things as they are? Do we revolt but with no adequate or suitable replacement? But why prolong the agony and the emptiness? There is simply no adequate alternative to the kingdom of God as proclaimed by

> *We have no absolute from which to face all the relativisms of today. We face relativisms with relativisms and end up relatively confused and paralyzed and frustrated.*

and illustrated in the person of Jesus. If God or man has a better alternative, let them trot it out for nature and man are crying out for that alternative. I believe that there is no alternative to the Unshakable Kingdom and the Unchanging Person. This kingdom is built into the foundation of the world, but not only built into the foundation of the world, but it is also built into us. The kingdom of heaven is within you. The laws of our being are the laws of the Kingdom of God; it is at our doorstep, ready to burst in upon us in the individual and in the collective with our individual and collective consent and cooperation. When you find the Kingdom, you find yourself — the Kingdom realization is self-realization; the Kingdom is our homeland; all else is alien and anti-life. This is life and you can bet your life on it? You will win. No matter the outer circumstances, you will win.

37. THE KINGDOM OF GOD — AND SENSE

After offering the kingdom of God as grace, "Ask and it shall be given you," Jesus gave a final warning about accepting the Kingdom as verbalism, of saying, "Lord, Lord," and expecting the fruits of vitalism. This is the kingdom of realism and an unreal attachment will bring nothing but unreality. A mathematician in India told us that he had learned three things from the study of mathematics: First, that you must be completely honest in mathematics, if you are going to get mathematical results. You cannot play any tricks. You must be completely honest in motive and method or you will not get results. Second, you must be faithful in the little, if you are going to be ruler over the much. You must prove your formulas in stages to get the final result. You cannot jump from the beginning to the end without patiently verifying your sums as you go along. Third, if you have a problem, then you know that just behind that problem is the answer, for if there were no answer there would be no problem. So the answer is embedded in the problem. God is the master mathematician in nature and in the Kingdom. You must be completely honest when you deal with both nature and the Kingdom. You must be faithful in the little to be ruler over the much and you must have the spirit of expectancy — for in the problem can be discovered the answer.

There is simply no adequate alternative to the kingdom of God as proclaimed by and illustrated in the person of Jesus.

Jesus says much the same in summing up the Sermon on the Mount, which unfolds the laws of the Kingdom: "Now, everyone who listens to these words of mine and acts upon them will be like a sensible man, who built his house on the rock. Down came the rain, floods rose, winds blew and beat upon that house, but it did not fall, for it was founded upon rock. And everyone who listens to these words of mine and does not act upon them will be like a stupid man, who built his house upon sand. Down came the rain, floods rose, winds blew and beat upon that house, until down it fell — and mighty was the crash!" (Matt. 7:24-27 Moffatt.)

Here Jesus is saying something that is breathtaking: "Try all the ways of life you may and in the end you will find that nothing comes out as solid reality but this way of mine — the Kingdom. Everything else is sand; this way is rock." In suggesting this way of putting this house of man-soul and of civilization under life to see what life will do to it, he was putting the Kingdom straight into the scientific method to get its verdict. Don't argue — try it. Put it under the microscope of life to see what life will do to it — will life confirm or deny what Jesus is affirming?

Jesus said that the testing of his affirmation will come from three directions — the floods will come from below, the winds will blow upon its sides, and the rain will descend from above, but the house will hold because Jesus is talking about reality. However, Jesus did not mention the potential for the Kingdom to be broken from within. That is the only direction from which the Kingdom can be broken, And that is what we can try to do and when we do we will end up broken. We can break it by not being true to it from within. But even that cannot ultimately break the Kingdom; we can break it as a force within our lives, but when we break it from within we only succeed in breaking ourselves on the laws of the Kingdom. The Kingdom is still there in spite of our betrayal. If you jump out of a ten-story building, you don't break the law of gravitation. You only illustrate it. You don't break God's laws, you only break yourself upon them. And those laws are color-blind, class-blind and religion-blind. Break them and you get broken. These laws also work in a profoundly positive direction. Obey those laws, align yourself with them, work with them and they will back you, sustain you and will further you. Confirm them and they will confirm you.

I write this passage while on a speaking tour in the Caribbean. As I have gone from country to country, I have seen an unfolding drama, a drama of the laws of the kingdom of God at work. The imperial powers of England, France, Spain, and Holland jostled and intrigued and fought over the possession of these Caribbean islands which they developed with slave labor imported from Africa. Nearly two centuries have gone by and the imperial powers have had to abdicate and these ex-slaves have moved into possession of their lands and into power. All of these beautiful tropical islands are now being run by independent governments and on the whole are being run well and there is peace.

> *Jesus is saying something that is breathtaking: "Try all the ways of life you may and in the end you will find that nothing comes out as solid reality but this way of mine—the Kingdom. Everything else is sand; this way is rock."*

As I have seen this drama unfold, the words of Dr. Charles Beard, the historian, have been running through my mind like a refrain. When asked what lessons he had learned from history, he replied he had learned four things. First, "when it gets darkest, the stars come out" — when everything seems lost there is a change, the stars come out. Second, "When a bee steals from a flower, it also fertilizes that flower" — when you steal away the rights of people you fertilize the people, you stimulate those whom you wrong. They overcompensate and move forward with their plans. Third, "whom the gods would destroy, they first make mad" — make mad with power. Fourth, "the mills of God grind slowly, but they grind exceeding small" — nothing escapes and nobody escapes. All four conclusions are important, but the second stands out: 'When a bee steals form a flower, it also fertilizes that flower." This is dramatically illustrated in the Caribbean. The colonial powers — Spanish, French, British, and Dutch each stole from the Africans and kept them as slaves on these islands. The years have turned into centuries and the ex-slaves have now become the rulers in nearly every Caribbean country, and the colonizer remnants are under them. The descendants of the people who used to sit under umbrellas with whips in their hands to see that the slaves did not pause in their work are now happy to sit under the umbrella of good government and peace and freedom supplied by these former slaves. "When a bee steals from a flower, it also fertilizes that flower" — you do a wrong to a people, steal away his manhood and his rights and all you succeed in doing is to make the wronged respond powerfully to regain his rights, and in the process often takes control of the situation leaving the prior colonial leaders out of power.

When Rhodesia (now Zimbabwe) was putting through a constitution patterned after South Africa, which put the Africans in a permanently inferior position with the white government over them, I read aloud in a cathedral the results of an examination, which took place in Old Umtali Mission Station. Thirty young African students took the Cambridge examination in a foreign language, English, and one hundred percent of them passed the examination, many of them with honors. Among the thirty were six girls, and one of the girls scored the highest among the thirty candidates. This occurred in the lifetime of a woman, still living who, when she went to school, produced a riot for girls were not supposed to be educated at all. I said to the cathedral audience: "This is the doom of your constitution patterned after South Africa's discriminatory policies. You can't permanently put down such talented and brilliant people such as I just described. "Whether you attempt to do so by whips or a constitution, there is something — something at the heart of things, the kingdom of God, which will upset your systems based on whips or unfair constitutions. You will end up stimulating the people you are suppressing. They will move forward instead of buckling under. So God is teaching us about race — teaching us by the hand of grace, and by the hand of judgment. If we won't take the teaching about race by the hand of grace then we have to be taught by the hand of judgment. Both are redemptive.

So behind the rise of man is the Son of man, and behind the Son of man is the kingdom of God, of which he is the embodiment. So love and law are one in him and his Kingdom, and when put together it all adds up to sense — total and final sense. There are two kinds of sense — one is a mathematical sense where having fulfilled the laws of mathematics, you come to mathematical sense, legal, and verbal sense. But there is another kind of sense where we put life under life, and see, by trial and error, which way of life is "approved." The Christian way is life. It is sense. "Now everyone who listens to these words of mine and acts upon them will be like a sensible man, who built his house on a rock." Note, a sensible man — not merely good man, but sensible, a wise man, who has tested life and found that it turns out to be "sensible."

Nothing, absolutely nothing, from the outside can cause the house of man-soul to fall for it is an Unshakable Kingdom and not merely an infallible kingdom. We noted earlier that collapse could only come from one direction from within. You can be a traitor to yourself and let the rains in, let the wind cause havoc within, and let the floods flood you. Then it can fall — then only. The Christian way has the sum total of reality behind it, everything behind it, except a traitorous will. It alone can let in the Trojan Horse. Nothing from without can overthrow it. It is rock solid and the best-tested fact in history. Tested in all ages by all men, of all types, simple and scientific, young and old, philosopher and peasant; everybody who tries it, honestly tries it, comes to the same conclusion: This is it—this is rock. A theologian put it this way: "The Christian way is sense, and if you take any other way, you are a fool, and I could add, you are a damned fool, and I wouldn't be swearing when I said it."

There is a dramatic passage in the book of Revelation of the progression of loss for the individual (or the group or the nation) when the individual begins life seated on the white horse of freedom, free to go forth "to conquer" (Rev. 6:2 NEB). This is the modern mood: Man has come to maturity—he can decide and shape his own destiny without God and without the Kingdom. He rides on the white horse of freedom, conquering the earth and the heavens and man.

The Christian way has the sum total of reality behind it, everything behind it, except a traitorous will.

However, the white horse, initially so resplendent and so self-confident, turns to a horse of another color—the red horse—"to its rider is given power to take peace from the earth and make men slaughter one another"; and "he was given a great sword" (vs. 4), in modern terms, nuclear weapons. Self-assertion in the individual and in society produces war.

This red horse of war changes its color again. It becomes the black horse of famine, "a whole day's wages for a quart of flour" (vs. 6). War makes everyone bankrupt and hungry.

Then the color of the horse changes again — a pale horse, pale as death — "its rider's name was Death" (vs. 8). So the modern white horse of freedom to conquer and to do as one likes is changing to the red horse of conflict and war, and the red horse of war is changing to the black horse of famine, and the black horse is changing into the pale horse of death. This parable, which began with the message about the illusory power of freedom, outside the context of the Kingdom, ends with death except to those who belong to the Unshakable Kingdom — the kingdom of God.

In the Unshakable Kingdom, they ride out on the white horse, not of personal freedom but of self-giving service. As a consequence, they do not produce the red horse of war but the red blood of human brotherhood. Instead of the black horse of famine, they produce an economy in which the goods that God produced for all are distributed to each according to his or her need and where each contributes according to his ability. Instead of a dog-eat-dog economy, there is a brother-help-brother economy. Instead of the pale horse of death being in the saddle, life rides us into freedom for all. Is it a dream? Well, the descending spiral in which we are currently caught is no dream; it is a dread reality — a fact. The dream is sense and what we have now is nonsense.

To work with the grain of the universe is sense; to work against the grain of the universe is nonsense. Sin is sinning against the law of the Kingdom, and hence, it is nonsense. Iniquity is (*harmartia*) — missing the mark — the mark of the Kingdom is written in the nature of things.

Africans have sensed that sin is not merely a private thing. It is cosmic. The ancestors have been entrusted with this potential for universal harmony. Sin is sin against that universal harmony and is not a private affair. Rather, sin is revolt against the universal harmony, a revolt against the Kingdom and its concerns such as God, nature, your family members, your fellow man and you. Sin concerns everything and everybody. So when the African sins, he asks pardon from his ancestors, the universal harmony, and from God. When we sin, we sin against God, against the Son of man, against our brother man, and against nature. Sin is lawlessness — in all directions, against everything and everybody.

Some look on the laws of the kingdom of God as foreign laws. That is not the case and that is not true. The laws of the Kingdom are not foreign laws, something imposed, and something frustrating to freedom. Rather, the fact that the God of the kingdom of God is the God of love which means that God is love — and he loves, and deeper still because God is love, he could not do an unloving thing without violating his own nature. That message was written at the very end of the Gospels, Acts, and the Epistles as the highest that could be said about God. But it could not have been said until the most loving

295

apostle, John, had looked long and lovingly into the face of the most loving Person, Jesus, and had seen there the express image of God, and had written of what he witnessed. He must have put down his head and wept— wept with joy, not merely because he wrote it, but because it was true. John had put his finger on the pulse beat of the universe and it spelled out the words, God is love.

God couldn't do an unloving thing without violating his own nature. So when God made the laws of the Kingdom and built them into the universe, he did it through Jesus Christ. "The Word, then, was with God at the beginning, and through him all things came to be; no single thing was created without him. All that came to be was alive with his life, . . . He was in the world, but the world, though it owed its being to him, did not recognize him" (John 1:24, 10 NEB). "He is the likeness of the unseen God ... for it was by him that all things were created both in heaven and on earth, both the seen and the unseen,... all things have been created by him and for him; he is prior to all, and all coheres in him" (Col. 1:1517 Moffatt). "... a Son whom he has appointed heir of the universe, as it was by him that he created the worlds" (Heb. 1:2 Moffatt). "These are the words of the Amen, the faithful and true witness, the origin of God's creation" (Rev. 4:14 Moffatt). So John, Paul, and the writer of Hebrews all say that God created the world through Christ and for Christ. With that backing, I repeat what I have said before in this book: Everything and every-body is structured to be Christ's. It is the destiny written in us: "Whom he did predestine to be made into the likeness of his Son." That destiny is written into our blood, our nerves and tissues and organs, and into our relationships. Everything works well in his way and works badly in some other way. The laws of our being are the laws of the kingdom of God. When we act according to them we fulfill our nature. When we act against them, we violate our nature. To say that sin is an affinity to human nature violates both Scripture and experience. It violates Scripture: "So God formed man in his own likeness, in the likeness of God he formed him" (Gen. 1:27 Moffatt). The statement is repeated for emphasis. Human nature was made by God, in the likeness of God *and* for God. The New Testament says that man was created by Christ and for Christ; for Christ is the express image of God. Now man, through his free will, has spoiled that likeness, spoiled it, but has not obliterated it. Sin is an alien intrusion. Sin is as "natural" as acid on a nerve, sand in the eye, a thorn in one's side. Sin may be the accustomed, but it is not the natural.

> *God couldn't do an unloving thing without violating his own nature. So when God made the laws of the Kingdom and built them into the universe he did it through Jesus Christ.*

297

Listen to this: "Lay aside the old nature which belonged to your former course of life [that course of life produced that old nature, i.e., the accustomed, but not natural] that nature which crumbles to ruin under the passions of moral deceit" (Eph. 4:22 Moffatt). Nature crumbles to ruin under the passions of deceit. The most verified fact in history is that sin is the enemy of human nature. In the book of Revelation there is this strange but pregnant sentence about a little scroll: "it did taste sweet, like honey, but when I had eaten it, it was bitter to digest" (Rev. 10:10 Moffatt). Sin tastes sweet when you taste it, but when you try to digest it, it turns bitter—life cannot digest or assimilate it; it rejects it. So evil is not merely bad, it is bad for us. It is life trying to live life against itself.

When Jesus said: "My yoke is easy and my burden is light," he said what "life" finds to be true when put under life and actually tried. Is it because he puts nothing on you that his yoke is easy? On the contrary, if you come to him he will put the world's troubles on your shoulders. Then are you burdened? No, for his yoke is your yearning, his burdens are your blessings. The happiest people in the world are the people who deliberately take on themselves the troubles of others. In the midst of it, their hearts sing with a strange and wild joy. One of the most important verses in Scripture is this one: "And his commandments are not burdensome" (I John 5:3 NEB). Why? Because what he commands, my human nature demands. His commandments are my *demandments*; they fit each other as light fits the eye, as truth fits the conscience, as love fits the heart. So when Jesus says, "Thou shalt love," my inner being says, "Thou shalt love" — not to get to heaven or to get a reward, for the reward is in the loving, the self is fulfilled in the loving, heaven and reward are thrown in. When the prodigal son, tired of bucking the laws of God and himself, came to himself, and turned from the unnatural way he was living, he went back to his father's house, his own home.

When you find Christ and his Kingdom, you find yourself. I only testify: Bound to him and his Kingdom I walk the earth free; low at his feet I stand straight before everything and everybody. I have served him these seventy plus years, but I have never made a sacrifice for him. Sacrifice? The sacrifice would be to tear from my heart this wonderful, increasingly wonderful, experience he brought me when I entered his kingdom. When my left hand begins to shake, as it has begun to shake at eighty-seven, I smile and say: "But I belong to an unshakable kingdom and to an unchanging Person, so shake on." And when the final shaking comes, falsely called death, but which I know to be only an anesthetic which God gives while he changes our bodies, I know this final shaking will only do what it did to Paul in prison: it loosed his fetters and bade him go to an awaiting home where love and joy abounds.

How can I be so sure? Suppose I find when I get to the end of life and face death, but see there is nothing there except a vast cipher — an eternal emptiness. I would look the universe in the face and say: "Well, I thought better of you. I thought you had meaning, value, goal, but I see you're empty with no meaning, value, goal; you have let me down, but I'm not down. Give me back my choices to make over again and I would make them as I have made them, with one proviso: that where I have been untrue I would be true, for this way is the way, heaven or no heaven, for I've had heaven within me — still have it within me. So as I would sink into universal nothingness, I would shout, "Jesus is Lord." Am I talking nonsense? Of course. For in a universe where there is conservation of energy, nothing is lost, but then will there be no conservation in value? The most valuable thing in life is character, moral character; would that be snuffed out just when it is at its best? I'm just learning how to live. I know better how to live at eighty-seven than I did at seventeen. Would the universe not preserve the most valuable thing in it — moral character? To me, heaven is inevitable, for I am in a state of heaven now. Like the old woman who said: "If they wouldn't let me in at the gate of heaven, I would shout all around the walls. Well, I've had a wonderful time coming anyhow."

Heaven is first of all a state and then it is a place. I have the state now, and later I will have the place. And so will everyone else who is sincerely belonging to the Way. What about people who have never heard of the Way? Everybody, I believe, will be given an adequate chance here or in the hereafter to say yes, or no, to the Unshakable Kingdom and to the Unchanging Person. I have seen the character of God in the face of Jesus Christ, and that character is pure love. Could love do less than that?

When people East and West, North and South, reject the Unshakable Kingdom and the Unchanging Person, they perish, now — they decay and go to pieces. "Who only hath immortality" (I Tim. 6:16); Who hath brought life and immortality to light through the gospel" (II Tim. 1:10). You find immortality when you find the Unshakable Kingdom and the Unchanging Person. Jesus ended the Sermon on the Mount with this important comment: "But what of the man who hears these words of

The most valuable thing in life is character, moral character...

mine and does not act upon them? He is like a man who is foolish enough to build his house on sand. The rains came down, the floods rose, and down it came with a great crash!" Can life end in a great crash? Yes.

Now what about rebirth? Is that possible? Is there a chance of another birth in this world? It is a slender possibility but with no scriptural or factual basis. The only factual surmise is that some people are supposed to remember such previous births. This is very questionable, for imagination can easily substitute for memory. However, if rebirths are a remedial system, everyone should be able to remember previous births. That would only be fair. What kind of a judicial system would it be if fault and punishment should have little or no memory connecting the two? You would be suffering, but you would have no knowledge of why? Additionally, you may be possibly rewarded in life, but again with no knowledge of why. It would all be a guess with no basis of fact. The answer, I believe, to rebirth is new birth in this birth. You have no need of the hypothesis of rebirth if you find the solid reality of a new birth now into the Unshakable Kingdom. "Except a man be born-again, he cannot see the kingdom of God" (John 3:3). "Unless you turn and become like little children, you will never get into the realm [kingdom] of heaven" (Matt. 18; 3 Moffatt). This is specific, and promising. The option of rebirth (reincarnation) is only a guess and an unpromising guess at that. When a man born-blind was brought to Jesus, and the disciples asked him, "Who did sin, this man, or his parents, that he should be born-blind?" Jesus answered, "Neither hath this man sinned, nor his parents: but that the works of God should be manifest in him" (John 9:23). Here Jesus dismissed rebirth as a cause and as a remedy and substituted the fact that the works of God could be manifested through the blindness.

A Japanese professor, a Buddhist, was stricken in midcareer with blindness. His Buddhist books told him he was blind because of sin in a previous birth. He couldn't believe it. He turned to the Christian Scriptures and found this account from John's gospel of the man born-blind and the answer of Jesus and asked, "Is it possible that the works of God could be manifest in my blindness?" It appealed to him, he surrendered himself to Christ and became a powerful evangelist. People crowded in to hear a man who took the worst that could happen to him, his blindness, and turned it into something good and significant. He went to Scotland and received graduate theological degrees, and returned to Japan to teach theology in Kobe Theological College. He also wrote fine books and was on top of his world. The works of God were made manifest in him. He pursued no fruitless speculation about the why of his blindness, rather, he took hold of calamity and turned it into opportunity.

Is it possible that we do not need to bear things, but to use them? That is the case. And the rebirth concept is unworkable speculation, and it leaves the individual and the civilization, which adopts it, smiting the forehead and saying, "my karma is bad." So when calamity strikes, it leaves the person in question helpless. But when calamity strikes the member of the Unshakable Kingdom, he surrenders the calamity to Christ and asks for wisdom and power to make something out of it, so the calamity can be used! This verse puts it this way: "I John, your brother, who share with you in Jesus the tribulation and the kingdom and the patient endurance" (Rev. 1:9 RSV). Note that tribulation comes to all with no exemptions, but note the second affirmation about the kingdom. Even in the tribulation, we are in the Unshakable Kingdom, and then note the outcome: patient endurance. When you are in the Kingdom, you can turn your tribulation into patient endurance. You can use tribulation and make it into a contribution. Everything furthers those who are in the Kingdom — good, bad, or indifferent, everything contributes. The good becomes better, the bad becomes good, and the indifferent becomes significantly different.

But suppose your efforts to sow the Kingdom fail? Jesus even said you would fail in three quarters of your efforts — some seed falling along the wayside, some on stony ground, some among thorns; only one-quarter would fall into good and receptive hearts. Now note the prepositions, which represent these four positions — *along* the wayside, *on* the stony ground, *among* thorns, and *into* good soil. Only the *into* is productive, but how does that happen? Some thirty fold, some, sixty fold, some a hundred fold. In other words, three thousand percent, six thousand percent and, ten thousand percent. Those are very large percentages and not exaggerations, for as you touch one person that person touches another one and then others and they touch others. It is never ending.

Our patient endurance comes from the feeling and the fact that being in the Unshakable Kingdom you have the universe behind you and the total of reality is behind you. No other worldview has such a cosmic backing. They are all fragmented, and hence, frail. They each collapse under the feeling there is little or nothing behind them — except their own shouting and anger.

There are occasionally fads in religion, founded on a marginal or fragmentary truth. They have their brief hectic day. The fads in religion and among people generally die because they are fads, not facts. The fact *is* the kingdom of God, and the Unshakable Kingdom. When that kingdom is lost and there is another replacement, for instance, the Church itself with its various doctrines, or the Kingdom as future when Jesus returns, there is inevitable decay. Now since the rise of the earth-born totalitarianisms — fascism, Nazism, communism — we have seen through their rising and their breakdowns, the absolute necessity of some total answer to man's total need, something cosmic and at the same time beyond the cosmic, something total and yet giving man total freedom when obeyed. We could not have seen this necessity of this total answer to man's total need had we not seen this necessity after the rise and fall of earth-born totalitarianisms. In the light of their blazing fall, we see the heavens and the earth light up with the necessity of God's Unshakable Kingdom. If there is no such Unshakable Kingdom then there

Everything furthers those who are in the Kingdom — good, bad, or indifferent, everything contributes. The good becomes better, the bad becomes good, and the indifferent becomes significantly different.

ought to be. God would be incomplete and frustrated without it. For God would be a Creator without a kingdom to rule his creation. So he created a kingdom built from the foundation of the world and not only built from, but also built into the foundation of the world, into the structure of man and of nature—and built in the way the universe is supposed to be run.

How could God show us the plan and pattern after which the universe is to be run? I see no other way than the one he apparently took. After various intimations among all nations about the coming kingdom, intimations written into nature and man, the best Man who ever lived announced it as his gospel—the gospel of the kingdom of God. And then one day after the disciples confessed that Jesus was the Christ, the Son of the living God, he immediately says: "I will give you the keys of the kingdom of heaven, and whatever you bind on earth shall be bound in heaven, and whatever you loose on earth shall be loosed in heaven" (Matt. 16:19 RSV). Peter had just confessed Jesus as the Son of the living God. "Now," said Jesus, "you have the keys of the Kingdom. You know who I am. I am the keys of the Kingdom." I am the Kingdom breaking through into time, the Kingdom personalized. My principles are the principles of the Kingdom and my character is the pattern of that kingdom. He that hath seen me, hath seen the Father and has seen the Father's kingdom embodied. The Father not only redeems by me, but he also rules by me. I am the key and the secret of the Kingdom." That is what he was apparently saying. Then we ask, "Could there be anything finer about the Kingdom than to say it is Christlikeness universalized?

So when we speak about the Unshakable Kingdom and the Unchanging Person we have to put them together. The Kingdom without the Person would run into many manmade patterns. What we need to grasp is that the Kingdom is God's lived-out pattern, which is Jesus.

This Unshakable Kingdom and the Unchanging Person are the two prongs of the anchor that reveal the nature of God's government and the nature of God's character.

38. THE KINGDOM OF GOD IS RELEVANCY

The great modern word in religion is relevancy: Is this relevant to modern life? If it is not related to life, it is of no use to life. This demand for relevancy is itself relevant. Is the kingdom of God relevant now to world conditions in the individual and in society, relevant everywhere and to everybody?

Pointing to the particular fact and place where a need is being met often satisfies this need for relevancy. But this piecemeal relevancy is not relevancy. We are grateful for these piecemeal relevancies, but not satisfied! What we need is a total relevancy, which makes everything within it also relevant because it is related to the total relevancy. Is there such a thing as a total relevancy?

The only total relevancy I can see or imagine is the Kingdom of God. The state is relevant in certain areas, the Church is relevant in certain areas and at certain times, and the school is a limited relevancy and for certain periods of life, but there is only one thing that is relevant in all situations, to all peoples, at all times, and in all ages, and that one thing is the Kingdom of God. Said Jesus to the Pharisees when being asked by them when the kingdom of God was coming: "The Kingdom of Heaven is within you" (Phillip's translation has "inside you"). Is the Kingdom of Heaven inside Pharisees? Yes, inside everybody as the law of his or her being. Break those laws and you get broken; obey those laws, consciously or unconsciously, and you are to that degree healed. For these laws are self-executing. Listen again to what Job says, "God's eye is on human life,... there is no darkness, there are no black shadows, where evildoers can ever hide. God has not to fix sessions, in order to bring men to justice; he shatters mighty men without a trial, and leaves their place to other men" (Job 34:2124, Moffatt). These self-executing laws are within you. They are the makeup of your being. You cannot escape or evade them. So these self-executing laws of the Kingdom for good or evil are unique — no other laws are thus built in, except the laws of nature around us. They, too, are built into nature, but these laws of the Kingdom are built into us as human beings. Therefore, the Kingdom is relevant to everybody, everywhere. No other such relevancy exists.

But this relevancy not only exists regarding you. It is relevant regarding relationships with other persons. A law of the Kingdom, called by James, the royal law: "If you really fulfill the royal law laid down by scripture: You must love your neighbor as yourself, well and good." Now note the rest of that passage: "But if you pay servile regard to people, you commit a sin, and *the Law* convicts you of transgression" (James 2:8-9 Moffatt). What law? Surely not the Jewish law, nor the state law, but the Law of the Kingdom written in us. It is the Law — self-operating, self-accusing, self-executing and self-punishing or self-rewarding. The quality of being goes up or down according to the obedience or disobedience to that law. This refers to the individual, to the group, to the nation, to total humanity. Listen to this: "Why break the commands of the Eternal? Why defeat yourselves?" (II Chron. 24:20 Moffatt.) Break the commands of the Eternal and you defeat yourself.

But there is only one thing that is relevant in all situations, to all peoples, at all times, and in all ages, and that one thing is the Kingdom of God.

So every revolt against the Kingdom has the doom of defeat and decay written on it. The analogy with cancer cells is relevant for just as every cancer cell has the doom of defeat written on it. Cancer cells are normal contributive cells turned selfish. They refuse to serve the organism and demand that the organism serve them, so they break the law of the Kingdom — loving your neighbors as you love yourself.

The cancer cells have the doom of their own ruin upon them.

The laws of the Kingdom of God are hedges put up along the precipices of human living to keep us from hurting or destroying ourselves. Their primary purpose is freedom. They are called the perfect laws of freedom.

The first relevancy of the Kingdom of God is that it is relevant to everybody everywhere in all stages of life, for it is the built-in way to live. Obey its laws, principles, and attitudes and you obey your own destiny written within you. This makes the Unshakable Kingdom and the Unchanging Person not only relevant, but also uniquely relevant. No other system of thought, philosophy, moralism, or faith gives two absolutes, which are universally relevant. Note this luminous verse, "The light was in being, light absolute, enlightening every man born-into the world" (John 1:9 Moffatt). Note, light absolute is a light, which lightens all lesser lights. We have a master light of all our seeing, an absolute from which we can work down to all the relativisms which confront us. Seek first, last, and always the Kingdom of God and all these things—the lesser demands and issues and needs—will be added to you.

So the Kingdom is the starting point of all your thinking, the beginning point of all your acting and the supreme point of all your affections. The Kingdom is a forced option in every situation, a forced option like eating. You don't have to eat, but if you don't eat you can't live. So the Kingdom is a forced option. You don't have to take it, but if you don't take it, you can't live, not well, or even not at all.

Take the matter of freedom, an issue with us all. There are two ways to try to be free. One is to do as you *like* and the other is to do as you *ought*. Which brings freedom? A pilot said to me: "We are free to fly if we obey the laws of flying every moment."

Take the royal law of loving your neighbor as you love yourself. That fits exactly my nature for in my nature are three driving urges—self, sex, and the herd, each partly self-regarding and partly others-regarding. So there are two directions—the self-regarding and the others-regarding. Now let's apply the two commands: love thy neighbor (the others-regarding urge) as thyself (the self-regarding urge). They exactly balance "as," and exactly fulfill the two urges within me. They fit. Now suppose I refuse to love my neighbor as I love myself, instead I hate him. What happens? I can't get along with my neighbor and I can't get along with myself. And moreover, I can't get along with God. So God has us hooked. If I won't live with God, I can't live with myself, and I can't live with my neighbor if I can't live with myself. So I'm hooked!

Perhaps the central verse in Scripture is: "Because the Lamb ... is at the heart of the throne" (Rev. 7:17 NEB). The big question in the universe is this: What is at the heart of the throne? What is at the center of power in the universe? Now hold your breath, for the most startling news ever announced is about to be recorded —the Christian faith says the Lamb—sacrificial love—is at the heart of the

311

throne; that the very center of power in the universe is sacrificial love. And that sacrificial love is not seen in sacrificing a lamb, but he is himself that lamb. Self-giving love is the final power in the universe. That is too startling to be imagined, it had to be revealed. And it could not be revealed in words. It had to be seen; that word had to become flesh—had to become flesh on a cross. Seeing is believing—we had to see it to believe it.

Why did God do it? I say he did it for "God was in Christ reconciling the world unto himself." God was not a spectator of the Cross—he was a participant. Why? He didn't have to do it—nothing compelled him, but his nature as love impelled him. He had to do it or he would not have been true to his nature.

Then why did God create man and make him free? That would be dangerous. Man might go wrong and break God's heart and his own. Break God's heart? Yes, for it is the nature of love to insinuate itself into the sorrows and sins of the loved ones. Then why did he create? The answer is in the question, "Why did parents create a child?" Because all love has the urge to have loved ones upon whom they can lavish their love and be loved in return. So they create a child on the understanding that anything that falls on the child will fall on them; its sorrows their sorrows, its sins their sins.

Would it be different with love in the Divine Parent? Would not that love want objects of love upon which he could lavish his love and be loved in return? And wouldn't parenthood in God say, "Anything that falls on them will fall on me; their sorrows are my sorrows; their sins are my sins." The moment man sinned, that moment there was an unseen cross upon the heart of God. The Lamb was slain from the foundation of the world —not merely two thousand years ago, but from the foundation of the world, the moment man sinned. But how would we know there is an unseen cross upon the heart of God? How indeed, unless an outer cross be lifted up in history to let us see the unseen cross upon God's heart. The outer cross lifted up on Calvary's hill lights up the nature of God as self-giving love. We now see that God redeems, recreates, and rules the world from a cross of self-giving love. The ultimate is good will toward everybody and everywhere.

Self-giving love is the final power in the universe.

Love is the highest in God and love is the highest in man. The universe is a universe and not a multiverse. The laws, which govern man, govern God for his laws are the projection of his character. They are not something imposed from without, but exposed from within. "Would I suffer for one I love, so wouldst Thou, so wilt Thou." Mr. C. T. Venugopal, a former member of the Indian Railway Board, heard me speak on the Cross in Madras when he was a Brahmin student, and his reaction was: "Well, if there isn't a God like that, there ought to be." Years later when Venugopal was in government, his Brahmin secretary heard me refer to Dr. Kagawa and the reaction of two pastors in America who heard him speak. One said, "Well, he didn't say much, did he?" The other replied, "When you are hanging on the Cross, you don't have to say much." The Brahmin secretary said, "When I heard of what was said of Dr. Kagawa, I thought of Mr. Venugopal. He too is hanging on the Cross, and he too doesn't have to say much." The Cross itself was speaking, speaking in the most authoritative voice in this universe.

Love is the most relevant thing in the universe. We said in the first part of this book that reality and love were always relevant. But reality without love is not relevant. The Hindu Vedantic philosophy posits *Brahm* in the *Nirguna* ("without bonds") state. There is no love. For love would create relationships, and relationships would involve *Brahm* with this world. But a God who doesn't care, doesn't count. So as someone has said: "The Advaitist philosophy is the philosophy of a few and the religion of none." For you cannot relate to the unrelated. So when the Christian faith puts love at the center of power, it makes that faith relevant in every situation. There is no unrelated love, for love by its very nature is related. So when in doubt as to what to do, do the most loving thing and you will always be right and redemptively relevant.

The head of the Canadian Ashram expressed this concept thusly, "If we do not work from the absolute, the Kingdom, down to all situations, then we react to the actions of others, and we are on the defensive; but working from the Kingdom, the absolute, we are on the offensive all the way down the line and, on all fronts. We set the stage and call the tune. We are on a loving offensive."

Working from the Kingdom down to all of life's fronts would mean what? It would mean loving your neighbor as yourself.

First, your nearest and most intimate neighbor is just yourself. To love yourself would mean that you would love the Kingdom of God supremely and seek it first, knowing that to surrender to God and his kingdom is your highest self-interest. Then you can accept yourself because it is an acceptable self. How can you reject what he accepts, loathe what he loves, look down on what he died for? When you love God supremely you can love yourself subordinately. The self is in its place and finds its freedom in supreme obedience. So all self-loathing, all self-hate, all self-depreciation drops away. Now you are a lovable self.

> *Working from the Kingdom down to all of life's fronts would mean what? It would mean loving your neighbor as yourself.*

Second, you must love your next nearest neighbor — your body. Your body is a part of a dedicated whole. It belongs to the Kingdom. It is a temple of the Holy Spirit. I will, therefore, reverence my body — reverence it so much that I will not tie it in knots by degrading habits, which

315

make my body a problem, instead of a possibility. I will discipline it so when I offer it at the marriage altar it will not be something of which I am ashamed.

Third, I will apply the love attitude to my husband or my wife. I will love the other as I love myself. I love myself sufficiently to surrender myself to God and now I can submit myself to husband or wife. "Be subject to one another, from reverence for Christ" (Eph. 5:21 Moffatt). Out of reverence for Christ—having submitted to him, you can afford to submit to each other without loss of self-respect. A husband and wife came to an Ashram making plans, as they drove along, to separate. They could not make a go of their marriage. At the Ashram they each surrendered to Christ and having done that, they found it easy to surrender to each other. They went back home as on a honeymoon.

Fourth, I will love my neighbor of whatever class or color— I will love him as I love myself. Every person is a person for whom Christ died. There are infinite possibilities in every race and every class. Put up no fences of exclusiveness because of race or class. Be a friend and you'll have friends. Love is race-blind and class-blind.

Fifth, your next neighbor whom you are to love as you love yourself is the business associate, either as employer or employee. This is a sensitive nerve center in modern life. Would loving your neighbor as you love yourself apply here? Personally, I do not see what else will apply. The alternatives are a dog-eat-dog economy instead of a brother-help-brother economy. The dog eat-dog economy is self-defeating. A new basis must be found and that is the kingdom-basis — loving your neighbor as you love yourself. Applied to industry, it would be a labor-capital division of the profits and losses — a cooperative order, with profit sharing, and significant sharing responsibilities between management and labor. Does it work? It is the only thing that really works without soul-tearing and economy-tearing friction.

Mr. Cromer, the head of the Avondale Mills, told me in answer to my question about how they ran their factory: "We give a basic wage equal to any union wage, then we set aside five percent for the investors, and then we go fifty-fifty for the rest of the profits between the business and labor. And we bring in labor and make it a part of management." "What about profits?" I asked. "We are one of the highest profit-earning companies in the country." This next comment comes from a banker: "We were interested in what you said in your Rotary Club presentation today about profit sharing.

When you love God supremely you can love yourself subordinately. The self is in its place and finds its freedom in supreme obedience. So all self-loathing, all self-hate, all self-depreciation drops away.

You may be interested to know that we as a bank, in taking over the financing of a business, we first try to get them to put in profit sharing. We don't do it as charity. We do it because it makes for better relationships and for better production." In other words, loving your neighbor as you love yourself is not mere sentimentality — it is sense and good business sense. It fits situations as the glove fits the hand. I believe that the free enterprise system can be converted from a ruthless dog-eat-dog economy to a brother-help-brother economy by the simple expedient of applying the principle of loving your neighbor as you love yourself to the economic life of America and it would be good business for everybody concerned.

Sixth, we now come to the crux of the application of the kingdom-gospel to America's relations with the Soviet Union, one representing roughly individualism and the other representing roughly collectivism. I say "roughly" for there is a great deal of collectivism in America, and there is some individualism in Russia. They are both half-truths. Individualism forgets that life is social; collectivism forgets that life is individual and personal. There is something beyond each struggling to be born-and that something is the kingdom of God, which fulfills the truth in each and eliminates the wrong in each. The kingdom of God is a society where you love your neighbor (the truth in collectivism) as you love yourself (the truth in individualism). The kingdom of God society fulfills the truth in each and eliminates the wrong in each. (Parenthetically, if I may add, I do not equate these two systems as having the same amount of good and evil in each. I said to the leading communist in India, "The two things in communism which make it float you "borrowed" from Christianity — to each according to need, 'distribution was made according to each one's need' [Acts 2:45], and contribution according to one's ability, 'If a man will not work, neither shall he eat' [II Thess. 3:10]. You have taken these two principles and have put force behind them and have ruined the principles and have ruined your people and have set the world into two camps of hate. You had better come back home." He laughed, but the laugh was not of derision, but one of desire, latent desire.) Now there are two ways to meet a confrontation between Russia and America: one way is to go to war and fight it out to determine which country will be the "top dog" in the world. If we take that option, there will be one result: nobody will win; both sides will be ruined.

The other alternative is to do what the kingdom of God commands, "Love your neighbor as you love yourself." Love Russia and the Russians as you love America and the Americans. Impossible? Well, the opposite is a forced option. You don't have to love your neighbor as you love yourself, but if you don't do it, there will be at the most, a ruined Russia and a ruined America.

Suppose we would go out and honestly love our neighbor, Russia, and try to help her with good will. Would her hate melt and would our hate melt? I believe it would happen. For mind you, the Russians are people and they are upset by the fact that nations are teetering on the precipice of war. But suppose there would be no response from people or government, would we be lost? No, remember the words of Jesus: "First say, 'Peace be to this household!' Then if there is a soul there breathing peace, your peace will rest upon him; otherwise, it will come back to you" (Luke 10:6 Moffatt). It will come back to you — you will be peaceful for having given the peace. The payoff would be in the nation. America as a nation would be more peaceful for having given the peace, and having meant it. Some respond, "But you are dealing with the Russians — they are implacable." They may be, but I doubt it. The early Christians went out in those early days and faced that Roman world, which was as challenging in that day as Russia is in this day. They went out armed with love and an infinite capacity to suffer and they overthrew that imperialistic Rome.

Our nation might be in a mood to try the kingdom way, as the alternative to the way of war, the way of futility, being now more chastened by the attempt to settle matters in Vietnam by military methods. These military methods are ending in disillusionment, as to the power of war, to settle problems and also ending up with a divided country, deeper in-debtedness and a reduced world image of America at home and abroad. Whatever role war may have served in the past, it has lost that power for now with such huge armaments in both countries that we have now less security. Never in the history of the world have we had so many armaments and never have we had so little security. Perforce, we are being driven to another approach and another way. The resources of the kingdom of God would be behind us, and if we failed, we would not fail for we would be the better for the trying. If we did succeed, we, and the world, would be better for the succeeding.

Seventh, the last area of applying the kingdom-principle of loving your neighbor is the area of the undertreated and the underprivileged of the world—the submerged half of humanity. Are they our neighbors? Jesus was asked, "Who is my neighbor?" And he replied in the parable of the Good Samaritan that the neighbor was any man in need. The answer could not be better, or clearer. Any man in need is my neighbor. And the answer to that need was to help the person set upon by robbers into safety and health. The underprivileged of the world are our neighbors and inescapably so. We can take one of two attitudes—the attitude of the priest and the Levite to pass by on the other side and be unconcerned. If we take that attitude, we too will pass by into oblivion just as the priest and the Levite did. If we don't attend to human

> *Whatever role war may have served in the past it has lost that power for now with such huge armaments in both countries, we have now less security.*

need around the world, then we will have to attend to nothing but needs — within us. We become the problems, which we refused to do anything about. The need-dodger becomes the need-filled. They are sooner or later in the hands of doctors or psychiatrists who treat them for mental and emotional illnesses, brought on by our self-centered preoccupations. You don't escape human need. You simply transfer it to within yourself. So it is good self-love to love your neighbor.

Then what would working from the Kingdom down to this human need mean? It would mean that government, industry, and the individual should each set aside, say two percent of their incomes for the underprivileged of the world, half of which should go to feeding the undernourished of the world and the other half go toward training the underprivileged and undernourished in arts and skills so they can stand on their own feet economi-cally and socially. Let those who believe in the kingdom of God give not two percent but three percent of their income, the extra third to go to introduce people everywhere to that king-dom and to its possi-bilities as God's total answer to man's total need.

One of the bright spots in the world situation is a growing feeling that we can do something positive for the world's under-privileged persons and that we *have* to do something about it. Hitherto, it was only the missionary-minded people who were involved in the educational, economic, social, and spiritual needs of humanity. Now this world-wide need is becoming a broad human concern. The time is ripe, very ripe, for some such proposal as noted above. If there is a growing feeling of involvement, there are also some feelings of non-involvement. The phrase that killed the old China was this: "It's not on my body," it is not my responsibility. Any crisis that arose would be met not by action, but by the shrugging of the shoulders and the words: "It's not on my body." Well, what was on nobody's body as responsibility was soon on everybody's body as calamity, which led to the country's downfall. That tragic noninvolvement is illustrated in the instance in a New York City where a hundred people stood around and watched as a man stabbed a woman to death, and nobody lifted a hand. If that spirit becomes dominant, we are in trouble as a nation. A kingdom-of-God caring would arrest this decay and start it on a new path the path of the Kingdom.

> *One of the bright spots in the world situation is a growing feeling that we can do something positive for the world's underprivileged persons and that we have to do something about it.*

39. THE KINGDOM OF GOD IS RELEVANT BECAUSE IT IS NATURAL

There is nothing more relevant than nature, human nature, nature around us, and ultimately Divine nature. It presses upon us from within and from without every moment of our lives. It also presses upon us from above as the kingdom of God. Is the kingdom of God an intrusion—an unnatural intrusion? Swinburne suggests that it is:

> And since my soul we cannot flee,
> To Saturn or to Mercury,
> Then keep we must, if keep we can,
> These foreign laws of God and man.

This is a modern perspective that the laws of God and man are foreign ones. I want to live out my own life and do as I please. That is the modern mood in its essence. But in Hosea's time, the note was the same: God's laws would be an intrusion (Hos. 8:12). But a lot of things intrude upon us. Food is an intrusion, a beneficial intrusion, if you don't take too much of it. Education is an intrusion, beneficial, if you get the right education, but it can poison if the information is incorrect. Marriage is an intrusion, a very blessed intrusion, if a good marriage. Social relations are intrusions—maybe irritating or irradiating. The most beneficent and blessed intrusions are God, Jesus, and the kingdom of God. Are they intrusions? In my view, they are not an intrusion but a homecoming. God made us and

324

made us for himself and for ourselves. When we find him, we find ourselves. When we lose him, we lose ourselves.

We have spoken previously of the five levels of life — the mineral kingdom, the vegetable kingdom, the animal kingdom, the human kingdom, and the kingdom of God. Each kingdom, up to the human kingdom, may think itself the highest and the ultimate. But mankind in the human kingdom stands between two worlds — the kingdom of the animal and the kingdom of God. He is pulled in two directions, toward his animal heritage and toward his divine heritage. He can be born-from below or born-from above. The kingdom of the animal stands for self against the rest, according to Darwin, the survival of the fittest in terms of the sharpest tooth and claw; or self for the sake of the rest, according to Kropotkin, in terms of mutual aid. The kingdom of the animal is life organized around the hunger motive; the kingdom of God around the love motive. The kingdom of the animal is red in tooth and claw; and the kingdom of God is red with the blood of the divine sacrifice, the Cross. The kingdom of the animal is a feud; and the kingdom of God is a family — the family of God. The lower kingdom is based on mutual destruction and the kingdom of God on mutual aid.

Now somewhere along the line when a body was prepared to be the vehicle of this kingdom, God must have breathed into man the breath of his own life, so that man became a living soul. For man is different from the animals. While he has many things in common with the animals, but man does something that animals do not do.

Man worships. Animals do not have a kinship with the Divine. However, mankind does and he has a central sickness, homesickness for God, his Heavenly Father. So man is incurably religious, and this is a hard-wired or a built-in desire for God and not built up by social custom. Some object to this perspective and suggest that men get along pretty well without God. But do they really get along without God? No one anywhere is getting along pretty well without God. Can the eye get along without light, the lungs without air, and the heart without love? If that is true, then possibly we can get along without God. I do not believe that is the case, for man is pressed on from above, and pressed on from within. That double pressure awakens men to prayer, to worship, to nostalgia and to restlessness for a God connection. While this restlessness might sometimes be unexpressed, it is always there. God responds to our human 'restlessness.'

God's answer to that upward desire and restlessness is Jesus and the Kingdom. For Jesus shows us what God is like. God is like Jesus, and the Kingdom shows us what God's reign is like and describes how we are to be and act in every conceivable circumstance and how we are to participate in this event called life. When Jesus performed miracles, they were simply a higher manifestation of the things God does in nature. Feeding the five thousand with a few loaves and fishes is what God does in nature. He turns a single grain into a hundred grains by sowing it. Jesus, the Lord of nature, hastened that process by his divine touch upon nature— not different, but more. He turned the water into wine, but God does that every day. He sends the water in the shape of rain. In the alchemy of the vine, the water is turned into the grape juice, which becomes the wine. His touch upon nature quickened that process and turned the water into wine. He cured disease, but God is performing that miracle every day, for he laid up within the body the healing forces that go into a healing process when needed. The physician or the surgeon does not heal; they simply clear away obstructions to allow nature or God to heal. Dr. Cannon, the great physiologist, in his book *The Wisdom of the Body,* shows how the body is structured to heal its own diseases. That is God's built-in wisdom. Now Jesus in healing diseases by touch or word was simply hastening a process that is really going on all the time. He walked on the water. We "walk" on water as we sail in our ships. Jesus as Lord of nature intensified the process and walked on water.

Every miracle was a heightening and intensifying of the processes of nature and never a so-called miracle of a god who twirled a mountain with the tip of his finger. Jesus never called those things miracles. He called them works. —"Greater works than these shall you do because I go to the Father." The works that God built into nature, the works Jesus revealed in his intensifying those laws by his direct touch upon them, and the works we can do through the Holy Spirit are all supernaturally natural. When he said greater works shall ye do because I go to my Father, what did he mean? Apparently this: "I am going to the Father to give you the Holy Spirit." Jesus healed comparatively few people. However, now and in his name and by his Spirit, his disciples through the ages, through hospitals and in other medical and surgical care settings, are multiplying the healings a thousand-fold or more. Jesus fed a few thousand people. Now, in his name, we feed millions—all of these things are a part of the "greater works."

All that Jesus said in his teaching, did in his doing, and shared in his unfolding of the Kingdom are all a part of a "whole." When Pilate looked at Jesus, he called out in admiration at his manhood shining through the mock royalty and said, "Behold the man." He had never seen such a man before. We look at Jesus as well with the background of the ages and say, "Behold the God," and thus God, the Man Jesus, and the Kingdom make sense to us. A teenager, after listening to this gospel of the Kingdom, said rapturously, "Now I can be a radical and a Christian."

This leads me to share something that Gandhi once said. Someone asked him, "Where would you begin if you were given the power to change the world?" He replied: "I would pray for power to renounce it." It was a noble reply and worthy of the Mahatma. But herein is a profound difference between Gandhi and Jesus. Gandhi felt rightly that he could not accept world power, even if offered. But Jesus did not hesitate to identify himself with world power and to accept it, for it was a different sort of power, a power based in love. Jesus went out preaching the gospel of the kingdom of God—that was his message, and he preached himself as the embodiment of that kingdom. Jesus and the Kingdom were one. He, himself, was the key to the kingdom of heaven — the master key. He was also the "secret" of the Kingdom — the open secret. Know him and you would have the secret of the kingdom of heaven. "All power is given unto me in heaven and in earth" (Matt. 28:19). The gospel of the Kingdom had become the gospel of the Person who embodied that kingdom. He used interchangeably "for my sake" and for "the Kingdom's sake."

The works that God built into nature, the works Jesus revealed in his intensifying those laws by his direct touch upon them, and the works we can do through the Holy Spirit are all supernaturally natural.

The transition from the gospel of the Kingdom to the gospel of the Person embodying that kingdom was done so seamlessly that we cannot mark a transition point. Jesus' role of being the Kingdom was required for it fixed the character of the Kingdom. The Kingdom was Christlikeness universalized. When you come into the Kingdom, you come into an order. When you come into Christ, you come into a Person who embodied that order. The Person and the order were one and yet each was distinctive —

individualism and collectivism were put together into a living blend.

The most natural person in the world is the Christian. He is at home anywhere and with everybody. He is relevant everywhere and in everything. But he must be a kingdom-of-God Christian, otherwise he will be anchored to some relativism, hence, not universal.

We have a motto on the walls of the Sat Tal Ashram: "There is no place where Jesus is out of place." We could have added, "even if that place be among sinners," for he would have been there redemptively. Here is a strange passage, "And when he returned to Capernaum, after some days, it was reported that he was at home" (Mark 2:1 RSV). But Capernaum was not his home city and the house was not his home; but wherever Jesus is, he was at home. (He is in my heart now and at home.)

Let us turn back to the miracles of Jesus for a moment. Jesus performed no miracle for himself—no miracle to extricate himself from a situation or to demonstrate or to show power. His miracles were all designed to meet human needs. They were to help others. There was a time in the history of Christianity when we leaned heavily upon the miracles of Jesus. Jesus was born in a super-natural way, did certain things called miracles, arose in a supernatural way, therefore, he was supernatural—the miracles carried Jesus. We now see the weakness of that view. I suggest that we let go of the miracles for a moment and go straight to the Person. Let his mind play upon your mind, his being upon your being. Then turn from

330

the Person to the miracles. Do they become credible in the light of this Person? Would a Person like Jesus do things like these? Yes, because he was the central miracle, a miracle of being. He rises in sinless grandeur above saint and sinner, a moral miracle. Then being a miracle would he perform miracles? The answer is that being a miracle it would be a miracle if he didn't perform miracles. So I don't believe in Jesus because of the Virgin Birth; I believe in the Virgin Birth because of Jesus. I don't believe in Jesus because of the Resurrection; I believe in the Resurrection because of Jesus. He, the miraculous, carries the miracles. They are the

> *When you come into the Kingdom, you come into an order. When you come into Christ you come into a Person who embodied that order.*

natural outflow of his Person. So the things that could seem "unnatural" in Jesus, namely, the miracles, become natural because of Jesus. He is supernaturally natural and so it is. So it is with his kingdom. It is heaven-born, but it is also earth-fitting. Everything — man and nature — are made in their inner structure to work in Jesus' way — the way of the Kingdom. "My kingdom is not of this world," said Jesus. It originated in the heart of God; it didn't come out of this world as its source. The "not of this world" is the genitive of source. But while it is not "sourced" in this world, it is *designed for* this world. May thy kingdom come and thy will be done on earth as it is done in heaven. This kingdom is built from the foundation of the world—but it is also built into the foundation of the world. For man and nature, it is the way to live, the natural way to live.

Nature awaits the redemption of the Kingdom: "Even the creation waits with eager longing ("on tiptoe," Phillips) for the sons of God to be revealed. The hope being that creation as well as man would one day be freed from the thralldom of decay and gain the glorious freedom of God's children" (Rom. 8:19-21 Moffatt). Man and nature have a destiny—to be the agent and illustration of God's kingdom. This eagerness for redemption on the part of nature is seen, for example, in the science of ecology. For when we are kingdom-of-God Christians we will treat nature in a Christian way—as a part of redemption. We often exploit nature, for instance, in strip mining, where we leave formerly beautiful farmland in heaps of rubble and do not even bother to level off the earth again. This behavior abuses nature. Nature is our blood brother and will be redeemed in the coming of the Kingdom.

The Kingdom-word is always relevant and is the issue now, everywhere in everything. For example:

(1) Take the Kingdom's relevant emphasis on the inner light, the inwardness of faith, that the Kingdom is within you—not as vague inner light, but a kingdom-of-God light, interpreted by and centered in Jesus Christ. You cannot

think a thought, or imagine an image without the approval or disapproval of the kingdom of God. And it is not vague light, but a vital, redemptive and relevant light. For instance, at my early morning "listening post" I recently heard this word from the Lord."I will take over your problems if you will let me, and you will!" That "and you will!" was redemptive for it illustrated not only my confidence in Him, but also His confidence in me."The life I now live, I live by faith of the Son of God."He believes in me even when I cannot believe in myself.

Jesus was the central miracle, a miracle of being. He rises in sinless grandeur above saint and sinner, a moral miracle.

(2) The kingdom of God is relevant to those who have a group mind and a group emphasis. Jesus planted the idea and fact of the kingdom of God in a small group of twelve persons. He said: "Fear not, little flock; for it is your Father's good pleasure to give you the kingdom" (Luke 12:32). Nothing seemed more absurd — the Kingdom entrusted into the hands of these uneducated disciples. But the principles and ideas entrusted into the hands of that group became the ruling ideas of civilization and when civilization lived according to those ideas and principles, it flourished. So people who are members of a "little flock" and with the Kingdom mind set may be very

important as they have hold of important ideas and principles.

Someone has said, "Five percent of the people think, ten percent think they think, and the rest would rather die than think." It's the five percent that rule the development of our society and culture. The kingdom of God is relevant to this group-minded five percent and can absorb them, use them as well as correct, and redeem them, for it links the group to the whole... the universal.

(3) The kingdom of God is relevant to the nation-minded. The nation as a nation has a destiny. Jesus said, "The kingdom of God will be taken away from you and given to a nation which will bring forth the fruits thereof." The nation as a nation has a destiny — of God; it should be built on the principles of the Kingdom; embody its spirit and attitudes and its loyalties; live its life and bring forth the fruits of the Kingdom. Is that too much to ask of a nation? Well, to take the opposite view is too tragic to imagine. For the opposite means decay and death. Everything against the Kingdom is self-doomed to decay and ultimate destruction.

There is a collective way to live, to live as a nation, and that way is the kingdom of God. Seek the Kingdom first and all these things — things needed for life — will be added. Seek something else first and all these things will be subtracted from you. This reality applies equally to the individual choice and to the collective choice. The Kingdom is relevant in public life.

When speaking to President Roosevelt on behalf of the National Christian Mission, I said: "Mr. President, you are trying to change the outer life of America. For that we are grateful. Some of us are trying to change the inner life of America — the character. We think that the outer life of a nation rests upon that imponderable thing called character. If the character breaks, the confidence breaks; if the confidence breaks, the country breaks. So if we can't do what we are trying to do, you can't do what you are trying to do." He nodded a hearty approval. The greatest enemy of America is not Russia. Our greatest enemy is the coming apart at the seams of our moral life.

(4) The kingdom of God is relevant to the secular-minded. The Christian faith is the most materialistic of faiths. It is the only faith that takes the material seriously. When God created the earth, he looked on it and saw that it was good. The earth was not perfect, but *good* for the purposes of redemption, with just enough resistance in the material upon which to sharpen our souls. The center of this materialistic faith is that the Word became flesh — the spiritual was to operate within the flesh and use it. The flesh was to be the vehicle of redemption — provided it obeys the Kingdom. The modern secularist has everything — and nothing, knows everything about life except how to live it. However, there is nothing richer than a man who turns the secular into the sacred — by dedication; who coins the base metal of the secular into the gold of the Kingdom — by dedication.

The dedication that I am writing about would mean having enough of material goods for one's own needs and the needs of his family with the rest belonging to the needs of others. That will be loving your neighbor as you love yourself, one of the marks of a kingdom-of-God Christian. When that dedication is present in your life, then you walk amid the secular world free, free to get and free to give—free! The kingdom-of-God emphasis is relevant in the secular.

(5) The kingdom-of-God emphasis is relevant to all ages from childhood to old age. It is relevant to the child. When the disciples pushed away the children who crowded about Jesus, he said to them: "Suffer the little children to come unto me, and forbid them not, for of such is the kingdom of God" (Mark 10:14). And then Jesus said this: "Except ye be converted, and become as little children, ye shall not enter the kingdom of heaven" (Matt. 18:3). What is there about the little child that makes the child represent the pattern of the spirit that enters the kingdom of God? It is their eager receptivity.

The kingdom-of-God emphasis is relevant to youth. Youth at its best is in revolt against things as they are on behalf of things as they ought to be. Jesus stands squarely in the midst of—youth in revolt against things as they are on behalf of things as they ought to be, for he presents in the kingdom of God the most radical revolt ever proposed to the mind of man. He proposed to replace the present world order founded on greed and exploitation and hate, with God's order, the Kingdom, founded on self-giving service and love, both in the individual and in the collective, and this apart from color or class or age or sex or race. And the proposal is a now-proposal, not to be indefinitely postponed: The kingdom of Heaven is at your doors — you can have it any time you want it — if you want it enough to pay the price for it — yourself. But when you pay that price — yourself — you find yourself again. You are free, free indeed.

Then the kingdom-of-God emphasis is relevant to what we call old age, but I call maturity on the way to further maturity — an eternal maturing. The book of Revelation says that the tree of life bears twelve manner of fruit, each month having its own fruit (Rev. 22:2). Is it possible that each month

Jesus stands squarely in the midst of — youth in revolt against 'things as they are on behalf of things as they ought to be, for he presents in the kingdom of God the most radical revolt ever proposed to the mind of man.

— each period of life — has its own fruit and beauty? Yes, I've found it so. I loved being seventeen (the year I entered the Unshakable Kingdom), twenty-seven, thirty-seven, forty-seven, fifty-seven, sixty-seven, and seventy-seven — and now I love most of all being eighty-seven. I name them off separately because each decade has been distinctive and progressive, each decade standing on the shoulders of the one preceding. I bet my life on the Unshakable Kingdom and the Unchanging Person and I've won—I've won, no matter what the future holds.

I have an ambition which I am not sure will be fulfilled, and it won't greatly matter if it can't be; but when some of my friends stand around when I pass over and say: "Well Brother Stanley has gone," I would like to wink at them, and if I had strength enough I'd like to put up my three fingers, which means Jesus is Lord. At any rate, if I can't actually do that, I am sure I will think it.

Since the passage of years carry us inevitably toward old age and death the relevancy of the Unshakable Kingdom and the Unchanging Person is clear. Cecil Rhodes while dying said: "God, it's dark, very dark ahead." It may have been for Rhodes, but not with the Kingdom that is unshakable by the coming of old age, or death. "For I am certain that neither death nor life, ... neither the present nor the future,... nor anything else in all creation, will be able to separate us from God's love in Christ Jesus our Lord" (Rom. 8:38, 39 RSV).

40. THE KINGDOM OF GOD AND GUIDANCE

Man is made in his inner structure for obedience and obedience is connected to receiving relevant guidance. The necessity for obedience is a built-in necessity, whether we have an earthly king or an earthly democracy. Obedience is fundamental.

Man is made in his inner structure for obedience. But obedience to what? That is the important question. There was a time when men looked for omens or signs for guidance and "obeyed" such "signs." For example, a ruler in India built a palace for himself. When he went to take possession of it, a black cat ran in front of his car. He turned around, never went into the palace, but turned it over to the government for another use. A black cat was his guidance and determined his destiny and his residence.

A superintendent of schools would not set out or return to his house unless a hawk, common to Indian cities, was sailing in an auspicious direction. A Kashmiri rajah tied up his houseboat for days until the stars were auspicious for travel. The business of state was tied up until the stars decided he should travel.

What is the alternative to receiving guidance from omens and stars? The modern mind seems to shy at absolutes, for we are so used to the relative. However, there are absolutes and the Kingdom of God is such an absolute. For example, all of the vast calculations of mathematics are built on absolutes. For when we come to the absolute two and two make four, then change and progress began. All the vast calculations in mathematics are built on absolutes. The discovery of the absolute is the beginning of progress. In algebra things equal to the same things are equal to each other — a fixed absolute, the same yesterday, today, and forever. But on that fixed absolute the vast algebraic calculations are made possible, the fixed becomes the progressive. In the realm of the moral and spiritual are there no fixed absolutes? The two we have selected, the Unshakable Kingdom and the Unchanging Person, we believe are absolutes. Beyond the kingdom of God as proclaimed by Jesus, the human race will not progress. Fascism, Nazism are gone; communism, as a political and military force, is still strong, but as a gospel of liberation to oppressed people, it has lost or is losing its appeal. Socialism is linked with political parties and hence, smacks of political methods and spirit. "Politics," says someone, "was invented by a grinning devil." Capitalism as a dog-eat-dog economy is unworkable. It destroys itself in the process of destroying others; converted into a brother-help-brother economy, it might survive, but it would not be the kingdom of God. All the world's Utopias have remained Utopian—passing visions. The Church contains perhaps the best life of the Kingdom, but it is not the Kingdom. It is relativism, related to the absolute, the Kingdom. Nowhere in the Scriptures are we told to build the Kingdom as we told people a generation ago: "Go out and build the Kingdom." We build the Church, but not the Kingdom, for the Kingdom is built from the foundation of the world, said Jesus. It is built into the nature of reality, is reality, and therefore, an absolute—an absolute and therefore, unshakable. Beyond the conception and fact of the Kingdom the human race will not progress. And beyond Jesus, as the embodiment and interpretation of that Kingdom, the human race will never progress. Coleridge said: "Beyond the life and character of Jesus of Nazareth, the human race will never progress," and this century is illustrating it, for every departure from Jesus has meant deterioration, inevitably with no exceptions.

So we must become disciples of the kingdom of God, make it our life study, and our life allegiance and our life plan of action in the personal and the social. A disciple to the kingdom of God is open to guidance, for he has the key to the Kingdom, and the open secret of the Kingdom is his. A pastor asked his church caretaker why he didn't come to church and the caretaker replied: "Have you had any fresh news from God? If so, I'll come." The disciple to the Kingdom has fresh news from God — he has the good news of the Kingdom, which is always

The Church contains perhaps the best life of the Kingdom, but it is not the Kingdom.

fresh and exciting because it is always relevant. In the words of Jesus: "If you dwell within the revelation I have brought, you are indeed my disciples; you shall know the truth, and the truth shall set you free" (John 8:31-33 NEB). Here, in this most important passage, Jesus marked out the sphere in which he was to operate and the sphere in which the disciples were to get their *guidance*: "If you dwell within the revelation I have brought." What was the revelation Jesus brought? He confined himself to two revelations: the message and the Man, the kingdom of

God and himself, the embodiment of that kingdom; the Unshakable Kingdom and the Unchanging Person.

Walter Rauschenbusch says that in Jesus' teaching the Kingdom is the vertebrae, the backbone, in which all the bones of teaching and action cohere and have their meaning. Remove the Kingdom and the 'bones of teaching' become incoherent, a mass of unrelated bones. But the kingdom of God would be meaningless and not understandable unless we could see in a Person, the order embodied and illustrated. Jesus did not give a diagram of future guidance, but a dynamic for life now: "But ye shall receive power to be my witnesses." Not scanning the heavens for signs, but looking at the earth for areas of service.

Paul preached the order (of the kingdom of God) and the Person dwelling within the revelation Jesus had brought. With those two things as a starting point and as the master light of all seeing, Paul faced life and all its issues with assured confidence. Jesus said, the revelation I have brought, — not taught, but brought, is brought in my own person. He was the revelation of what God is like and what the Kingdom is like. And there is more guidance: When "you dwell within the revelation I have brought ... you shall know the truth, and the truth will set you free ... If then the Son sets you free, you will indeed be free" (John 8:31,36 NEB). Here Jesus equates the revelation he has brought with the truth, not truth nor a truth, but the truth.

Johns Hopkins University, a scientific institution, put over the portals of its gate as its motto and as the motto of science: *You shall know the truth and the truth shall make you free.* Here science and faith coincide and offer guidance.

So dwell — dwell, do not run in and out, but dwell within the revelation Jesus brought and you will be guided in keeping your life straight and if you make mistakes, you can absorb them and go on your way rejoicing. Absorb your mistakes by his forgiveness and by forgiving yourself. Can you really go on your way rejoicing? Yes, with this passage ringing in your ears: "For whatever is born-of God conquers the world" (I John 5:4 Moffatt). This Unshakable Kingdom and this Unchanging Person were both born-of God and are our absolute necessities.

The guidance available to use through the unshakable Kingdom is the open door for the future: "Behold I have set before you an open door which no man can shut." The open door is a total message for the total man and total society in their total relationships. We can't offer less, for he offered us this 'word.' "He that gathers not with me scatters." The time has gone for trifling, but the time is ripe for testimony. Here is the place for the laity.

I believe that the next great spiritual awakening is going to come through the laity. We ministers, pastors or evangelists, like myself, are not going to save the world — we are too few and besides it wouldn't be good if we could do it, for it would take away from the laity that spiritual and moral growth which comes through sharing one's faith. The lay witness movement is the brightest spot on the spiritual horizon and the world is ready for it.

Two laymen went out for visitation evangelism. They were a little frightened for the first prospect was a leading lawyer in their community. They began the encounter this way: "We've come to ask you to join the Church." And the lawyer replied: "Is that all you want of me? If so, I'm not interested. Many people through the years have asked me to join the Church, so that if that is all you want, I'm not interested." The layman replied: "Well, there is this other part of being a Christian and it involves surrender to Christ, but frankly, we don't know much about this ourselves, so we have come on the only level we know asking you to join our— church." The lawyer replied: "Well, I'm interested in this other part, (of being a Christian). Haven't you got a card?" They fished out a "decision card"[4] from their pockets and handed it to him. He read it slowly, pulled out his pen and signed it with this remark: "I've always wanted to do that, but no one has ever asked me to do it. They have always asked me something else, such as joining the church. Where do you go next? I'd like to go with you." And he went right out with them to the next prospect. In fact he went with them through the whole of the evangelistic lay- campaign. It created a sensation. Now when people come to him for legal advice about a potential divorce he gives them a copy of *Abundant Living* and tells them to read it for a

---

[4] A 'decision card" was often used to formalize a person's decision to surrender her life to Christ and to follow Jesus."

week and if they still want a divorce to come to see him again. "Then I'll talk about it, but not now." Now note the lawyer's powerful comment, "Is that all you want from me—church membership?" If that is all we have to offer this empty-hearted and confused generation then we are irrelevant. Our 'ask' is not big enough or demanding enough. Even surrender to Christ personally is not big enough or consuming enough if it stops at personal surrender. Rather, the "ask" must be related to the gospel of the Unshakable Kingdom and the Unchanging Person. The laity can be effective messengers to share this gospel!

> *I believe that the next great spiritual awakening is going to come through the laity. We ministers, pastors or evangelists, like myself, are not going to save the world.*

The hour for effective Christian witnessing has come and —was never as great as now. Modern man is empty — he knows everything about life except how to live it. And this emptiness is increasing and will increase. For the modern man stands between two worlds— one dead and the other not yet born. That emptiness is the greatest mission field we have ever had since the world began.

For this witness to be effective it must be a witness to individual and collective need minute enough to change the individual and magnificent enough to change the nation, a total answer to man's total need. Man, the individual, must be the proving ground for anything that is to be universal. If it won't work in the individual, it won't work in the collective. Jesus intended his kingdom for the collective: "Full authority in heaven and on earth has been committed to me. Go forth, therefore, and make all nations my disciples" (Matt. 28:18, 19 NEB). Note, "nations my disciples" — the nation as a nation was to be the disciple — the corporate life was to be a disciple. Note further, it doesn't say, your disciples, meaning the disciples of the disciples. The individual and the nation are to be primarily attached to Jesus and secondarily to a body of believers, the Church. This is important, for if you make the individual and the nations disciples of disciples, then that makes them denomination-minded instead of kingdom-minded. You can be kingdom-minded first and secondarily denomination-minded because your primary allegiance determines and controls your secondary alle-giance. But you can't be primarily denomination-minded and secondarily Kingdom-minded, for you've lost the Kingdom in making it secondary. I am a grateful member of the Methodist Church, for in that fellowship I found the Lord, or he found me. But I don't belong to the Methodist Church. I belong to the Unchanging Person and to the Unshakable Kingdom, but I am a member of the Methodist Church.

The biggest betrayal of the Kingdom is to hold it as a primary belief but a secondary allegiance, and the Church as the primary, as the working way to live. The Kingdom is cancelled and the secondary takes over. In making the Church primary, it saves its life and it loses it. For the Church then stands for nothing except itself. When the Church stands for itself, it has little to stand for — its world significance is gone. But when you make the Kingdom absolute, the absolute allegiance and all else, including the Church, is relative. Then your values are clear, and all the values you hold turn valuable because they are related to the utterly valuable, the Kingdom. They all have the value of that kingdom. For you take on the significance of that which you hold primary. In this case, you have the significance of the kingdom of God; when you speak the Kingdom speaks, when you act the Kingdom acts — the ultimate acts in the relative.

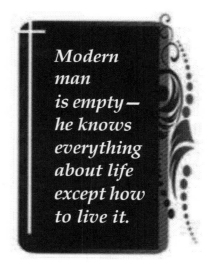

Modern man is empty — he knows everything about life except how to live it.

A few days ago, a man from NASA came to visit in the midst of my writing this book and said: "As you see from my card, I'm a chief of a bureau at NASA. We've succeeded in going to the moon and we may go to Mars, but I've recently come into the kingdom of God, and I am so excited about it that I want to give my whole life to witnessing to the Kingdom. It is more exciting than

NASA." I commented: "NASA is good, but this is it." And this is freedom.

The Unshakable Kingdom will shake into dust all the shakable kingdoms founded on blood and fear. The meek will inherit the earth — inherit it through the blood of the Lamb, what he has done, and by the word of their testimony — what we do. We can fairly shout our answer from the housetops, for if we hold our peace, the stones will cry out — the hard bare facts of life will cry out for the Kingdom.

41. THE KINGDOM OF GOD AND PHYSICAL HEALTH AND HEALING

Here we come to the acid test of the workability of the kingdom of God in what it does for the human physical frame, called the body, in which we live, and live very intimately day-in and day-out for an average of sixty-nine years for men and seventy-two for women. Does it matter to the human body whether you live by the kingdom of God principles and spirit or whether you live by the ordinary secular codes without that kingdom? Or whether you do just as you please with your body apart from secular codes or the Kingdom? Does the body have anything to say about the treatment it gets from within or without, or both? I believe that it certainly does. Our bodies react into health or sickness according to the within and without treatment. Of course this is modified by the kind of body you inherited from your parents. But apart from that, does it matter to the body how you act and react in this thing called life? It certainly does. The British Medical Association reports that there is not a single cell of the body totally removed from the influence of mind and emotion. The American Medical Association reports that fifty percent of diseases are rooted in the mental and spiritual and fifty percent rooted in the physical. Yesterday I spoke with a missionary doctor, returned from India, about a patient in her hospital where a Hindu wife was so anxious to have a baby that she produced all the symptoms of pregnancy, including a much-distended abdomen. She was put under an anesthetic and the

The Unshakable Kingdom will shake into dust all the shakable kingdoms founded on blood and fear.

abdomen flattened out and the symptoms disappeared. "Yes," said the doctor, "that happened in my hospital, and it happens in America too." A famous surgeon said to me: "You could have headed off, with the kind of religion you are proclaiming, eighty-five percent of the cases that come to me for surgery. They begin with functional disturbance through wrong mental and spiritual attitudes and actions, then the functional passes to the structural, and then we surgeons get them."

I have often imagined a convention of bodies talking about the people who inhabit them. We have often had conventions of people who talk about their bodies—I'd like to see that conversation reversed. A body stands up and says: "Oh my, it's awful to live with the man I have to live with. He ties me in knots by his wrong mental and emotional and spiritual attitudes. I can't function normally, so I'm sick and in revolt half of the time. Then he doses me with all kinds of medicines that have no relationship to what's the matter with me. I wish he knew how to live, for he makes me sick." Another body stands up and says: "My, it's wonderful to live with the woman I live with. She is rhythmical and harmonious and disciplined and happy. We are a team and you should see what I do for her—prodigious things. It's a joy to do it." Suppose your body would stand up and talk about you— would you wish to have a sudden engagement elsewhere? But your body does talk about you. "That the life of Jesus may be manifest in your mortal body"—manifested as health. Suppose something other than the life of Jesus were at the center such as —fear, anger, and a self-centered preoccupation. Would that be manifested in your mortal flesh? Yes, it would as disease. Every thought and attitude is registered in your mortal body. You, in large measure, make your own body—from within.

If that is true, then does the kingdom of God make for health or illness, or is it neutral? God wills health, and the kingdom of God is God's total program for health— health to the mind and the soul, to the body and to society.

Every single principle and attitude of the Kingdom is health producing and health maintaining. Call the roll of those principles and attitudes and every one, if practiced, would produce health: "love, joy, peace, good temper, kindliness, generosity, fidelity, gentleness, self-control" (Gal. 5:22 Moffatt). These are called the fruits of the Spirit; those fruits are fruitful in producing health, every one of them.

Some doctors went around the world to find out the attitudes and actions that make for health. After searching in many nations and many cultures and faiths, they came back and found in the Beatitudes the best list of attitudes and actions to produce and maintain health. A medical convention, after debate, adopted a resolution agreeing with the doctors who said the Beatitudes are health-giving, but they would use "healthy" instead of "blessed," so they would read: "Healthy are those who know they are poor—poor enough to receive the receptive. Healthy are those who mourn—those who care about the wrongs of the world; Healthy are those of a gentle spirit—not lording it over others and pushing them around. Healthy are those who hunger and thirst to see right prevail—those who care enough about the wrongs of the world to do something about it. Healthy are those who show mercy—the compassionate. Healthy are those whose hearts are pure—are undivided in heart. Healthy are the peacemakers—those who bring about peace between man and himself, man and man, and man and God. Healthy are those who suffer persecution for the cause of right—

if you don't stand for something, you will fall for anything. Healthy are those who suffer insults and every kind of calumny and can accept it with exultation — no self-pity — they don't bear trouble, they use it."

So the medical profession when truly scientific is truly aligned to kingdom-of-God attitudes. Those attitudes are built in instead of built up — they are inherent. Every departure from that kingdom results in physical upset. Note these passages: "Some, weakened by their sinful ways were sick and suffering through evildoing, had a loathing for all food, and were on the verge of death" (Ps. 107:17,18 Moffatt). "They would take their own rebellious way till evildoing wasted them away" (Ps. 106:43 Moffatt). "Your own wickedness will punish you, your apostasy will chastise you" (Jer. 2:19 Moffatt). "But if evil men whoever in a good land will not learn to be good, they cease to be" (Isa. 26:10 Moffatt). "My health pines away under my trouble" (Ps. 88:9 Moffatt). "Such is the fate of the self-satisfied, the end of all whose faith is in themselves; death shepherds them un-checked" (Ps. 49:13,14 Moffatt). "When my heart was sour, when I felt sore, I was a dull, stupid creature, no better than a brute before thee" (Ps. 73:21-22 Moffatt).

Into that morass of ancient and modern living was projected a new order of life, the kingdom of God. Would it have anything to do with physical healing? Since the physical and the spiritual are so intertwined, I do not see how physical and spiritual healing could be avoided. So when Jesus came on the scene "he made a tour through the whole of Galilee, teaching in their synagogues, preaching the gospel of the Reign and healing all diseases and sickness among the people." The gospel of the Kingdom and the healing of diseases and sicknesses were inseparably connected. Physical healing wasn't his whole gospel for the above verse is followed by this: "When he saw the crowds he went up the hill," and then the Sermon on the Mount follows and he shares the total message of the Kingdom in its relationships to the individual and society. So if you pick out one item, physical healing, and make that your gospel, it is off center, for that makes you the center and God your servant. He keeps you in repair — and anything that makes you the center is off-center. You are using God for your purposes. God is the center and reconciliation with God is the center of our emphasis. But reconciled with God, you are reconciled with yourself, and reconciled with yourself, you are reconciled with your body. Many diseases drop off by that reconciliation. For

Some doctors went around the world to find out the attitudes and actions that make for health. After searching in many nations and many cultures and faiths they came back and found in the Beatitudes ...

353

the body falls in line with the purposes of the Kingdom, becomes truly natural and is, therefore, rhythmical and happy and healthy.

We cannot be absolutists in this matter of healing. By absolutists, I mean those who say that all diseases and sicknesses must be cured in this life or else there is sin or lack of faith. If you take that position, you leave a lot of wreckage behind, for many saints were never cured in this life. Did they have sin or lack of faith? Paul had a thorn in the flesh, and in Gal. 4:13-15 (Moffatt) he tells what that thorn was. "It was because of an illness that I first preached the gospel to you ..., and though my flesh was a trial to you, you did not scoff at me, or spurn me, but you welcomed me like an angel of God, like Christ Jesus... (I can bear witness that you would have torn out your very eyes ... and given me them.)" Obviously the thorn had to do with his eyesight—a sore trial to a public speaker. Three times he asked God to take that thorn away but God said, "My grace is sufficient for you, for my strength is made perfect in weakness." I'll give you power to use it. So Paul said: "Then I'll glory in my infirmities, for when I'm weak, then I am strong." He would not just bear it—he would use it. So when his eyesight went bad, his insight went better. So some diseases and infirmities must await the final cure in the resurrection when we get our resurrection body. The Christian answer seems to be: God will cure the disease now in some of the ways I shall mention, or give you power to use the disease till the final cure in the resurrection. But having said that, I hasten to say that disease is not the will of God. Nowhere in the New Testament does it say that God sends disease. Disease is an enemy. The evil of the mind is error, the evil of the emotion is suffering, the evil of the will is sin, and the evil of the body is disease. So God is out to abolish all evil, up and down the line, but some diseases must await the final cure in the resurrection. This is a mortal world and we were not intended to be immortal in a mortal world. Some time or other the mortal body breaks down. Death is a part of life. It is appointed unto men once to die.

Jesus was Lord of sickness and disease while here. Interesting that Jesus was never sick. Once it was said that he was wearied by walking all morning, but it was a good healthy tiredness, no tiredness from his inner conflicts or worries or fears, no home grown weariness. And none of his disciples was apparently ever sick. Why? Because the Kingdom they had entered offered a climate of health. The King of that kingdom was the King of health. Health irradiated from him. But—and this is important—when he went up to give the Sermon on the Mount, it was preceded by "He went around... preaching the gospel of the kingdom and healing every disease and every

> *Some diseases and infirmities must await the final cure in the resurrection when we get our resurrection body.*

infirmity among the people. Seeing the crowds he went upon the mountain." Then follows the Sermon on the Mount, and yet in that sermon he never mentioned physical healing—it was all moral and spiritual attitudes from beginning to end. Why? Because Jesus knew what science and medicine and personal and corporate experience are just beginning to discover: that many diseases (not all, for there are contagious diseases and germ diseases, and they are real) are rooted in the mental and spiritual, and every single thing he emphasized in the sermon would be health producing if applied to life. Not one single thing is questionable. All his moral and spiritual attitudes and teachings contribute to health. And the opposite can occur, for example, every single attitude, which goes against the Sermon on the Mount, produces ill health.

The Mayo Clinic suggests *"Steps to a Long Life,"* and includes the following guidance, "Be optimistic." Physiologically happiness is healthy. A man who is depressed suffers from a slowdown of all his metabolic processes. A case of nerves is not just in your head, but is as real as a heart attack. The nervous system has a job to do just like the heart and its functioning is affected by stress, such as extra responsibility and futile worry. We are certain some of our patients die young because they lack a positive attitude. A physician friend had a myocardial infarction and literally died of fright.

There are two great approaches to life, the Christian and the scientific. The Christian approach works from revelation down. And the scientific approach works from the facts up. Do these two approaches come out of two conclusions about life, or only one? When I say revelation I mean the revelation which Jesus brought — the revelation of what God is like and what God's kingdom is like. We see both are Christ-like — God is a Christ-like God and the Kingdom is a Christ-like kingdom. Between that revelation and current science, the gap is increasingly narrowing. In my opinion, science is discovering that the laws of health are the laws of God written in flesh and blood and nerves and tissues. They are the laws of the Kingdom. A doctor said to a clergyman: "You're a Christian, aren't you? Why don't you act on your Christianity and you'd be well." A surgeon said: "If you don't surrender to God, you'll probably have to surrender to me as a surgeon."

One of the central things in the Christian faith is the Word become flesh. An aluminum plant, put up by Canadians in India, had a unique way of telling the engineer its needs. A machine would put out an arm on which was painted: "I need oil." "My wires are crossed," and so forth. If the human body were so constituted that it could put out an arm with a need painted on it, there would be many specific needs painted on it. But the need of needs, which the body would express, would be this: "Please, oh please, be Christian. I work well that way. If you try to work me some other way, I work my own ruin." Every cell of your body dances with glee when you enter the Kingdom.

Are Jesus and his kingdom a stimulus to health? Yes, the greatest stimulus in this world. He stimulates the mind, the emotion, the will, and the total person. Jesus stimulates the body — every cell responds to its Master's voice and is alive and alert. The need for stimulants is removed with Jesus. Here is a powerful example: A woman went to her handbag after surrendering to Christ and picked out a whiskey flask, a cigarette case, and bottle of tranquilizers and handed them to me with, "I won't need them anymore." And she didn't. Jesus takes the place and more than the place of narcotics, cigarettes, drugs, tranquilizers, and stimulants. All substitutes are unbelievably unnecessary. Jesus is health. He is health, not only to the mentally and emotionally afflicted, but to the structurally afflicted as well. I am not a healer and I've never asked for or wanted the gift of healing, lest the single eye of evangelism be clouded by the subordinate gift of healing, but I've been called on to pray for the structurally afflicted and I've seen tuberculosis, cancers, club feet, heart and liver and kidney ailments, skin afflictions, and cysts — the whole gamut of structural afflictions — cured, and cured unmistakably, by prayer in his Name and by his power.

Some of these healings have taken place with a laying on of hands, but some have come without any human intervention. For instance, a college professor, during a healing service, felt he could not come to the altar. He remained in his seat, but surrendered a pain in his back, which he had for ten years as a result of a war injury. He was immediately and permanently healed. I rejoiced over this for it was accomplished without any human mediation—it came directly from God.

But one of the most unencumbered and clear-cut healings took place recently with my evangelistic colleague, Mary Webster. She had a fractured elbow which even after medical and physical therapy treatments left her with the arm bent, four inches shorter than the other, and unable to move except in a restricted way. While she was praying for others, a voice said pre-emptorily, "Stretch forth your arm." Surprised at the abrupt command, she obeyed. The arm had been set for a year and a half since the accident and the ligaments were fixed, but as she obeyed, though it caused pain, she could

> *Science is discovering that the laws of health are the laws of God written in flesh and blood and nerves and tissues.*

hear the cracking of the ligaments in the shoulder and the elbow. Another woman watched the arm straighten out and cried out, "O Lord, don't make it longer than the other one." It stopped at the exact length of the other arm and the arm was free to move in any direction exactly the same as the other. The after-pain soon subsided. This was a sovereign and clear-cut intervention of Divine healing power.

If at eighty-seven I can still carry the same load of engagements that I carried forty years ago without exhaustion, it is because of "grace, grass, and gumption." But grace is first. (Lately I've had to change the word "grass" to "grasses" — the cereal grasses — because of the current use of the word "grass" as a term for marijuana.) Under gumption I include the three exercises I take just before I go to bed at night. When I was fortyish I wrote to a friend in India saying, "I don't know how long I can keep up this pace. Not beyond sixty, I suppose, for by then I'll have burnt up myself for God." But I've found to my glad surprise that Jesus Christ is energy, stimulus, and fire, and like Moses' burning bush, the "bush" of my body is not consumed. So his fire is not fever, his energy is not enervating, his stimulus is not just stimulating but provides for an increase in energy. It's real, lifelong and dependable and it works. My body is at home in the kingdom of God. I am often asked, "How long are you going to keep this up?" I don't know, but I know one thing: I'm going to go full steam ahead until the boiler bursts. And I hope my last cry will be, "I commend my Savior to you."

42. THE UNSHAKABLE KINGDOM APPLIED
TO LIFE HERE AND NOW

I am picking out now an apparently ordinary account of an apparently ordinary group of people who went through an ordinary situation, but were the center of extraordinary events because they embodied extraordinary principles and attitudes.

They were the center of nine revolutions, quiet revolutions, but ones which changed humanity because they went about preaching and bringing the gospel of the kingdom of God. The whole account reads this way: "Soon afterwards, he went on through cities and villages, preaching and bringing the good news of the kingdom of God. And the twelve were with him, and also some women who had been healed of evil spirits and infirmities: Mary, called Magdalene, from whom seven demons had gone out; Joanna, the wife of Chuza, Herod's steward; Susanna, and many others, who provided for them out of their means" (Luke 8:13 RSV). Contained in this simple narrative were nine distinct, quiet revolutions — embodied revolutions, which have changed the world's outlook on life and changed the world's character, consciously or unconsciously.

Perhaps we can see in these subtle actions the method of embodying kingdom of God attitudes and acts, and thus we too can become centers of quiet revolutions, which might change the world around us and beyond, and perhaps even the world as a whole. For the world now is in a fluid state, often called chaotic, and it may be that as the Spirit of God in the beginning moved upon the face of that chaos and out of it came a cosmos, so out of the welter of this current world chaos will come God's cosmos, the kingdom of God on earth— if it can see the pattern. And we may be that pattern. We will begin at the last verse and work back to the first verse and discover the climax of these quiet revolutions.

(1) Here is illustrated a mastery of the material by the spiritual. "Some women who provided for them out of their means." Here is a statement about the mastery of the material by the spiritual, an important mastery in life. For if we don't master the material, it will master us. One man's grave site read, "Born a man and died a money bag." Here the women mastered the material by its dedication—they dedicated their money, invested it in the greatest movement that ever struck our planet, the movement of the kingdom of God. Their money contributed to the fruitfulness of the kingdom. How much shall we dedicate? Since the kingdom of God principle is, "to each according to his need," a disciple to the kingdom of God would ask, "What financial resources do I need to make me more fit mentally, physically, and spiritually for the purposes of the kingdom of God?" This would include providing for herself and those dependent on her, including the education of her children. The remaining resources, after one's own needs are met, belong to the needs of others. Each person in the light of her own needs and the needs of others must draw that line before God

and her own conscience. Blessed is she who comes to mastery at that point.

Now note that it was the women who had the privilege of providing for the disciples out of their means. This applies today. The women of America now hold seventy-five percent of the wealth of the wealthiest country of the world. (A woman corrected me, "You're wrong—it's eighty-two percent.) "Love left it to us," said a woman. So women hold seventy-five to eighty-two percent of the wealth of America. Will they wisely invest it as did these early Christian women, or will they assume the vices of men? It is fine with me for women

For if we don't master the material, it will master us.

to be different from men. Be different and stay on your pedestals! We love you that way! I said that to a couple of thousand high school students and the male portion roared its applause. It was advance notice to the females in the audience. There must have been a divine purpose in entrusting this money into the hands of women. You have come, as Esther, to the Kingdom for such a time as this.

(2) There was a mastery of status in that group. For there was Mary Magdalene, a woman out of whom seven devils had gone. They may have been devils of impurity and perhaps of low social status. Then there was Joanna, the wife of Herod the king's steward, probably high in

social status. They were brought together in this fellowship of the Kingdom and neither one was identified as of high or low social status. They were both equal in the sight of God and in this new emerging social order of the Kingdom. Status was eradicated. Everyone was a person for whom Christ died. A new sense of human values had come into society and status symbols were out of place.

When I came back from India on my first furlough, an old schoolmate called me up on the West Coast and said: "Hello, Stanley, welcome back. I'm coming to see you in my Cadillac." I inwardly laughed. He thought I would be impressed and bend the knee when I heard that he was driving a "Cadillac." It was laughable, but tragic for it became the stumbling block over which he stumbled to his downfall. He was an effective evangelist, but trying to add a cubit to his stature by outer status symbols—a mansion of a home with mahogany staircases, a motorboat, and a plane and then the Cadillac. His marriage ended in a quarrel over these status symbols with his wife chasing him around the palatial home with a butcher knife. Over against that put this: "Jesus, knowing that the Father had given all things into his hands, and that he had come from God and was going to God, rose from supper, laid aside his garments, and girded himself with a towel and began to wash the disciples feet" (John 13:3-5 RSV). The consciousness of greatness—Jesus came from God—was the secret of his humility. His status symbol was a towel, used to be the Servant of all. But the Servant of all became the greatest of all. The two status symbols of that early kingdom of God society were a towel and a cross. The final status was this, "The conqueror I will allow to sit beside me on my throne, as I myself have conquered and sat down, beside my Father on his throne" (Rev. 3:21 Moffatt). Those who were girded with a towel and carried a cross found to their surprise that they were sharing in the ruling of the universe. God and Christ had moved over and let them help them run the world.

(3) There was a mastery over race by the spiritual. (Here I am importing into this account something in line with this mastery. While it was a later development of the kingdom-of-God spirit, as a spiritual illustration, it belongs here.) "Now there were in the church that was at Antioch certain prophets and teachers; such as Barnabas, Simeon, that was called Niger [literally, "the black"]" (Acts 13:1). There was in that early church Simeon, the black man. Simeon was not on the edges, but at the center as a prophet or teacher, and he with others laid hands on Paul and Barnabas to send them forth to preach the gospel of the Kingdom to white Europe. This illustrates the powerful place of the African in the early Christian society of the Kingdom. After wandering in the wilderness of racism for two thousand years, we are coming back to the place where we began and we think we are doing something extraordinary. No, this was the early Christian "ordinary." Segregation is out of line, a departure from the Christian faith and practice. It is anti-kingdom. Therefore, it is anti-good for everyone concerned. Segre-

gation is against the good of the black man, but it is also against the good of the white man. For when the blacks are fully and freely integrated into our society, we will all be richer from the contribution that they will bring to the total society. They have enriched science, writing, athletics, and religion and their gifts are felt in academia as well, commerce and politics. When the black man is not fully participating in society, we are the poorer.

So the third thing in this mastery sequence was the mastery of race— in the Kingdom race was not wiped out, but transcended and used, so that in this new order a man was a son of the Kingdom with regal blood in his veins.

(4) The next mastery was the mastery of the sexual by the spiritual. Note straight off that in the kingdom of God, the sexual is God-created and God-approved. "So God formed man in his own likeness, in the likeness of God he formed him, male and female, he formed both" (Gen. 1:27 Moffatt). Sexuality is an approved part of creation and has a destiny and is to be used as a part of the kingdom of God. The intention seems to be this: One man and one woman are to live together until death parts them either by physical or spiritual death. The purpose of that relationship within the home seems to be: procreation and fellow-ship. Outside the home sexual energy can be sublimated into creative energy, creating new movements, new hopes, newborn souls, and new life. These people seemed to have fulfilled these purposes constructively. Single and married men and women

moved night and day together through Galilee. Now that wasn't usually done in those days. The disciples marveled that Jesus at the well talked with a woman—not the woman, but a woman (any woman at all) in public this way. It wasn't done. If a wife should meet her husband on the street, she was supposed to turn and look the other way. The holiest among the Pharisees were called the bleeding Pharisees. They went around with bleeding foreheads because they always looked at the ground so as not to see a woman, hence, they were bumping their foreheads against trees, walls, and posts and so had bleeding foreheads. In modern life, sexuality has often moved into the center and

Segregation is out of line, a departure from the Christian faith and practice. It is anti-kingdom. Therefore, it is anti-good for everyone concerned.

produced a society considerably preoccupied by the sexual. I doubt if this emphasis is producing more intimate sexual enjoyment, and perhaps it is quite the opposite. The divorce parade in our culture, with one of three marriages ending in divorce, demonstrates the misery and consequent breakdown of morality.

On the other hand, these kingdom-of-God Christians did not try the way of the bleeding Pharisees, nor the sexuality dominated moderns. They lived together quite normally and naturally and enjoyed each other, but—and this is the point—the breath of scandal never touched them. Jesus and his disciples were accused of many things, but never of immorality. Purity had moved to the inside of them. They enjoyed life with a pure and unalloyed joy. That joy is expressed in these words: "Whereas the aim of the Christian discipline is the love that springs from a pure heart, from a good conscience, and a sincere faith" (I Tim. 1:5 Moffatt). Note that a pure heart (the emotions), a good conscience (the will), and a sincere faith (the mind), results in love springing from all three and the whole person is alive with love.

(5) There was a mastery of sickness and disease— "women ... who had been healed ... of illnesses." A new healthy society was emerging for two reasons. They were in the presence and under the power of a healing person— Jesus. He radiated health and he cured disease by his command and touch. Jesus was the holiest, healthiest, and "healingest" Person who ever lived. Just being in his presence was healing. And they found healing by living in the holiest, healthiest, and "healingest" order that ever existed—the kingdom of God. And note it was the women who ministered to them out of their means and it was the women who were healed of illnesses.

(6) There was the mastery of sin and evil by the spiritual— "women who had been healed of evil spirits."

I am not sure what evil spirits mean, but I suppose this can be applied to the whole world of sin and evil. Dean Church, the historian, says: "A solemn joy goes through that ancient world: sin and evil had met its match. Man could attain to that hitherto impossible thing for the multitudes, not merely here and there, but on a wide-scale — the soul's attainment to goodness." That was good news. We are now discovering through trial and error that sin and human nature are antithetical. It is said that "the Son of Man ..., will gather out of his Kingdom whatever makes men stumble, and all whose deeds are evil" (Matt. 13:41 NEB). Does evil cause offense? Yes, evil is an offense to God and his kingdom. It is an offense and it is offensive. Does God have to punish sin? No, sin and its punishment are one and the same thing. You don't have to punish the eye because it has sand in it, a body because it has a cancer in it.

It was said that Jesus healed "those who were annoyed with unclean spirits" (Luke 6:18 Moffatt). If sin and evil are natural, why should evil spirits annoy people? They should blossom and bloom under evil spirits. Evil spirits produce annoyance in human nature. They always have and always will. They annoy human nature, annoy relationships between persons, and annoy society. Goodness is an affinity. Evil is an annoyance. Of all the things that produce unhappiness, sin and evil are responsible for ninety percent. The gospel of the Kingdom brought release from sin and evil and is, therefore, the greatest producer of happiness and joy on this planet. I don't try to have a good time, I just have a good time, constitutionally. I don't know what it is to have a blue hour or a discouraged one. I haven't had one, say, for forty years. Not because I have been good, but I had sense enough to align myself to a good Kingdom and a good Redeemer. And his goodness is joy, joy, and joy!

(7) There was a mastery of noncreative waste material by the spiritual. The account says, "with him were the Twelve." Now Twelve begins with a capital T in the New English Bible. That is significant. When the disciples came to Jesus, they were just twelve men—they had little or no significance; but coming to Jesus and aligning themselves to him and his kingdom, they could no longer be characterized in any way other than as the Twelve. They were important, not in themselves, but in the movement and the Person to whom they were aligned. They now represented the cause, which Jesus represented—the cause of the kingdom of God. If they hadn't become his disciples, their biographies could have been summed up something like this: Born in a fisherman's home, as boys they caught fish, grew up, married, they caught more fish, when children came they had to catch still more—thus it went until old age and then death. They had the significance of family and fish. Now they had the significance of a universal kingdom, which was to replace the present world order with God's order. The "no-bodies" had become the "somebodies." They were now the Twelve. Jesus heightens everything he touches. He turns all our common nouns into proper nouns. It was heady wine and

initially it went to their heads. They quarreled over who was to be first in this new kingdom. Peter said: "Although they all betray thee, yet not will I" — it was an I-They relationship; I'm superior, they are inferior. Peter stood against the eleven. Following his denial and the weeping, Peter stood up among the eleven (Acts 1:15); then the Holy Spirit moved within him and at Pentecost he stood up along side the eleven (Acts 2:14). And at that point Peter said we — "we cannot give up speaking" (Acts 4:20). He had come from an I-They to a *we* relationship, and it was the Holy Spirit cleansing him from within, from pride and self-assertion, that brought him to the *we* relationships. A more astonishing gift of power

Of all the things that produce unhappiness, sin and evil are responsible for ninety percent. The gospel of the Kingdom brought release from sin and evil and is, therefore, the greatest producer of happiness and joy on this planet.

was seen in these words: "The conqueror I will allow to sit beside me on my throne, as I myself have conquered and sat down beside my Father on his throne." This sharing of power by Jesus Christ and the Father with the disciples is breathtaking for it was not marginal power. It was central and universal power. It was God moving over and asking man to help him in the running of the universe. How dare God do it? He did it because the Lamb was at the heart of the throne—"the Lamb who is at the heart of the throne will be their shepherd." Self-giving sacrificial love is at the heart of the throne, so those who take that attitude toward life—God and man—can be entrusted with ultimate power. They would never use it for their own purposes, but only for the good of others. That kind of power can be entrusted to that kind of person. Another passage shows the complete trustability of people in the Kingdom: "I saw thrones with people sitting on them" (Rev. 20:4 Moffatt). So in the end, the people rule. The emperors, kings, princes, and potentates have departed and the people rule. Democracy can be an ultimate power only with trustable persons. Trustable persons can be entrusted with power as it will not corrupt them, but consecrate them.

I was invited for dinner by a highly sophisticated member of New York society. At the close of the dinner, served by a French chef, the hostess asked me if she could talk with me. She said, "I had never had any contact with religion except to take a cocktail with my rector in my country home, but one day I was given your book, *The Christ of the Indian Road*, and I took it to bed with me to put me to sleep. However, I did not go to sleep, but finished the book at 4 a.m. and got up and sat before the fire in meditation. A warm, living Presence came into my heart. I call that hour my shining hour. People seem to think that I have found something, for they come to me with their problems. Some time ago I was asked to head an important society in New York City, but I turned it down because I would have to meet so many un-sophisticated persons. But now since this change in me has come, I feel I would like to meet those people and I have accepted the position. Now what do you think has happened to me?" My reply, "I think you've been converted." She replied, "I agree with you—I have been converted. Now that I'm a Christian, how do you act as a Christian? What's the technique of being a Christian? I'm a musical professional. In music we have technique—what is yours?" I was on the spot and said, "You will have to work out a technique as you go into this society of yours. Write about it in the language you used at the dinner table tonight." I threw out that suggestion and went back to India. A year later, I received a manuscript from her entitled *Technique*. With a sigh, I began to wade through it and was stabbed wide-awake. She really had something. It was published under the title of *I Follow the Road*[5] and went into several editions. Another book followed, *The Rule of the Road*.

Now, and this is the point, "Up to age sixty "she wrote, "I created nothing. My biography could be summed up in three words: 'fashionable, fleshy, and futile.'" After sixty she began to be creative. In a kingdom of values she

---

[5] *I Follow The Road: A Modern Woman's Search For God* Paperback – by Anne Byrd Payson (Author), E. Stanley Jones (Introduction). See, https://archive.org/details/ruleoftheroad012290mbp.

was valuable. Until sixty, nothing was behind her except herself. When she stepped into the Kingdom, the sum total of reality was behind her. She counted because she cared.

(8) There was a mastery of environment by the spiritual. The account says: "they went through cities and villages." That, too, is important. Many are caught and confined by their environment. Some people feel they have to live in a city to provide a background of greatness for their own supposed greatness. Others prefer the village — where they can perhaps be a "big fish in a small pond." These people were not caught or confined, neither by the city nor by the village. They belonged to both. They were not afraid of the city, nor did the village degrade them. They belonged to something bigger than each — the Kingdom. So both city and village were kingdom-opportunities.

I was about to get on a train in India. I asked an Indian gentleman on the station platform whether he was going on this train. "No," he said, "there is nothing but third-class carriages on it." "But I'm going on it," I replied. "Yes," he said, "you are a religious man. If you go first-class, it doesn't exalt you, and if you go third class, it doesn't degrade you. You are lifted above these distinctions, but I have to keep them up." I could have danced on the platform, *but* I felt sadness for the gentleman. First-class didn't exalt me, nor did third-class degrade me, for I didn't belong to first-class or third class. I belonged to the kingdom of God, which was a classless society. I was at home anywhere because I was at home everywhere. When the Kingdom is your home then every home is your home. When you are at home with yourself, you are at home anywhere. For if you can't draw anything from your circumstances, you can always draw water from your inner-stances. You can always do what Proverbs suggests: "Drink fresh water out of your own well" (5:15 Moffatt). And this: "Happy are they who, nerved by thee, set out on pilgrimage! When they pass through Wearyglen, fountains flow for their refreshing, blessings rain upon them; they are the stronger as they go, until God at last reveals himself in Zion" (Ps. 84:57 Moffatt).

Someone once said to me: "It must be wonderful to be on the mountaintop all the time in these Ashrams and evangelistic campaigns." I replied: "I'm not on the mountain top and I'm not in the valley. I'm on the Way and the Way is a gentle upward." That way may lead through city or village, but in both it is the Way. And it is the way of joy even in Wearyglens.

A little girl writing on true greatness said she had a canary, which broke its leg. They thought they would have to put it out of its misery, but when they came down the next morning, the canary was sort of propped up with the broken leg against the bars singing at the top of its voice. "That," she said, "was true greatness." Here is another illustration: A man was told by the doctors that they would have to take out one of his eyes and put in a glass eye, and his reply was, "Doctor, if you do have to put in a glass eye, please put a twinkle in it." So the happy sons and daughters of the Kingdom going through city or village, take what comes and make something out of it. They use everything, for they are backed by everything. They are happy in spite of, when they can't be happy on account of.

(9) There was a mastery of themselves by the Kingdom. "They went preaching and bringing the good news of the Kingdom of God." This is the climax — they *preached* the Kingdom and they *brought* the Kingdom. Where was it? Inside of them and outside of them in their relationships. This translation of Martin Buber: "The Kingdom of Heaven is between you" — in the relationships you have with others — it is between you. So the kingdom of Heaven was in them and between them — it was both. They preached that kingdom and they brought that kingdom. The word of the Kingdom had become flesh in the individual person and in the group. It was personal and it was social. They had surrendered to the Kingdom — it mastered them. The word of the Kingdom had become flesh in them. That was the first and most crucial revolution. The other eight revolutions followed as cause and effect. Self-surrender is primary, all else is secondary.

So the kingdom-mastery of the self-showed itself in the mastery of economics, social status, racial factors, sexuality, illness and moral evil. Silent, but dynamic, revolutions were wrapped up in the ordinary, and they became the extraordinary. They set the standards of life, which have permeated the world. And where humanity has lived according to those standards, it has risen, and where it has lived against those standards, it has fallen. So the statement of Jesus has come to pass: "Fear not little flock, it is your Father's good pleasure to give you the kingdom." The kingdom disciples have become the rulers of humanity—ruling its development by the principles and standards they embodied.

This has happened in a period of half-discovery, half-realization, and a half-application of the kingdom of God in history. "What will happen when there is a full discovery, a full realization and a full application of the Kingdom to human affairs, as there is bound to be, or we will perish? What will happen? We turn now to our last section and to our conclusions.

43. OUR CONCLUSIONS CONCERNING THE UNSHAKABLE KINGDOM AND THE UNCHANGING PERSON—THE ABSOLUTE ORDER AND THE ABSOLUTE PERSON

If there isn't such an order and if there isn't such a Person, there ought to be. "There ought to be a plan in the universe," said a newspaper editorial. He who put plan and purpose for the cell, into the minute, would he have no plan for the magnificent, in the whole? Certain tribes in Africa believe that God is good and wise, but that he has a half-witted brother who spoils God's creation. Well, if God has no plan—no overall plan for the universe, then — and I say this reverently — then, God himself must be that half-witted brother — for God to set forces at work in the universe and to have no plan for their use is unthinkable for God. There ought to be a plan. I believe that God has a plan.

Could we imagine a better plan than the Kingdom of God? And can we imagine a better person to inaugurate it and be its illustration than Jesus Christ? If so, why hasn't man with all his progress in science and technology and knowledge brought out the plan and presented it? We believe that it couldn't be imposed on man as a code, for man is to develop in freedom as a moral being if he is to accept such a plan as his own. Therefore, this Kingdom must be hidden in the nature of things, and await man's discovery and acceptance. The Kingdom must be revealed in two ways — "the glorious Father, grant you the Spirit of wisdom and revelation" (Eph. 1:17 Moffatt) — through wisdom as in — man's search from below; and revelation — God's unfolding from above. It can't be man's wisdom from below alone, or God's revelation from above, alone. It must be a joint revealing and unfolding — God's revelation and man's discovery. These two "efforts" must sooner or later coincide. That is what is happening. We are discovering that what God has unfolded in nature, he is unfolding in Christ. The God of nature and the God of grace is the same God. The laws of our being are the laws of the kingdom of God. Could you improve on that? And can we find any better illustration and meaning of the kingdom of God than in the person of Jesus Christ? He made himself and the Kingdom one—*auto-basilea*—himself the Kingdom.[6] Would you want or could you imagine a better order than an order in which the spirit of Jesus Christ pervades, guides, and illustrates? And could you find anything more satisfactory to human personality than to find that the laws of the kingdom of God are the laws of our own being, so that when we obey those laws of the Kingdom, we discover ourselves and when we obey those laws, we find our own freedom? This Kingdom is built from the foundation of the world

We are discovering that what God has unfolded in nature, he is unfolding in Christ.

and not only built from it, it is also built into the foundation of the world so that it includes our human nature. We are structured to belong to Jesus, and when we find him and his kingdom, we find our homeland, our natural way to live, so that we are supernaturally

---

[6] *Autobasileia* is as Origen describes, the "Kingdom in person." It is Jesus. Pope Benedict writes in his book *Jesus of Nazareth,* "Jesus himself is the Kingdom; the Kingdom is not a thing, it is not a geographical dominion like worldly kingdoms. It is a person; it is he. On this interpretation, the term "Kingdom of God" is itself a veiled Christology. By the way in which he speaks of the Kingdom of God, Jesus leads men to realize the overwhelming fact that in him, God himself is present among them, that he is God's presence." (p. 49). http://dulmer.blogspot.com/2007/09/autobasileia.html (Accessed 7/28/2017).

natural. Does that make any difference to human life—not to be fighting human nature, but fitting into human nature with the sum total of reality behind you, so that you are living with the grain of the universe and not against it, so that you have cosmic backing? Wouldn't it be good news that the far country was truly alien to the prodigal son and his father's house was natural, his homeland? Does it make any difference to you to know that all coming to Jesus has the feeling of a homecoming upon it and all going away from him has the feeling of estrangement upon it?

Is it good news to learn that the kingdom of God and Jesus are both called the Way? We noted that the kingdom of God is called the Way, and that Jesus is called the Way—"I am the way, and the truth, and the life." Does it mean anything to you that the experiment (of living upon the Way), wherever tried, is saying the same thing and illustrates that Jesus and the Kingdom are turning out to be the Way? An African explorer was being guided through a trackless jungle. He began to have doubts and said to his guide: "Is this the way?" The guide responded: "There is no way—I am the way." Does it mean anything to you that Jesus, the Person, (i.e., the guide) and the Kingdom, the order, are both the Way?

When you think of goodness, you don't add virtue to virtue, you think of Jesus of Nazareth. When we think that the good is not only good, it is good for us, then when we say, "May Thy kingdom come," we really say, "May our highest good come." Again, is it good news that the kingdom of God is not offered to the good nor to the worthy, but to the willing? *Nowhere are we taught in Scripture to build the Kingdom, as we were taught a generation ago.* We build the Church, which is relativism, but the Kingdom is built from the foundation of the world. It is an absolute. You don't build an absolute. You receive an absolute and accept it as a gift. "How blest are they who know they are poor" — poor enough to receive — "the kingdom of heaven belongs to them." "Let us be grateful for receiving a Kingdom which cannot be shaken" (Heb. 12:28). We receive it — as a gift, free to anyone poor enough to receive. But it isn't a cheap gift. It is very expensive, for if you take the gift, you belong forever to the Giver. You will be bound with silken cords of love forever to his heart. But this bondage is the perfect law of freedom.

This gift of the Kingdom is open then to the morally unfit, but in the taking of it they become the morally fit. Here is an example, Admiral Sato, commander of the Japanese submarine fleet at Pearl Harbor, told me that the verse that got him and opened the door into the Kingdom for him was this one: "He sends the rain on the evil and on the good and wishes his sun to shine on the just and the unjust." He said to himself, "If I can't get into the Kingdom because I'm good, but maybe I can get in because I'm evil." And he lifted the latchstrings and was in. Jesus said, "The least in the kingdom of God is greater than John the Baptist." Why? Because John preached the gospel of a demand — you can't do this, you must do that, whereas the good news of the Kingdom was the gospel of an offer. So the least in the Kingdom of an offer was greater than the greatest in the gospel of a demand. You don't climb the ladder and find the Kingdom at the topmost rung of the ladder of worthiness. The Kingdom is the ladder put down from God and you receive it at the bottom most rung of willingness.

A businessman said, "For fifty years I've been trying to climb the ladder to God to find him and his Kingdom at the topmost rung and now you tell me I'm wrong. It is a gift at the bottommost rung of willingness. Well, this is good news." As I look at it, I ask, "Could the invitation to the Kingdom be more generous and more demanding and more freedom-giving?" No, it is perfect as it is offered.

Another consideration and conclusion. This kingdom is bound up with no culture, no nation, no race, and no religion. It is open to everybody, everywhere on equal terms. Jesus never used the word religion, for he was not founding a new religion to set over against other religions. Religion is man's search for God. The Gospel is God's search for man. So anything good in any race, religion, or culture, which is worth preser-ving, will not be lost in the Kingdom. "I come not to destroy but to fulfill."

Where does the Church come in? The Church contains the best life of the Kingdom. It has the clearest and most authoritative account of the revelation of the Kingdom through the New Testament. The church is the best serving institution on earth. It has many critics, but no rivals in the work of human redemption. However, the Church is not the exclusive agency of the coming of the

Kingdom. Wherever men bring forth the fruits of the Kingdom, there the Kingdom is, inside of the Church or outside of the Church. "The kingdom of God shall be taken away from you and given to a nation that will bring forth the fruits thereof."

Some of those who call themselves atheists see this kingdom dimly written in themselves and in the nature of things, and therefore, unconsciously have their fingers on the latchstrings of the Kingdom. Here are some examples."Dr. Alfred Adler, a non-Christian psychiatrist, as noted earlier said: "I suppose all the ills of human personality can

Jesus never used the word religion, for he was not founding a new religion to set over against other religions. Religion is man's search for God. The Gospel is God's search for man.

be traced back to one thing, not understanding the meaning of the phrase: 'It is more blessed to give than to receive.' "But that is a basic principle of the Kingdom. Alder's hand, was on the latchstring. Soviet Premier Alexei Kosygin praised the non-aggression agreement, which had been signed by West Germany and the Soviet Union, praised it as "a very important decision, dictated by life itself." "Dictated by life itself?" Then there is something in life itself, not built up, but built in, which favors good will, not ill will, love and not hate—the Kingdom is that life itself.

Richard Rubenstein, a fine Jewish thinker,[7] came to the conclusion that an all-encompassing nothingness is the ultimate, yet paused to contend that "the new freedom allows us to discover not that all things are permissible, but rather a natural morality which inheres in the very character of life. We are to discover that moral limits are inherent in the very structure of possibilities available to man as a social and biological being and even when all is permitted, the body has its own morality." So the body has its own morality? A built-in morality? And what is that built-in morality? It is the kingdom of God built into nerves, tissues and organs of our body. They are kingdom of God laws. "The body is ... for the Lord; and the Lord is for the body" (I Cor. 6:13). The Hindu president of a college in Trinidad and an authority on the Bhagavad Gita, the sacred book of the Hindus, told me he ends up his lectures with this: "But there is no one who has ever fulfilled the ideal of the Bhagavad Gita except Jesus Christ." A mimic depicting the gods of the Hindus before an audience of Hindu lawyers made them rock with laughter, but when he began to do the same with Christ, they hissed him off the stage.

---

[7] Richard Lowell Rubenstein (b. January 8, 1924 in New York City) was an educator in religion and writer in the American Jewish community, noted particularly for his contributions to holocaust theology. See, https://en.wikipedia.org/wiki/Richard_L._Rubenstein (Accessed 10/27/2017).

I now repeat what I've said before, this time from a statesman with his finger on the pulse of the modern world, Adolf Berle, Jr., "No individual, or group of human beings, however implemented, have been able to challenge the great design." That great design is the Kingdom. Jesus said quietly: "He that gathers not with me, scatters," and the ages have corroborated what he said in essence. If you try to work life in the way of Jesus, it works—if you try to work life some other way, then life scatters, goes to pieces. Here are no exceptions for the individual or for society.

Does it matter then whether we live life in the Kingdom or against the Kingdom and does it matter now? Does life work well in his way, and badly and sadly in any other way? A young woman in Latin America, brilliant and cultured, said at the close of my address: "You have told us how to be happy in Christ, now tell me how I can be happy without Christ." I had to answer: "I'm sorry, but I don't think it can be done." It apparently can't be done. I sit here after writing that sentence to try to think back over my life of over half a century of traveling to find in memory an authentically happy person apart from Christ. I have never met one. I have seen people who were momentarily happy through happenings — receiving a gift or seeing a friend — but people who are happy, not merely on account of, but in spite of as well, only the Christian faith in Christ produces that. But if faith in the Unchanging Person, Christ, produces that happiness, incorrigible happiness, what kind of joy would be produced when the Unshakable Kingdom is added? That brings a sense of security to the joy, you have cosmic backing for your joy. That brings grace upon grace and joy upon joy, security upon security.

That brings me to another conclusion: The Christian faith has often been trying to fly with one wing—the living Christ as experience or the living order, the Kingdom as a task and hope. We are now seeing more clearly that to fly with one wing is to go round in circles, be that one wing the Person *or* the order. It must be both — the Person and the order. Each is unique, but coming together they make unparalled uniqueness. There is no person in any faith comparable to Jesus Christ. Jesus alone is the Spotless Incarnation, in any clime, in any age, in any faith. When I see God in the face of Jesus, I am not blinded, for Jesus is the human-divine transformer. I can look on the face of God and live—and how!

The Kingdom of God as preached and illustrated in his own Person by Jesus is also unique. No age, no clime, and no faith have presented anything like the kingdom of God. And both of them are realism, not idealism. They are the Word of God become flesh—Jesus shows us what God is like and he shows us what God's government, God's kingdom, is like. "He that hath seen me, hath seen the Father," and he that hath seen me, hath seen what the Father's kingdom is like. They are both Christ-like.

Is anything higher, anything imaginably higher? If so, I've never seen it or heard of it. It hasn't been on the scene and I suspect that it won't be on the scene. This is it! Jesus is said to be the origin of God's creation—God created the world through Christ and for Christ, everything is made to work in his way and when it does, it works well, and if it works in some other way, it works its own ruin. "I am the first and the last"—the Alpha and the Omega—"I have the first word in creation and I will have the last word in creation." If it doesn't come out at his feet, it doesn't come out. It perishes. I pause now to make a prophecy: The greatest discovery in science and in religion in the years to come will be that all humans and nature have a destiny and that destiny is this, that all things work well in a Christian way and badly in some other way, and that destiny is written in human and nature and is therefore inescapable.

I have seen the inklings of the truth of my "prophecy." For example, a physician, the editor of a national medical science journal said to me: "Why this idea that human nature is structured to work in the Christian way and works well and adjustably when it does so, and badly when it departs from it, and that the Christian way is the natural way is startling. Why I see that in my medical practice. It is true. And it is exciting. But why hasn't the Church told us this before? This is really exciting." Jesus said that the kingdom of God will be discovered in two ways—one, like a man going across a field who stubs his shoe on what turns out to be a hidden treasure, sells all, and buys that field. This is what happens for the person, who in a moment of insight, discovers the Kingdom, and commits himself to its possession. This is the sudden, decisive type of discovery—in one divine moment he sees, decides, and commits himself for life. The other way (of discovery of the Kingdom) is like a merchant seeking good pearls, who finds one of great price, sells all, and buys that one pearl. This is the careful, weigher-of-values type; he finds the pearl of the greatest value and sells all and buys it. The first is the emotional discovery of the Kingdom and the second is the hardheaded, businesslike, show-me-your-value discovery of the Kingdom. Jesus welcomed both "discoverers"and both approaches. The intellectual climate of the world has changed. It used to be very traditional, and we simply took what was passed on from generation to generation without question. Now the world climate is increasingly scientific.We test, try, prove, and only act upon the proven. The Kingdom welcomes that approach, even eagerly welcomes it, for we are persuaded that when we throw on the scale of value all the various interpretations and explanation of life—the philosophical, the religious, the secular, the moralistic, the scientific, the militaristic—all those views and ways of life—the kingdom-of-God way will outweigh any one of them *and* all of them combined.

Let me offer my reader an example from the militaristic view of life. I was at a luncheon in the Pentagon with some officers and I asked them: "Is religion growing in the armed forces, just holding its own, or going down?" A colonel spoke up and said, "Among the thoughtful it is growing. And the reason seems to be this: We have tried everything else and nothing else works. We are now trying Christ and it is working, working to the degree that we work it."

Out of sheer human necessity, we *will* take the kingdom of God. We have to or we will perish. This is the hour of the *great shaking*. What is shakable, will crumble to the dust or rubble and the Unshakable Kingdom will not only prove its survival value, but its value for survival. It will not only be the strongest, but also the fittest system to survive. This crucial moment had to come after the earthborn totalitarianisms have been given a chance to prove their efficacy for beneficent survival. They have failed, are failing, and will fail. For they have put force behind their revolutions and that has corrupted them. The wrong means get to wrong ends, for the means preexist in and determine the ends. Democracy, too, will fail to the degree that we use force for the gaining

> *The greatest discovery in science and in religion in the years to come will be that all humans and nature have a destiny and that destiny is this, that all things work well in a Christian way and badly in some other way, and that destiny is written in human and nature and is therefore inescapable.*

of democratic ends. It has failed in Indochina, showing us that the United States is not to be the policeman of the world, spreading democracy by force and corrupting ourselves in the process. We are destined to be an instrument of the kingdom of God and to use kingdom-of-God methods to reach kingdom-of-God ends. We had to experience the breakdown of other totalitarianisms and of democracy gone astray before we were prepared to accept the kingdom of God as God's way out, and ours! I want to make a final comment about the significance of the laity to Christianity. I believe that the future of the Christian church will not be from the pulpit, but from the pew. There is a current cleavage among the laity and clergy between the individual and the social gospel. This is an unfortunate dispute, which could contribute to a permanently divided church. I speak now to those persons who stand only in one camp (the individual Gospel) or the other, (the social gospel). These opposing stances are unnecessary. The gospel of the kingdom of God, the message of Jesus and his Gospel brings together these two emphases in a living blend, sums up the truth in each and goes beyond each in the process. The gospel of the kingdom of God is God's total answer to man's total need, individual and collective. God is not a half-god ruling over a half-realm, the individual or the collective. He rules over both, both in a living blend. He lays his hand upon the individual will and says, "Repent, be converted, enter the Kingdom and obey it." He lays His hand upon the collective will and says, "Repent, be converted, enter the

Kingdom and obey it." So, I'm no longer interested in an individual gospel or a social gospel—I want one gospel that demands and offers conversion for both. "Woe unto you Capernaum;" "the kingdom of God will be taken away from you and given to a nation that will bring forth the fruits thereof;" "Go forth, therefore, and make all nations my disciples." The corporate entity, the city, the nation, must be disciples and bring forth the fruits of the Kingdom.

If we start with the absolute of the Kingdom and work down to all life, individual and collective, The oneness of the individual and the social emphases is seen in the final scene, "I was hungered, and you gave me meat, ... Naked, and you clothed me, I was sick and you visited me. Then shall the righteous answer him saying, Lord, when saw we thee hungered, and fed Thee?" The reply of the Lord, "Inasmuch as you have done it unto one of the least of these my brethren, you have done it unto me" (Matt. 25:35-36, 40). Here social service and spiritual service were one— to do it to them was to do it to him.

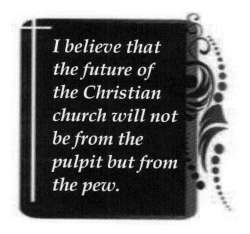

I believe that the future of the Christian church will not be from the pulpit but from the pew.

This cleavage between the individual and the social emphases fades out if we start at the place Jesus started—

the Kingdom. Transformation (conversion) for the individual and for society is a necessity for both — for all.

We come now to our final conclusion — at the place of this question, How do we begin and where? We can't wait until everyone is ready. To begin our acceptance and application of the Kingdom, we must begin with ourselves. "Religion that doesn't begin with the individual doesn't begin, but if it ends with the individual it ends." The saintly Bishop Pakenham-Walsh of the Anglican Church raised that question after my address on the kingdom of God in Bangalore, India. "Brother Stanley, how do we begin?" I pondered a moment and then replied: "Bishop, I suppose we must go out and begin to think and act as though the Kingdom were already here. And as far as we are concerned, it will be already here." He said, "All right, I will invest my life, the rest that there is left, to try to act as if the Kingdom of God has already come."

So that would mean that if we are to think and act as though the Kingdom were already here, if we have said personally that Jesus is Lord and have made a personal surrender to him with all we know and all we don't know, then we belong to the Unchanging Person and, *therefore*, we belong to the Unshakable Kingdom. As a person who belongs to the Un-changing Person and the Unshakable Kingdom, I can prayerfully consider how I can apply the Kingdom spirit and principles to all my relationships, to my personal thoughts, life, actions, and habits, to my family life, to my professional or business relationships, to my class and race relationships, and to my national and international relation-ships, to my recreational relationships, and to my church relationships. We can't change everybody, but I can change my relationships and me as far as they depend on me. In each of these relationships I can say: As far as I am concerned, the Kingdom is already here. In the light of its being already here, how do I think and act? I am certain of one thing about that kingdom, that the Kingdom is the kingdom of love. So I will begin to love, if not by my love, then with his love — for everybody, everywhere, I am a disciple to the Kingdom of God, under its tutelage and control and unfolding sovereignty. I may make blunders and fall, but if I fall, I will fall on my knees, and if I stumble, I will stumble into the arms of Jesus. I have a destiny — I am a seed of the new order — "the good seed means the sons of the kingdom" (Matt. 13:38 RSV). I am sown in this particular place to be the interpretation and meaning and message of the new order. I know the seed and the soil are affinities, so that all the resources of the Kingdom are at my disposal. So "in Him who

> *How do we begin and where?... I suppose we must go out and begin to think and act as though the Kingdom were already here. And as far as we are concerned it will be already here.*

strengthens me, I am able for anything" (Phil. 4:11 Moffatt). I have a total Gospel, for man's total need, for the total world. I ought to be happy and I am!

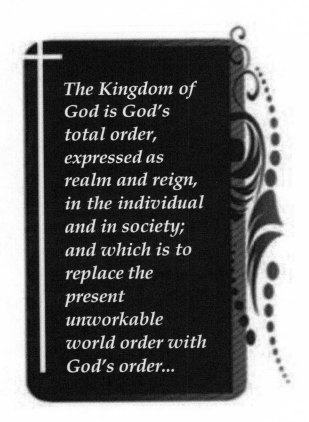

The Kingdom of God is God's total order, expressed as realm and reign, in the individual and in society; and which is to replace the present unworkable world order with God's order...

AFTERWORD

By Ron Crandall

IN 1967 I RETURNED from a year of missionary work in Vietnam trying to discern God's design for my life. Many things contributed to my decision to drop out of seminary and make the trip to that distant land and its turmoil, but at the top of my list was frustration. I felt stymied by the intrusion of "middleclass," "western," "American," and "church" into the radical gospel of the Jesus who had captured my heart.

Among villagers and Vietnamese Buddhist lowlanders, I came to recognize my longing for *The Christ of Every Road* and the larger shape of the gospel as the *Kingdom of God*. I began to consume Jones' writings. I finally found a truly integrated approach to our Trinitarian faith and an answer to all the issues confronting us at every level of the human condition. I was hooked.

In this book, written near the end of his life Brother Stanley, as he preferred to be called, sets forth the core message of his 50 years of seeking. My desire for living within both an evangelistic and social gospel would no longer be impossible. They were two wings of the same message, the same Bird. Through Jones the gospel invitation was no longer simply a way to a personal encounter with God and the hope for life after death. It was now "walking in the Way"—the Kingdom of God within us and among us. Perhaps no single text from this book captures this more than these powerful words.

> Jesus didn't define the Kingdom in precise terms, perhaps because he was the definition. We may define the Kingdom because he has shown us what it is—shown us in his own person, as: The Kingdom of God is God's total order, expressed as realm and reign, in the individual and society; and which is to replace the present unworkable world order with God's order in the individual and in society; and while the nature of the Kingdom is social the entrance into it is by a personal new birth now; the character of that kingdom is seen in the character of Jesus—the Kingdom is Christlikeness universalized.

In his day, some saw Jones as a dreamer, an idealist, a humanist, a universalist, and even a communist. He was in fact a realist! Jones believed that the seed of the Kingdom of God was planted within the very fabric of the universe and inside every human being.

So, this book is about the "How" as much as it is the "What." It tackles the issues faced by individuals as we seek to live with ourselves and others across our globe, to deal with the urges within us that can conspire to destroy us and our relationships or to lead us to a wonderful new focused energy and freedom. Jones discusses economics, politics, social order (and its opposite), cultural and religious conflicts, racial and gender turmoil. His primary source is the New Testament, but it is impossible to read a single page of this book without encountering two or three stories and illustrations from his world travels and his coming to know representatives of our human family.

The Bible translations Jones used were those of his day—The Revised Standard Version, King James Version, New English Bible, Moffatt's Translation, and even JB Phillips Paraphrase. Nevertheless, you won't find a better description of how the Sermon on the Mount and the Beatitudes actually reveal secrets to living in the Kingdom than those that are on these pages. In reading E. Stanley Jones, you read not only history, but about that which is always contemporary and ultimately eternal.

If you have a heart for all of God's world and long to find answers about *how* to make your own life a life in Christ, you owe it to your dreams to read and learn, and find the transforming freedom of *The Unshakable Kingdom* and *The Unchanging Person*.

"the time is fulfilled, and the Kingdom of God has come."
(Mark 1:15)
"abundantly far more than we can ask or imagine..."
(Ephesians 3:20)
"from one degree of glory to another..."
(2 Corinthians 3:18)

DR. RON CRANDALL
Professor Emeritus and Retired Dean
E. Stanley Jones School of World Mission and Evangelism,
Asbury Theological Seminary
Wilmore, KY

ABOUT THE AUTHOR

E. STANLEY JONES
(Portrait by Shivraj Mahendra, 2017)

E. STANLEY JONES (1884-1973) was described by a distinguished Bishop as the "greatest missionary since Saint Paul." This missionary/evangelist spent seventy years traveling throughout the world in the ministry of Jesus Christ. Jones wrote and spoke for the general public and there is little doubt that his words brought hope and refreshment to multitudes all over the world. As a well-known, engaging, and powerful evangelist, Jones delivered tens of thousands of sermons and lectures. He typically traveled fifty weeks a year, often speaking two to six times a day.

Jones worked to revolutionize the whole theory and practice of missions to third world nations by disentangling Christianity from Western political and cultural imperialism. He established hundreds of Christian Ashrams throughout the world, many of which still meet today. E. Stanley Jones was a crusader for Christian unity, a nonstop witness for Christ, and a spokesman for peace, racial brotherhood, and social justice. He foresaw where the great issues would be and spoke to them long before they were recognized... often at great unpopularity and even antagonism and derision to himself. Many consider Jones a prophet and his honors – and he did receive them – were all laid at the feet of Jesus Christ. Jones would readily admit that his quite ordinary life became extraordinary only because he fully surrendered his life to Jesus Christ!

Jones' writing and preaching did not require people to leave their intellect at the door; his presentation of Jesus engaged both the intellect and touched humanity's desire to experience the living Christ in their lives. When Jones wrote or talked about Jesus, it was as if he knew Jesus personally and could reach out and touch him. Jones described himself as an evangelist... the bearer of the Good News of Jesus Christ. The countless illustrations found in his books and sermons speak to a cross section of humanity and demonstrate, in a multitude of ways, the transformative impact of Jesus Christ on human existence. Few readers or listeners could miss identifying with one story or another – virtually all would find stories that touched their lives. All were offered hope that they, too, could experience the transformation available through self-surrender and conversion.

In presenting Jesus as the redeemer of all of life Jones used his wide ranging study of the non Christian religions, medicine, psychology, philosophy, science, history, and literature to make the case that the touch of Christ is upon all creation — that the totality of life was created by Christ and for Christ. We were all created to live upon Christ's Way. Jesus' Sermon on the Mount lays out both the principles and the Way.

Jones wrote twenty-seven books. More than 3.5 million copies of his books have been sold and they have been translated into 30 languages. All proceeds from his books have gone into Christian projects. He gave all of his money away! Now more than 40 years after his death – his books and sermons (many written in the 1930s and 40s) are not out of date and with few exceptions are entirely relevant to today's world.

According to his son in law, United Methodist Bishop James K. Mathews, "the most salient and spiritually significant characteristics of Stanley Jones were the spiritually transparency, clarity and persuasiveness of his personal witness for Christ. For thirty five years I knew him intimately and had occasion to observe him closely for prolonged periods. He rang true! Once when I asked a Hindu how he was, he replied, 'As you see me.' So it was with Brother Stanley, as he was called. He was as you saw him."

Even after a severe stroke at the age of 88 robbed him of his speech, Jones managed to dictate his last book, *The Divine Yes*. He died in India on January 25, 1973.

Jones' monumental accomplishments in life emerged from the quality of his character cultivated through his intimacy with Jesus Christ. As he lived in Christ, he reflected Christ. That experience is to us when we invite Christ to live in us!

Follow E. Stanley Jones on Facebook, Twitter and Amazon

ABOUT
THE E. STANLEY JONES FOUNDATION

The E. Stanley Jones Foundation is dedicated to bold and fruitful evangelism which shares the life-changing message of Jesus Christ to persons of all ages, backgrounds, life situations and locations. The Foundation is also dedicated to preserving and extending the legacy of the late E. Stanley Jones who blessed millions of people around the world with his preaching, teaching and prolific written words proclaiming Jesus is Lord! Our vision is to reach every generation with the message of Jesus Christ; enlighten spiritual growth through education and inspiration; prepare both Christian leaders and laity to be followers of Jesus Christ, and make known the Kingdom of God today.

For more information and our current programs, kindly visit us at:

www.estanleyjonesfoundation.com

Follow us on
Facebook, Twitter and Amazon

Thank you!

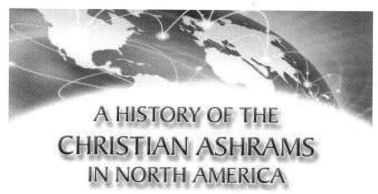

Anne Mathews-Younes, *A History of the Christian Ashrams in North America*. Potomac, MD: The E. Stanley Jones Foundation, 2017, 528 pages.

Anne Mathews-Younes, *The Life and Ministry of Mary Webster: A Witness in the Evangelistic Ministry of E. Stanley Jones.* Potomac, MD: The E. Stanley Jones Foundation, 2017, 286 pages.

E. Stanley Jones, *A Working Philosophy of Life: Exploring the Sermon on the Mount*. Reprint of *The Christ of the Mount*. Potomac, MD: The E. Stanley Jones Foundation, 2017, 312 pages.

OTHER BOOKS BY THE AUTHOR

Christ of the Indian Road
New York, Grosset & Dunlap, 1925.

Christ at the Round Table
New York & Cincinnati, Abingdon, 1928.

The Christ of Every Road:
A Study in Pentecost
New York, Cincinnati & Chicago, Abingdon, 1930.

The Christ of the Mount:
A Working Philosophy of Life
New York & Nashville, Abingdon-Cokesbury, 1931.

Christ and Human Suffering
New York, Cincinnati & Chicago, Abingdon, 1933.

Christ's Alternative to Communism
New York, Cincinnati & Chicago, Abingdon, 1935.

Victorious Living
New York & Nashville, Abingdon-Cokesbury, 1936.

The Choice Before Us
New York, Cincinnati & Chicago, Abingdon, 1937.

Along the Indian Road
New York, Cincinnati & Chicago, Abingdon, 1939.

Is the Kingdom of God Realism?
New York & Nashville, Abingdon-Cokesbury, 1940.

Abundant Living
New York & Nashville, Abingdon-Cokesbury, 1942.

The Christ of the American Road
New York & Nashville, Abingdon-Cokesbury, 1944.

The Way
New York & Nashville, Abingdon-Cokesbury, 1946.

Mahatma Gandhi: An Interpretation
New York & Nashville, Abingdon-Cokesbury, 1948.

The Way to Power and Poise
New York & Nashville, Abingdon-Cokesbury, 1949.

How To Be A Transformed Person
New York, & Nashville, Abingdon-Cokesbury, 1951.

Growing Spiritually
New York & Nashville, Abingdon, 1953.

Mastery: The Art of Mastering Life
New York & Nashville, Abingdon, 1955.

Christian Maturity
New York & Nashville, Abingdon, 1957.

Conversion
New York & Nashville, Abingdon, 1959.

In Christ
New York & Nashville, Abingdon, 1961.

The Word Become Flesh
New York & Nashville, Abingdon, 1963.

Victory Through Surrender
New York & Nashville, Abingdon, 1966.

A Song of Ascents:
A Spiritual Autobiography
New York, & Nashville, Abingdon, 1968.

The Reconstruction of the
Christian Church
Nashville, Tennessee, Abingdon Press, 1970

The Unshakable Kingdom
and the Unchanging Person
New York & Nashville, Abingdon, 1972.

The Divine Yes
New York, Cincinnati & Chicago, Abingdon, 1975.
(Posthumously published).

Made in the USA
Columbia, SC
29 January 2023

10690223R00245